22

Campaign Atlas
to
The Second
World War

Campaign Atlas to The Second World War

Thomas E. Griess
Series Editor

DEPARTMENT OF HISTORY
UNITED STATES MILITARY ACADEMY
WEST POINT, NEW YORK

AVERY PUBLISHING GROUP INC.
Wayne, New Jersey

Contents

Part One:
Campaign Atlas to Europe and the Mediterranean

Part Two:
Campaign Atlas to Asia and the Pacific

Foreword

Cadets at the United States Military Academy have studied military campaigns and institutions for almost a century in the course entitled History of the Military Art. Not until 1938, however, was that study supported by carefully integrated narratives and geographical portrayals. That year, T. Dodson Stamps, head of the Department of Military Art and Engineering, introduced an atlas specifically designed to support the study of the campaigns of the American Civil War. Shortly thereafter, additional atlases were devised to support the study of other wars.

During World War II, members of Stamps' department hurriedly prepared pamphlets on operations as they progressed. Eventually those pamphlets, revised and corrected, became the basis for a departmental text entitled *A Military History of World War II*, which first appeared in 1953 and was jointly edited by Stamps and Vincent J. Esposito. A number of serving officers in the department wrote that text and designed its accompanying atlas. In 1959, Esposito served as chief editor for *The West Point Atlas of American Wars*, which included coverage of the Second World War and made use of carefully revised maps from the 1953 departmental atlas. That last text served its purpose well in a time which required expanding coverage of military history. But as the course in the History of the Military Art, taught in the newly created Department of History since 1969, required modification to include new events and more than purely operational military history, the treatment of the Second World War has been compressed and accommodated to new themes. Such changes required the development of new texts.

This atlas, which has been designed to support these new texts, *The Second World War: Europe and the Mediterranean* and *Asia and the Pacific*, depicts primarily strategic coverage of the major campaigns of the war. Both text and atlas are original works written by officers in the Department of History, who extensively researched primary and secondary sources in preparing the narrative and developed new geographical depictions of the campaigns. The undersigned served as editor for the finished products. We are indebted to those officers for their dedicated work on the text and atlas alike. The following individuals contributed to coverage of the war in Europe: John A. Hixson (Poland and Campaigns in Norway and the West), David R. Mets (The Battle of Britain), Bruce R. Pirnie (Campaigns in Finland and the Balkans and the Russo-German War), Clifton R. Franks (Campaigns in North Africa, Sicily, and Italy), Thomas R. Stone (Campaign in Western Europe), Thomas B. Buell (Battle of the Atlantic), and James F. Ransone, Jr. (Grand Alliance). John H. Bradley prepared all of the material covering the war in the Pacific and Jack W. Dice prepared the chapter and maps pertaining to operations in the China-Burma-India Theater.

We are also indebted to Mr. Edward J. Krasnoborski and his assistant, Mr. George Giddings, who drafted the maps in final form. Mr. Krasnoborski, an unusually gifted and imaginative cartographer, supervised the drafting effort and did the majority of the maps; his effort and skill are imprinted everywhere on the finished product.

Thomas E. Griess
Series Editor

CHRONOLOGY OF EVENTS OF THE SECOND WORLD WAR

1939	POLAND	NORWAY	WESTERN EUROPE	BALKANS	NORTH AFRICA	RUSSIA	EAST ASIA AND THE PACIFIC	ALLIED CONFERENCES
SEPT.	Invasion							
OCT.	Surrender							
NOV.								
DEC.			Minor Operations					
1940 JAN.								
FEB.								
MAR.								
APR.		Invasion						
MAY			German Invasion of France					
JUNE		Allied Evacuation	French Surrender					
JULY								
AUG.							Sino-Japanese War (1937–1945)	
SEPT.			Battle of Britain		Graziani's Advance			
OCT.								
NOV.								
DEC.				Italian Invasion of Greece				
1941 JAN.					Wavell's Offensive			
FEB.								ABC-1 (Washington)
MAR.								
APR.				German Invasion of Yugoslavia, Greece and Crete	Rommel's First Offensive			
MAY								
JUNE					Wavell's Counteroffensive	Invasion, Bialystok, Minsk		
JULY						Smolensk		
AUG.						Uman and Gomel		
SEPT.						Kiev		
OCT.						Vyazma and Bryansk		
NOV.					Auchinleck's Offensive	Approach to Moscow		
DEC.						Russian Counterattacks	Pearl Harbor; Malaya; Philippines	

CHRONOLOGY OF EVENTS OF THE SECOND WORLD WAR

1942-43

1942 / 1943	NORTH AFRICA	SICILY AND ITALY	RUSSIA	EAST ASIA AND THE PACIFIC	ALLIED CONFERENCES
JAN.					ARCADIA (Washington)
FEB.			Russian Counterattacks	Singapore	
MAR.					
APR.	Rommel's Second Offensive			Fall of Bataan	
MAY			Kharkov	Corregidor; Allied Retreat from Burma	
JUNE			Sevastopol	Midway; Kiska	
JULY					
AUG.	Alam Halfa		Caucasus	Guadalcanal Landing; Kokoda	
SEPT.					
OCT.	El Alamein				
NOV.	Allied Invasion; Race for Tunis		Stalingrad	Buna-Gona	
DEC.					
1943 JAN.			Russian Leningrad Offensive		Casablanca
FEB.	Kasserine Pass		Russian Campaign in Ukraine	Japanese Evacuate Guadalcanal	
MAR.	Mareth				
APR.	Bizerte; Tunis Surrender				
MAY					TRIDENT (Washington)
JUNE					
JULY		Invasion of Sicily	Kursk; Orel	New Georgia	
AUG.		Salerno	German Withdrawal	Salamaua	QUADRANT (Quebec)
SEPT.		Naples; Volturno River		Lae	
OCT.					
NOV.		Winter Line Campaign	Russian Winter Offensive	Bougainville; Tarawa; Stilwell's Burma Campaign	Cairo-Teheran
DEC.				Arawe; Cape Gloucester	

CHRONOLOGY OF EVENTS OF THE SECOND WORLD WAR

1944-45

1944	WESTERN EUROPE	ITALY	RUSSIA	EAST ASIA AND THE PACIFIC	ALLIED CONFERENCES
JAN.		Anzio Landing			
FEB.			Leningrad	Kwajalein	
MAR.		Attack on Cassino	Ukraine	Stilwell's Burma Campaign; Manus; Japanese Imphal-Kohima Offensive	
APR.			Crimea	Hollandia	
MAY				Biak; Saipan	
JUNE	Normandy Landing	Rome Campaign		Guam	
JULY	Avranches		Latvia; Warsaw		
AUG.	Southern France; Westwall	Attacks on the Gothic Line	Rumania; Bulgaria		
SEPT.	Arnhem			Morotai; Palaus	OCTAGON (Quebec)
OCT.	Aachen			Leyte	
NOV.	Metz			Slim's Burma Offensive	
DEC.	Ardennes		Budapest; East Prussia; Poland	Landing on Luzon; Mindoro	
1945 JAN.					
FEB.	Advance to the Rhine			Manila; Shimbu Line; Iwo Jima	Yalta
MAR.	Remagen; Ruhr Encirclement; Advance to the Elbe				
APR.		Allied Spring Offensive; German Surrender (2 May)	Vienna; Berlin; German Surrender (8 May)	Okinawa; Borneo; Mindanao and the Visayas	
MAY	German Surrender (8 May)				
JUNE					
JULY					Potsdam
AUG.				Japanese Surrender (14 August)	
SEPT.					

TABLE OF SYMBOLS

BASIC SYMBOLS

Battalion	II
Regiment	III
Brigade	x
Division, air division . . .	xx
Corps	xxx
Army, air force, fleet . . .	xxxx
Army group	xxxxx
Airborne	⌒ (in box)

Air Force unit	⊗
Armor	⬭ (in box)
Artillery	• (in box)
Cavalry	╱ (in box)
Infantry	⊠
Mechanized	⬰
Naval troops, ground employment	⊥ (in box)
Special naval landing force .	SNLF

EXAMPLES OF COMBINATIONS OF BASIC SYMBOLS

Small British infantry detachment .	Br ⊠
34th Regimental Combat Team . .	⊠ 34 RCT (III over, x under)
Combat Command C of 1st Armored Division .	C ⬭ 1 (xx)
82d Airborne Division	⊠ 82 (xx)
1st Motorized Division	⬰ 1 Mtz (xx)

2d Marine Division	⊠ 2 Mar. (x x)
French Second Corps less detachments .	FR ☐ II (−) (xxx)
Third Army	THIRD (xxxx)
First Air Force	∞ FIRST (xxxx)
Bradley's 12th Army Group . . .	12 ☐ BRADLEY (xxxxx)

OTHER SYMBOLS

	Actual location	Prior location
Troops on the march	(solid arrow)	(dashed arrow)
Troops in position	(solid curved)	(dashed curved)
Troops in bivouac or reserve . .	(solid oval)	(dashed oval)
Field works	Occupied ⋀⋀⋀⋀	Unoccupied ⋀⋀⋀⋀
Strong prepared positions . . .	⊔⊔⊔⊔	⊔⊔⊔⊔
Airfield	◎	○
Covering force, armor or foot . .	• • • • •	• • • •

Troops in position under attack .	(curved arrow with arrows)
Route of march or flight . . .	(dashed line with arrows)
Boundary between units . . .	—— xxx —— (Appropriate basic symbol)
Fort	⋈
Fortified area	(oval shape)
Fuel pipeline	—•—•—
Minefield	—○—○—
Airborne landing	⌒

Part One
Campaign Atlas
to
Europe and the Mediterranean

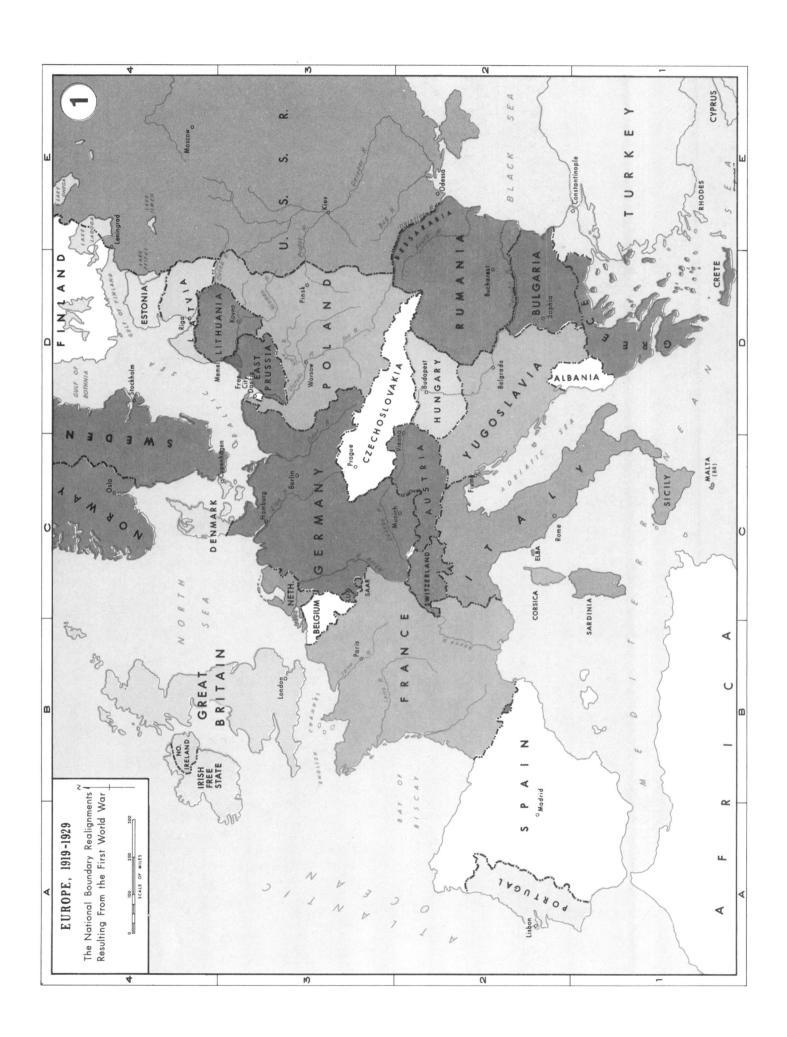

EUROPE, 1919-1929

The National Boundary Realignments
Resulting From the First World War

SCALE OF MILES
0   100   200   300

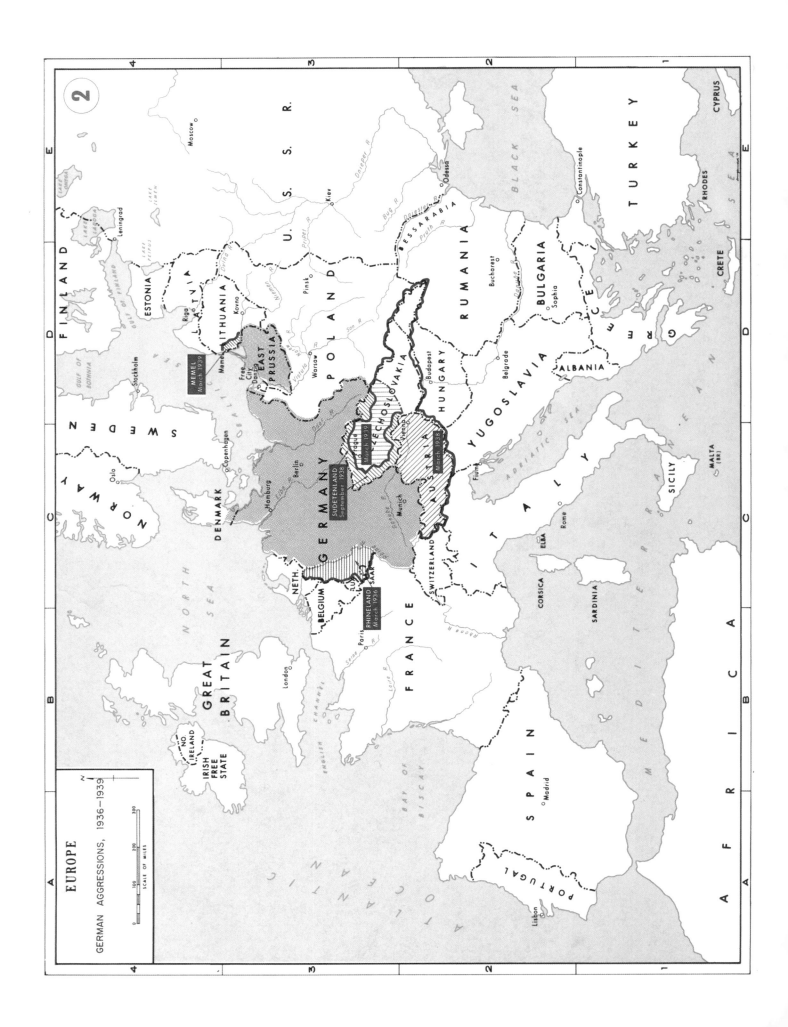

EUROPE

GERMAN AGGRESSIONS, 1936–1939

SCALE OF MILES
0   100   200   300

MEMEL
March 1939

SUDETENLAND
September 1938

AUSTRIA
March 1938

SAAR

RHINELAND
March 1936

March 1939

March 1938

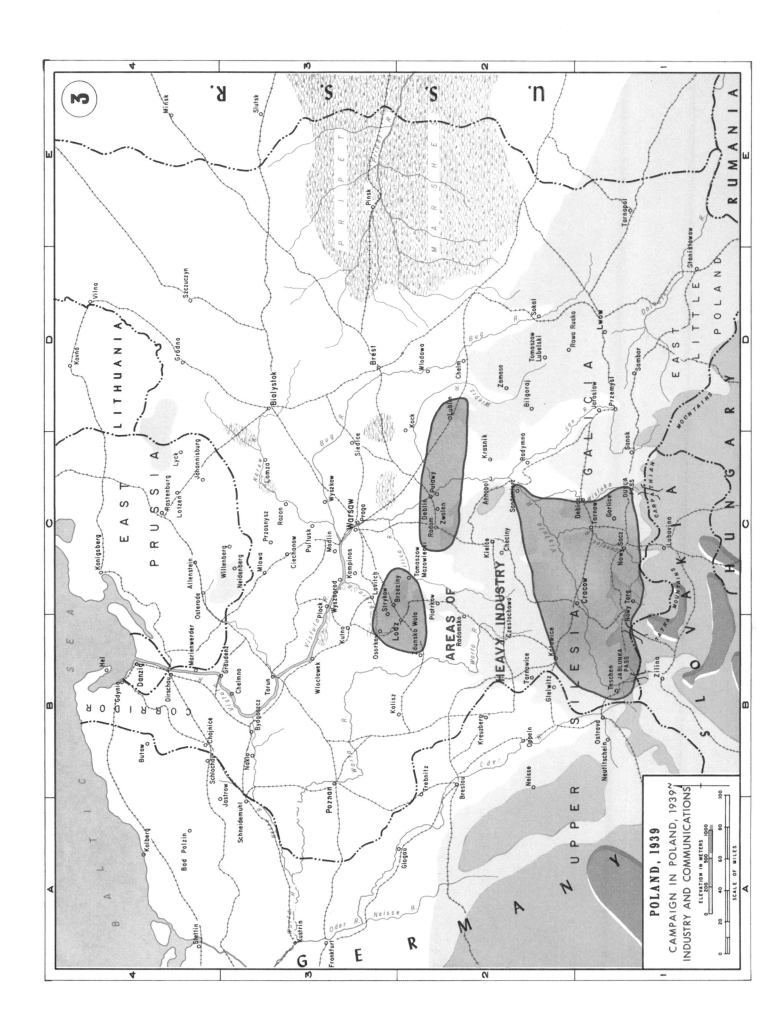

POLAND, 1939

CAMPAIGN IN POLAND, 1939
INDUSTRY AND COMMUNICATIONS

ELEVATION IN METERS
200 500 1000

SCALE OF MILES

AREAS OF
HEAVY INDUSTRY

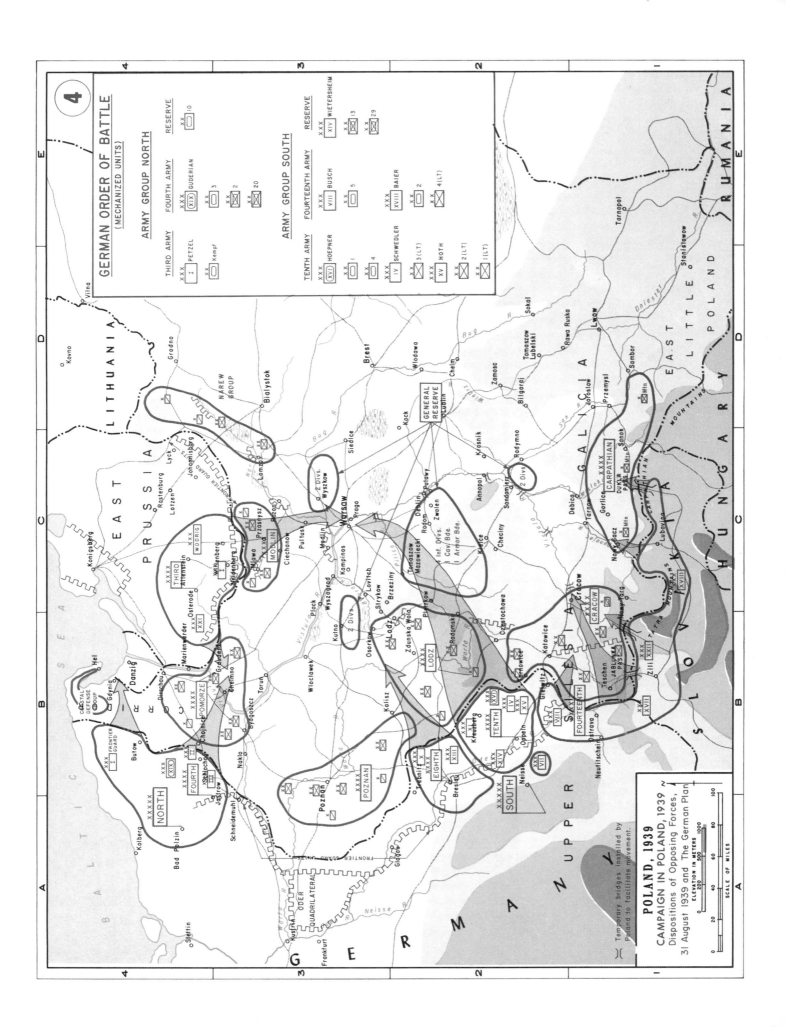

GERMAN ORDER OF BATTLE
(MECHANIZED UNITS)

ARMY GROUP NORTH

THIRD ARMY	FOURTH ARMY	RESERVE
PETZEL	GUDERIAN	10
Kempf	3	
	2	
	20	

ARMY GROUP SOUTH

TENTH ARMY	FOURTEENTH ARMY	RESERVE
HOEPNER	BUSCH	WIETERSHEIM
1	5	13
4		29
SCHWEDLER	BAIER	
3 (LT)	2	
HOTH	4 (LT)	
2 (LT)		
1 (LT)		

POLAND, 1939
CAMPAIGN IN POLAND, 1939
Dispositions of Opposing Forces,
31 August 1939 and The German Plan

ELEVATION IN METERS
200   500   1000

SCALE OF MILES
0   20   40   60   80   100

Temporary bridges installed by
Poland to facilitate movement.

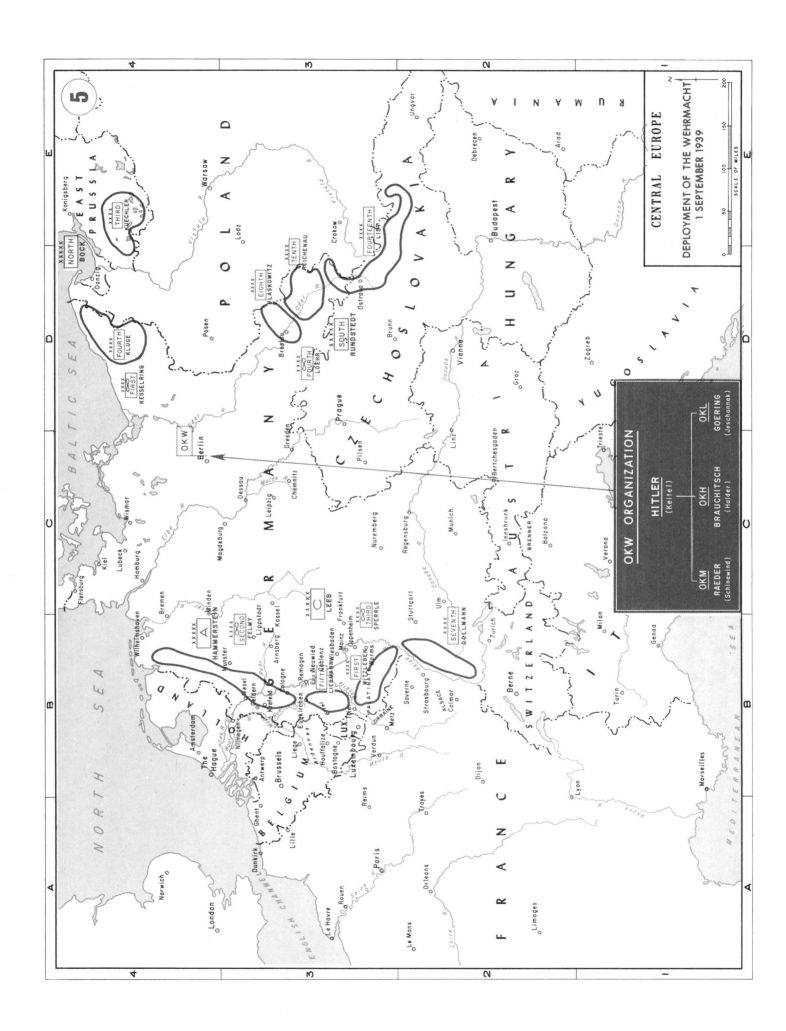

CENTRAL EUROPE

DEPLOYMENT OF THE WEHRMACHT
1 SEPTEMBER 1939

SCALE OF MILES
0   50   100   150   200

OKW ORGANIZATION

HITLER
(Keitel)

OKM   OKH   OKL
RAEDER   BRAUCHITSCH   GOERING
(Schinewind)   (Halder)   (Jeschonnek)

OKW
Berlin

xxxxx
NORTH
BOCK

xxxx
THIRD
KUECHLER

xxxx
FOURTH
KLUGE

xxxx
FIRST
KESSELRING

xxxx
EIGHTH
BLASKOWITZ

xxxx
TENTH
REICHENAU

xxxx
FOURTEENTH
LIST

xxxxx
SOUTH
RUNDSTEDT

xxxx
FOURTH
LOEHR

xxxxx
A
HAMMERSTEIN

xxxx
SECOND
FELMY

xxxxx
C
LEEB

xxxx
FIFTH
LIEBMANN

xxxx
FIRST
PALATINATE

xxxx
THIRD
SPERRLE

xxxx
SEVENTH
DOLLMANN

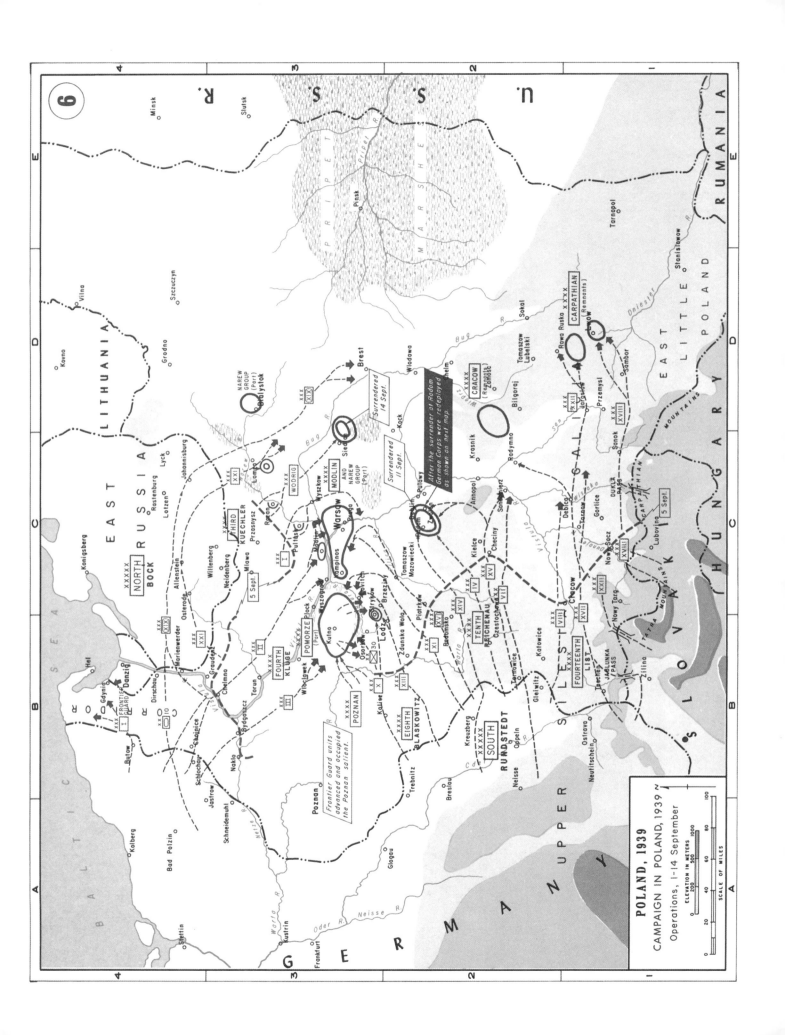

POLAND, 1939
CAMPAIGN IN POLAND, 1939
Operations, 1-14 September

ELEVATION IN METERS
SCALE OF MILES

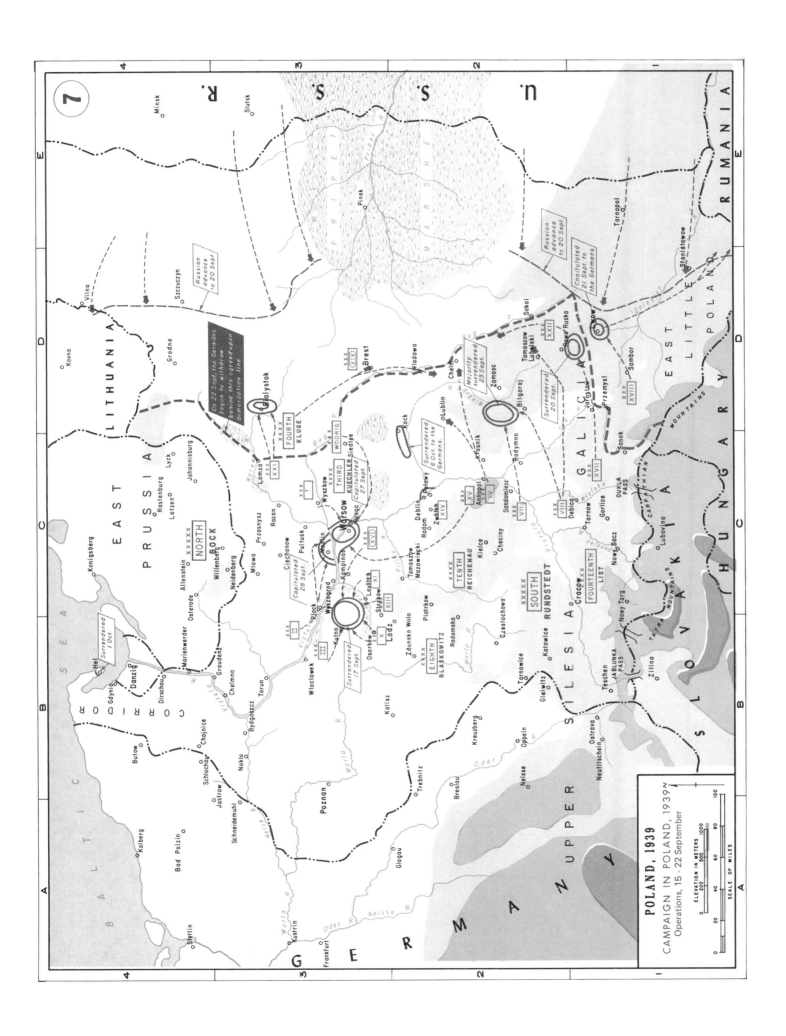

POLAND, 1939

CAMPAIGN IN POLAND, 1939
Operations, 15 - 22 September

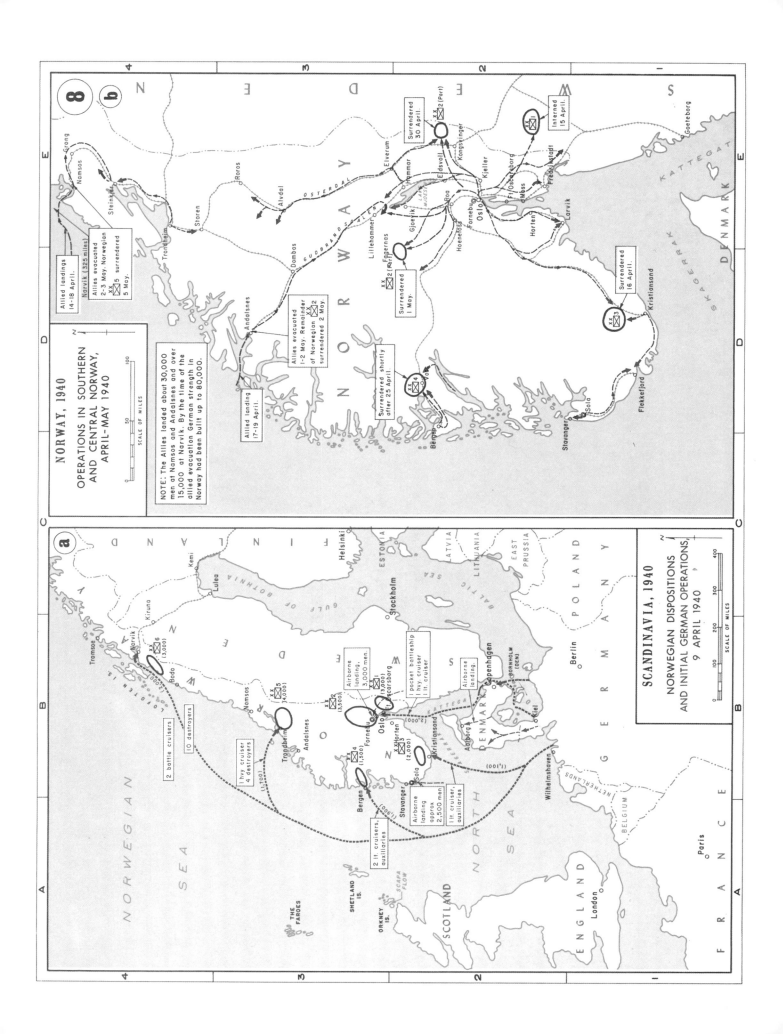

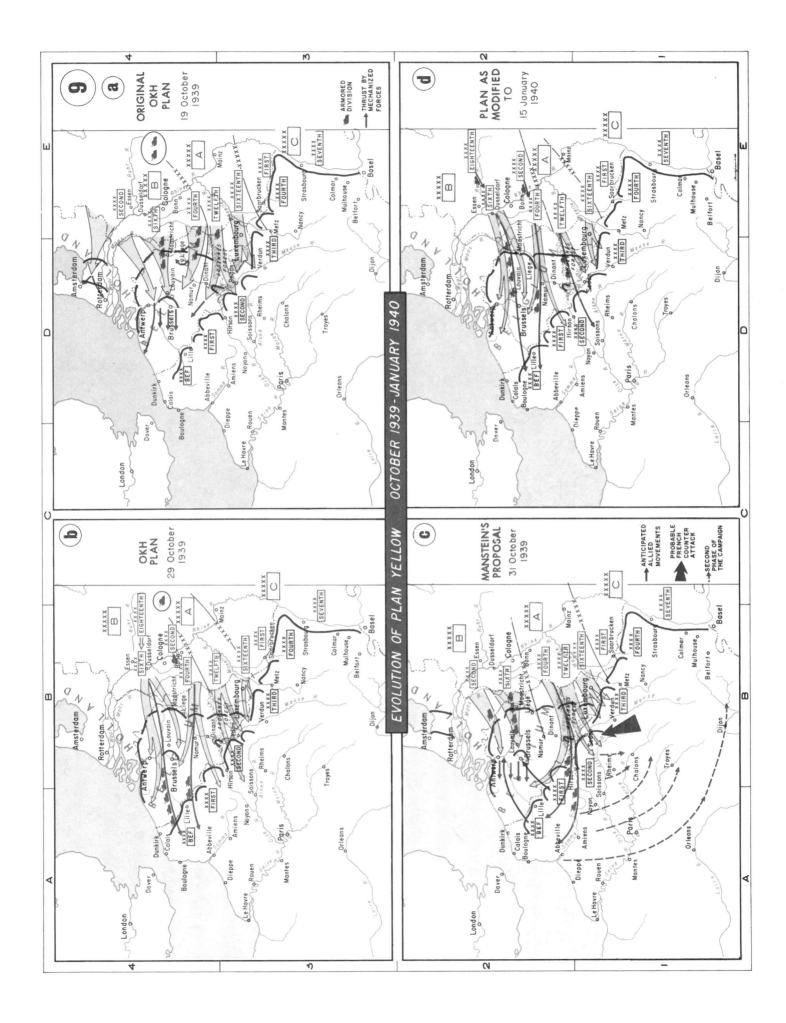

EVOLUTION OF PLAN YELLOW: OCTOBER 1939 - JANUARY 1940

9

a ORIGINAL OKH PLAN 19 October 1939

ARMORED DIVISION

THRUST BY MECHANIZED FORCES

b OKH PLAN 29 October 1939

c MANSTEIN'S PROPOSAL 31 October 1939

ANTICIPATED ALLIED MOVEMENTS

PROBABLE FRENCH COUNTER ATTACK

SECOND PHASE OF THE CAMPAIGN

d PLAN AS MODIFIED TO 15 January 1940

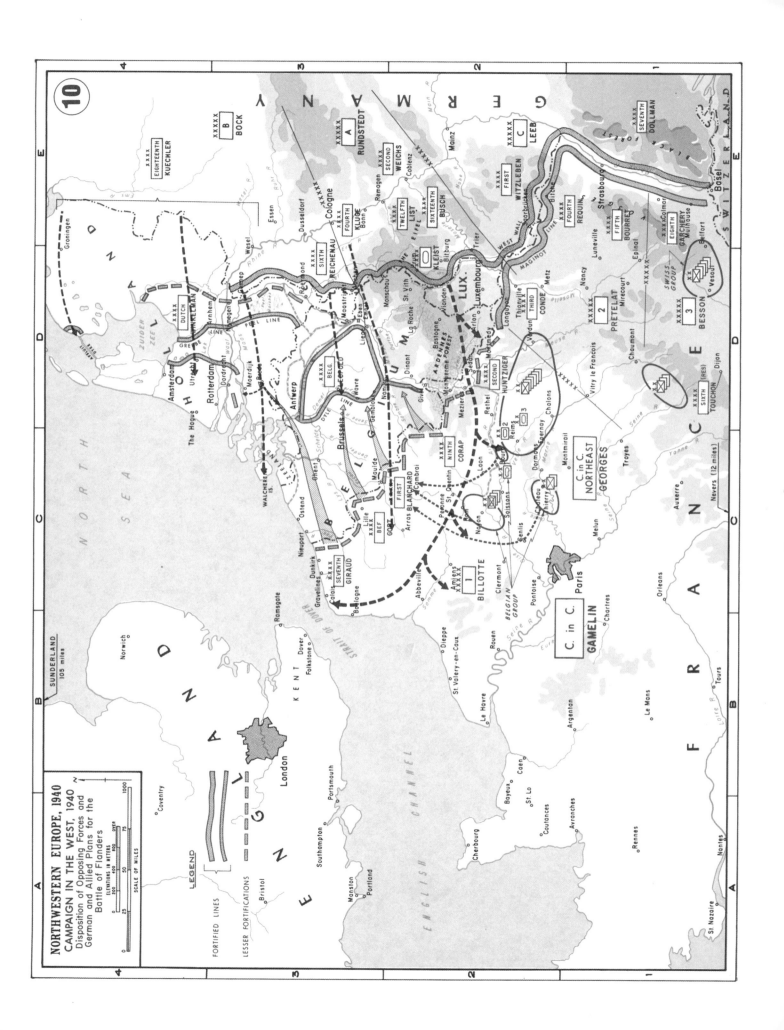

NORTHWESTERN EUROPE, 1940
CAMPAIGN IN THE WEST, 1940
Disposition of Opposing Forces and
German and Allied Plans for the
Battle of Flanders

LEGEND

FORTIFIED LINES

LESSER FORTIFICATIONS

ELEVATIONS IN METERS
200 400 600 800 1000 OVER

SCALE OF MILES
0 25 50 75

10

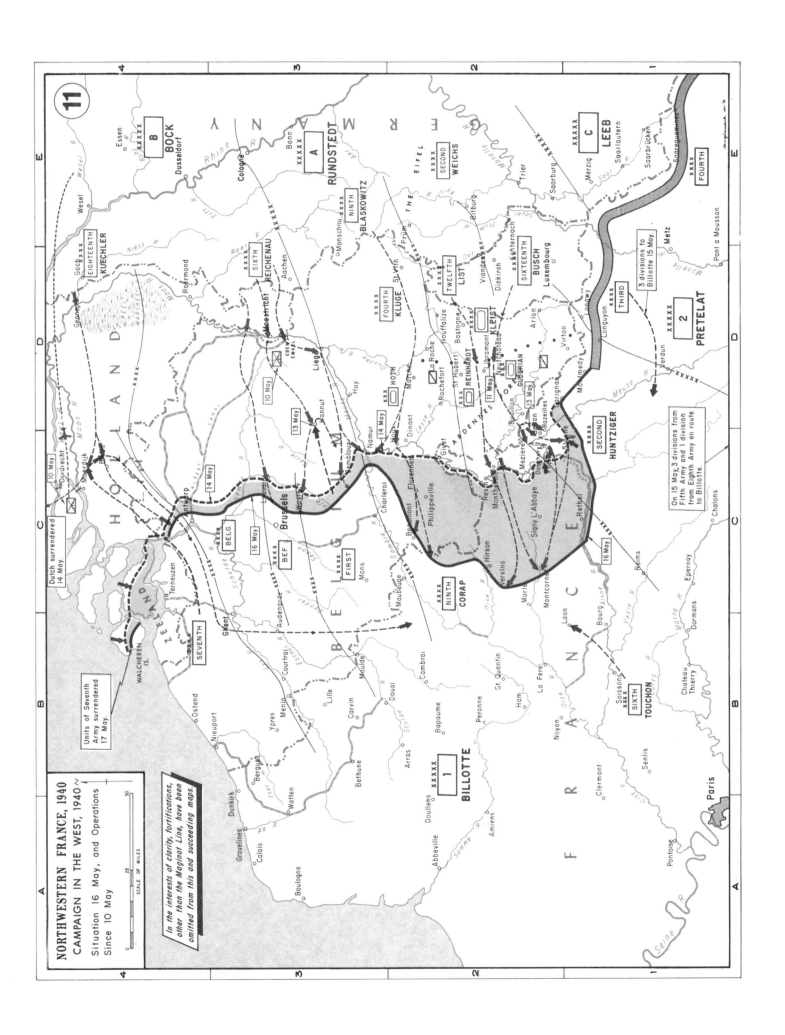

NORTHWESTERN FRANCE, 1940
CAMPAIGN IN THE WEST, 1940
Situation 16 May, and Operations
Since 10 May

SCALE OF MILES

In the interests of clarity, fortifications,
other than the Maginot Line, have been
omitted from this and succeeding maps.

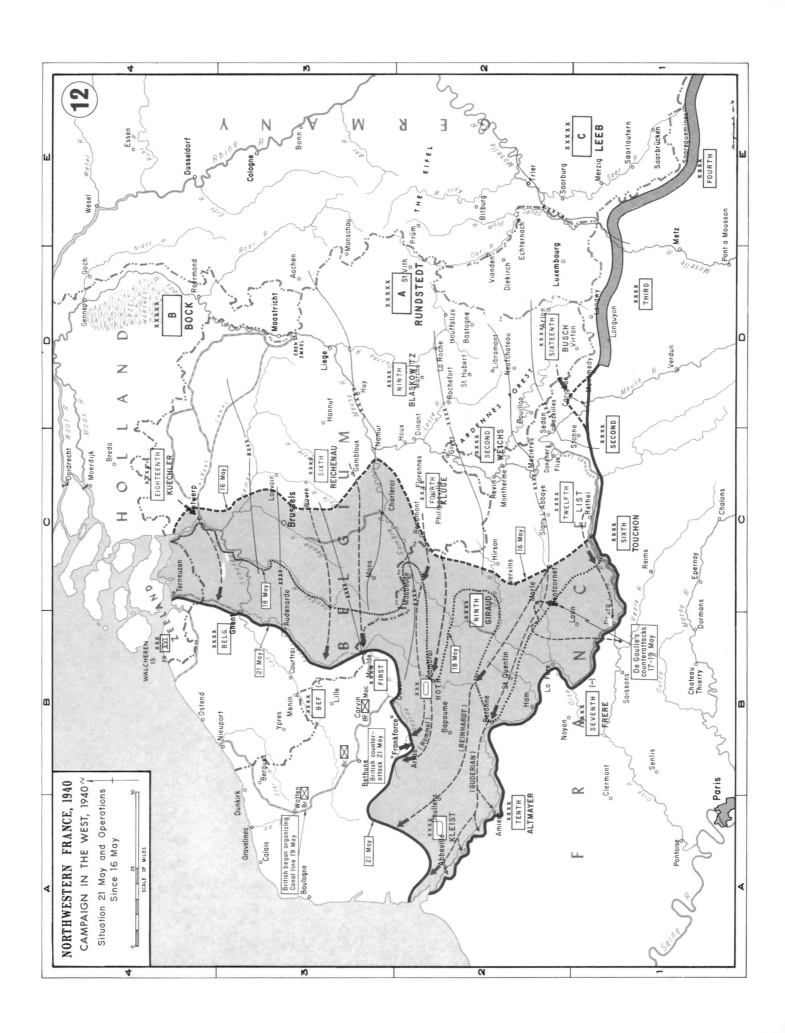

NORTHWESTERN FRANCE, 1940
CAMPAIGN IN THE WEST, 1940
Situation 21 May and Operations
Since 16 May

SCALE OF MILES

12

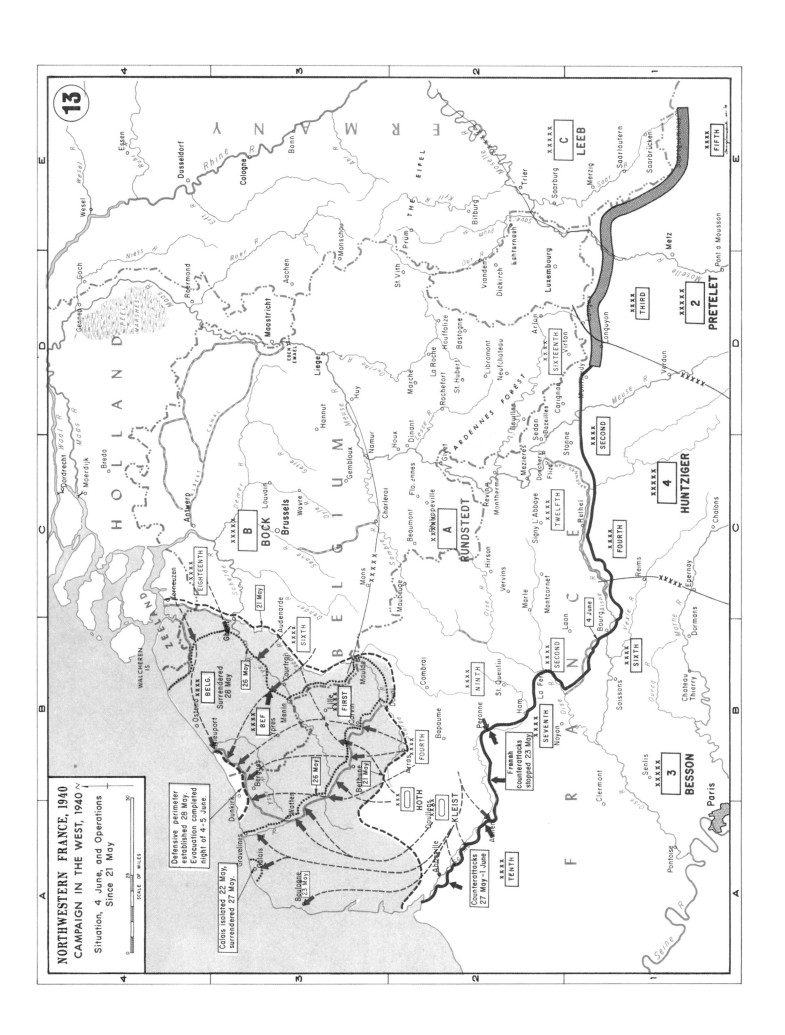

NORTHWESTERN FRANCE, 1940
CAMPAIGN IN THE WEST, 1940

Situation, 4 June, and Operations
Since 21 May

SCALE OF MILES
25   50

Defensive perimeter
established 28 May.
Evacuation completed
night of 4-5 June.

Calais isolated 22 May,
surrendered 27 May.

Boulogne
23 May

Counterattacks
27 May-1 June

French
counterattacks
stopped 23 May

13

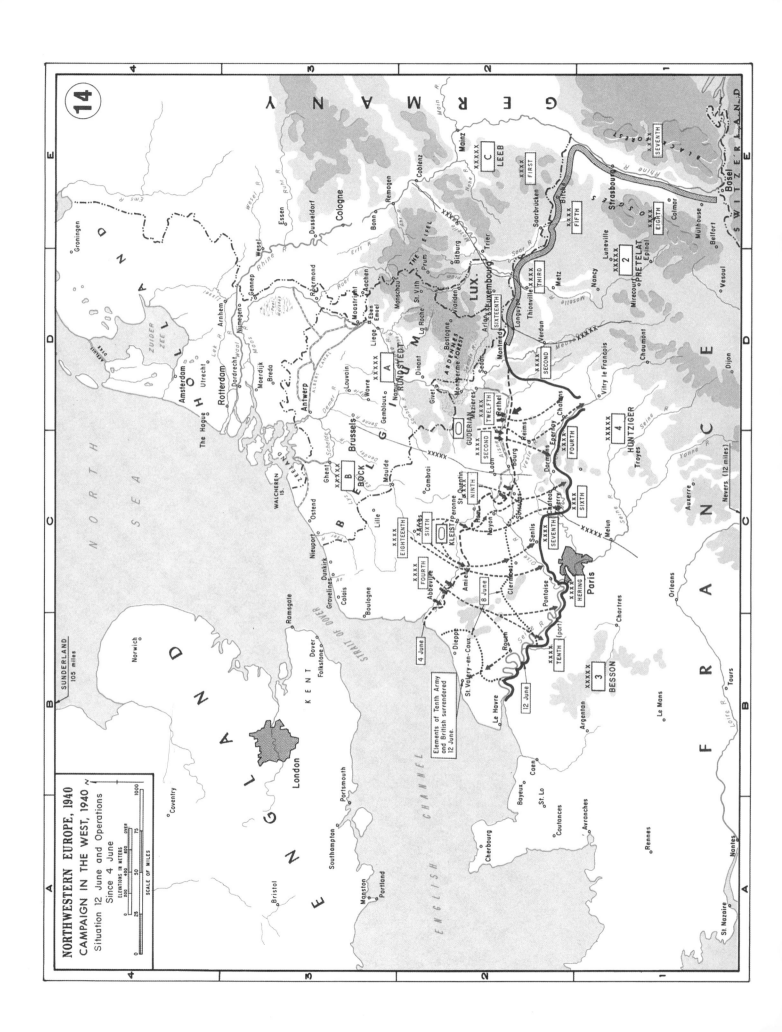

NORTHWESTERN EUROPE, 1940
CAMPAIGN IN THE WEST, 1940
Situation 12 June and Operations
Since 4 June

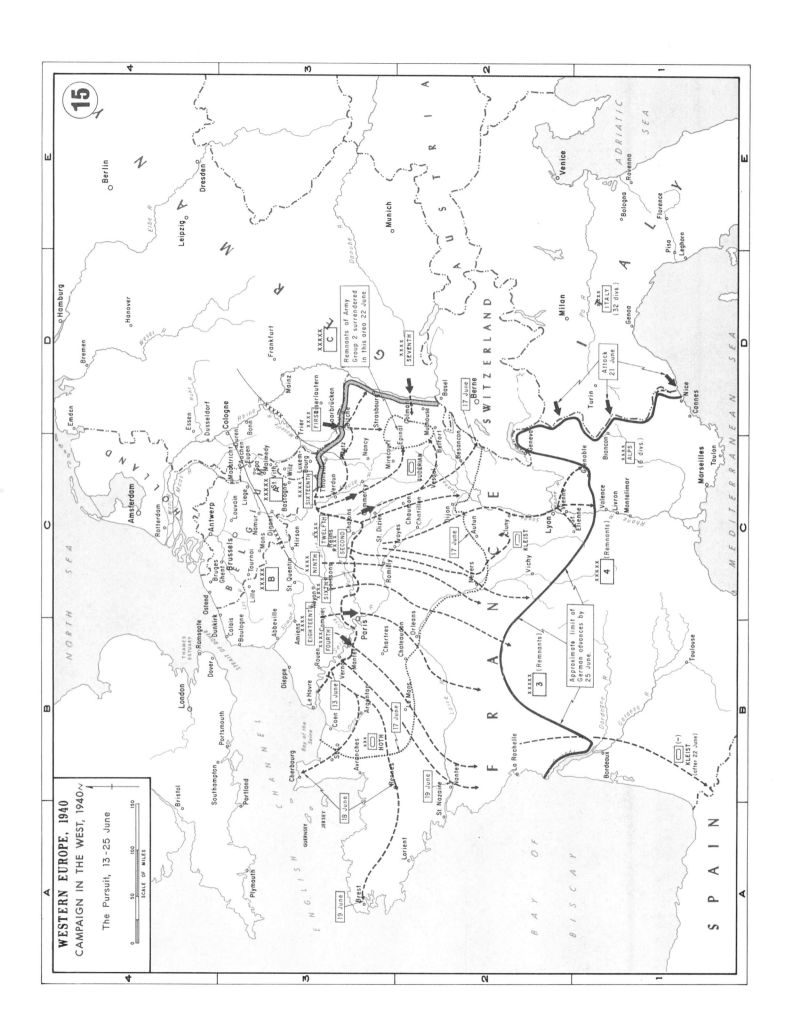

WESTERN EUROPE, 1940
CAMPAIGN IN THE WEST, 1940

The Pursuit, 13-25 June

SCALE OF MILES
0   50   100   150

15

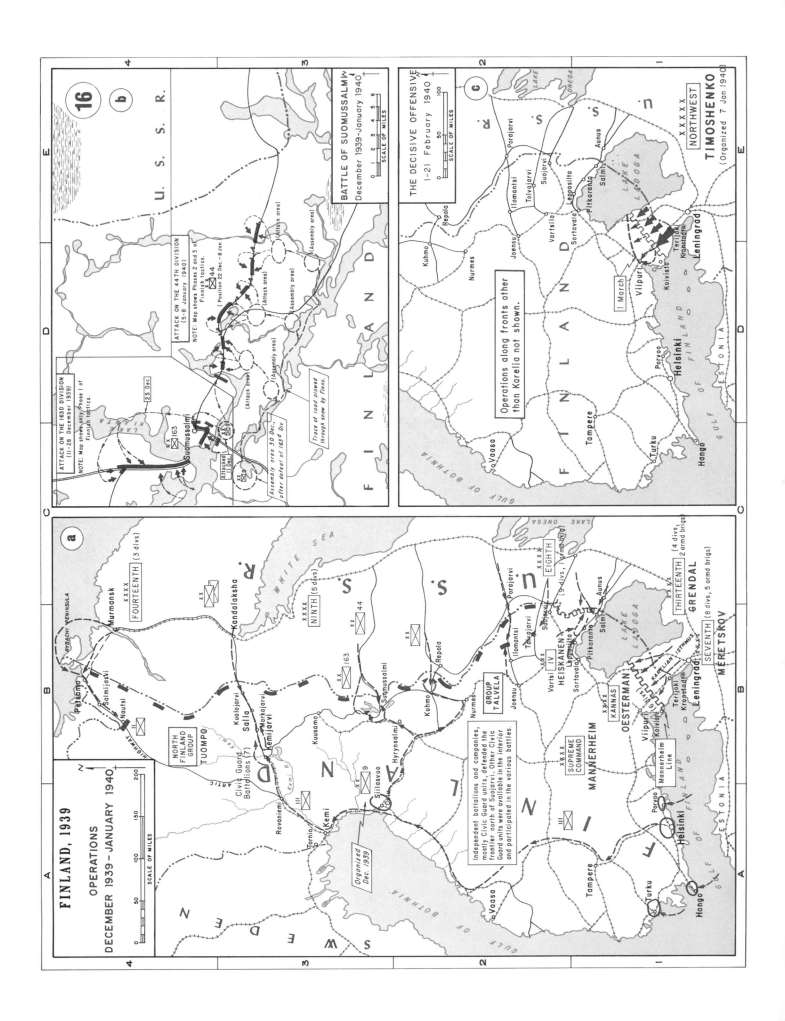

FINLAND, 1939
OPERATIONS
DECEMBER 1939–JANUARY 1940

SCALE OF MILES
0   50   100   150   200

a

XXXX FOURTEENTH (3 divs)

NORTH FINLAND GROUP
TUOMPO

XXXX NINTH (5 divs)

GROUP TALVELA

XXXX EIGHTH (9 divs, 1 armd brig)

HEISKANEN

XXX IV

XXX KANNAS

XXXX SUPREME COMMAND
MANNERHEIM

OESTERMAN

XXXX SEVENTH
MERETSKOV

THIRTEENTH (4 divs, 2 armd brigs)
GRENDAL (8 divs, 5 armd brigs)

Mannerheim Line

KARELIAN ISTHMUS

Organized Dec. 1939

Independent battalions and companies, mostly Civic Guard units, defended the frontier north of Suojärvi. Other Civic Guard units were available in the interior and participated in the various battles.

Civic Guard Battalions (7)

Rybachi Peninsula · Murmansk · Petsamo · Salmijärvi · Nautsi · HIGHWAY · Kuolajarvi · Salla · Markajarvi · Kemijärvi · Kuusamo · Rovaniemi · Kemi · Tornio · Siilasvuo · Suomussalmi · Hyrynsalmi · Kuhmo · Repola · Nurmes · Joensu · Ilomantsi · Tolvajärvi · Suojärvi · Porajärvi · Aunus · Värtsilä · Sortavala · Pitkäranta · Salmi · Viipuri · Koivisto · Terijoki · Kronstadt · Leningrad · Porvoo · Helsinki · Tampere · Turku · Hango · Vaasa

Kandalaksha · R. Kem · WHITE SEA · LAKE ONEGA · LAKE LADOGA · GULF OF BOTHNIA · GULF OF FINLAND · ESTONIA · SWEDEN · S S U R · F I N L A N D

b

ATTACK ON THE 163D DIVISION
(11–28 December 1939)
NOTE: Map shows only Phase I of Finnish tactics.

25 Dec

Assembly area 30 Dec., after defeat of 163d Div

XX 163
Suomussalmi
Attacked 11 Dec.

ATTACK ON THE 44TH DIVISION
(5–8 January 1940)
NOTE: Map shows Phases 2 and 3 of Finnish tactics.
(Position 22 Dec.–8 Jan.)

XX 144
XX 44

(Attack area) (Assembly area) (Attack area)

Trace of road plowed through snow by Finns.

16

BATTLE OF SUOMUSSALMI
December 1939–January 1940

SCALE OF MILES
0 1 2 3 4 5 6

U. S. S. R.
F I N L A N D

c

THE DECISIVE OFFENSIVE
1–21 February 1940

SCALE OF MILES
0   50   100

XXXXXX NORTHWEST
TIMOSHENKO (Organized 7 Jan 1940)

Operations along fronts other than Karelia not shown.

1 March

Repola · Kuhmo · Nurmes · Joensu · Ilomantsi · Tolvajärvi · Suojärvi · Porajärvi · Aunus · Vartsilo · Sortavala · Leppäsilta · Pitkäranta · Salmi · Viipuri · Koivisto · Terijoki · Kronstadt · Leningrad · Porvoo · Helsinki · Tampere · Turku · Hango · Vaasa

LAKE ONEGA · LAKE LADOGA · GULF OF BOTHNIA · GULF OF FINLAND · ESTONIA
U. S. S. R. · F I N L A N D

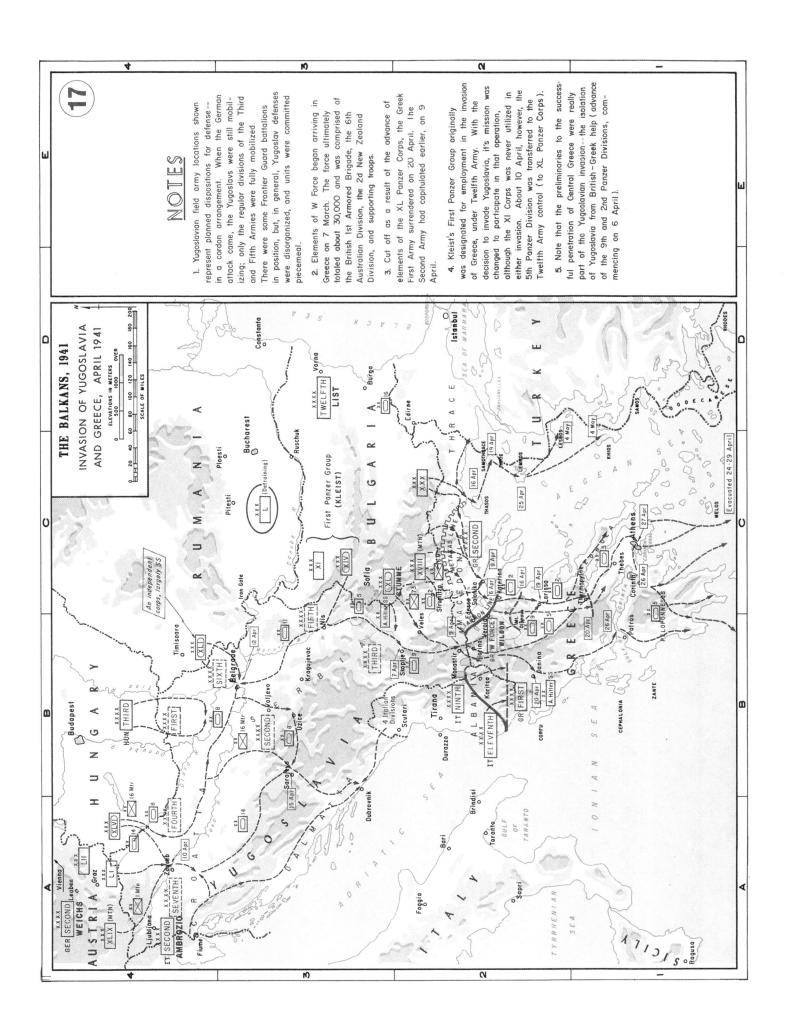

THE BALKANS, 1941
INVASION OF YUGOSLAVIA AND GREECE, APRIL 1941

ELEVATIONS IN METERS

0   500   1000   OVER

SCALE OF MILES
0   20   40   60   80   100   120   140   160   180   200

NOTES

1. Yugoslavian field army locations shown represent planned dispositions for defense—in a cordon arrangement. When the German attack came, the Yugoslavs were still mobilizing; only the regular divisions of the Third and Fifth Armies were fully mobilized. There were some Frontier Guard battalions in position, but, in general, Yugoslav defenses were disorganized, and units were committed piecemeal.

2. Elements of W Force began arriving in Greece on 7 March. The force ultimately totaled about 30,000 and was comprised of the British 1st Armored Brigade, the 6th Australian Division, the 2d New Zealand Division, and supporting troops.

3. Cut off as a result of the advance of elements of the XL Panzer Corps, the Greek First Army surrendered on 20 April. The Second Army had capitulated earlier, on 9 April.

4. Kleist's First Panzer Group originally was designated for employment in the invasion of Greece, under Twelfth Army. With the decision to invade Yugoslavia, it's mission was changed to participate in that operation, although the XI Corps was never utilized in either invasion. About 10 April, however, the 5th Panzer Division was transferred to the Twelfth Army control (to XL Panzer Corps).

5. Note that the preliminaries to the successful penetration of Central Greece were really part of tho Yugoslavian invasion—the isolation of Yugoslavia from British-Greek help (advance of the 9th and 2nd Panzer Divisions, commencing on 6 April).

17

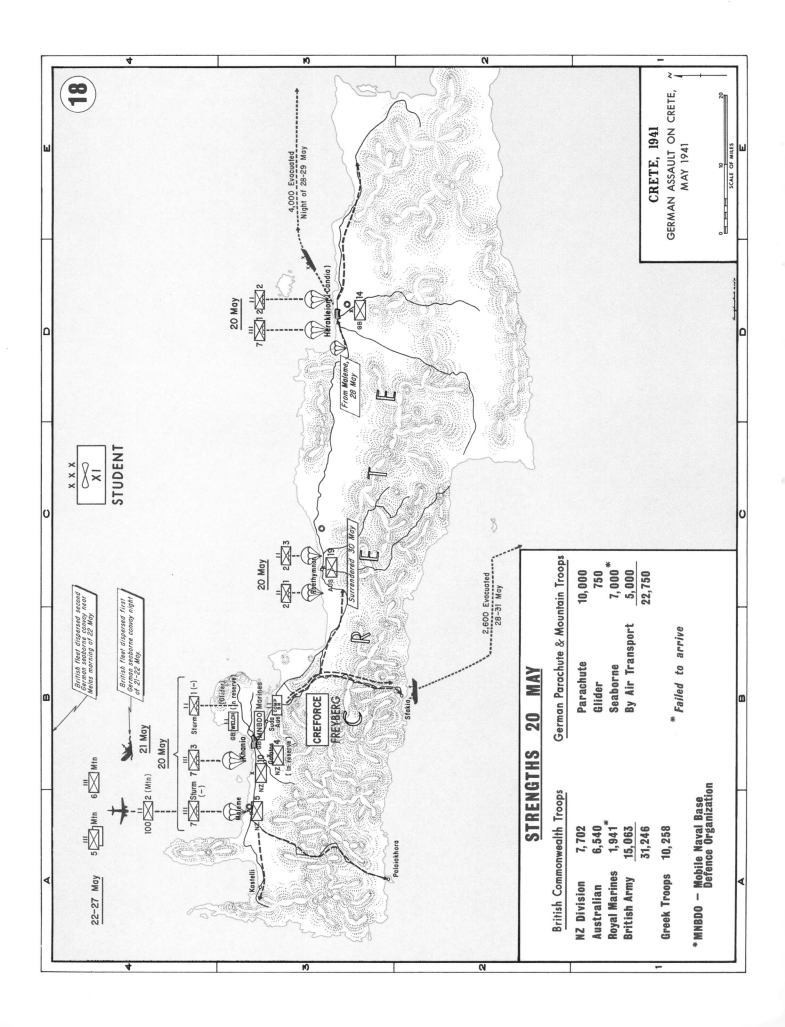

CRETE, 1941

GERMAN ASSAULT ON CRETE, MAY 1941

SCALE OF MILES

STUDENT

STRENGTHS 20 MAY

British Commonwealth Troops	
NZ Division	7,702
Australian	6,540
Royal Marines	1,941*
British Army	15,063
	31,246
Greek Troops	10,258

German Parachute & Mountain Troops	
Parachute	10,000
Glider	750
Seaborne	7,000*
By Air Transport	5,000
	22,750

*Failed to arrive

*MNBDO – Mobile Naval Base Defence Organization

British fleet dispersed second German seaborne convoy near Melos morning of 22 May.

British fleet dispersed first German seaborne convoy night of 21-22 May.

22-27 May

21 May
20 May

20 May

20 May

From Maleme, 28 May

Surrendered 30 May

4,000 Evacuated Night of 28-29 May

2,600 Evacuated 28-31 May

CREFORCE
FREYBERG

CRETE

Kastelli
Maleme
Khania
Suda
Rethymnon
Herakleion (Candia)
Sfakia
Palaiokhora

18

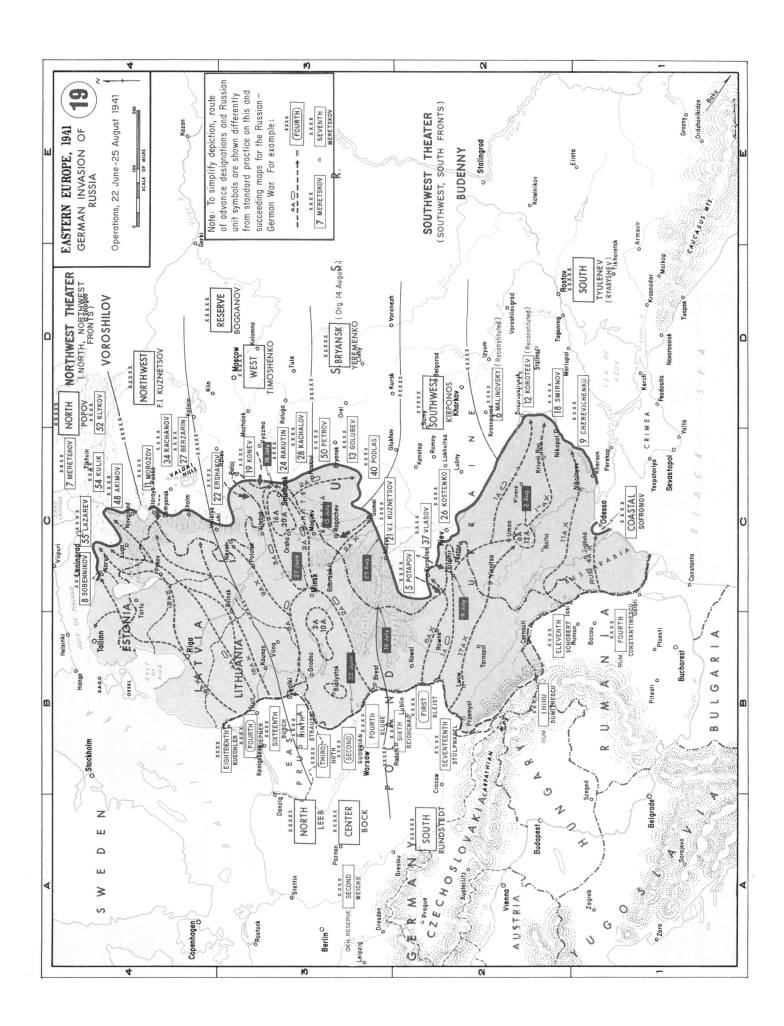

EASTERN EUROPE, 1941

19

GERMAN INVASION OF RUSSIA

Operations, 22 June–25 August 1941

SCALE OF MILES
0   100   200

Note: To simplify depiction, route of advance designations and Russian unit symbols are shown differently from standard practice on this and succeeding maps for the Russian–German War. For example:

4 A ▷ = FOURTH

7 MERETSKOV = SEVENTH MERETSKOV

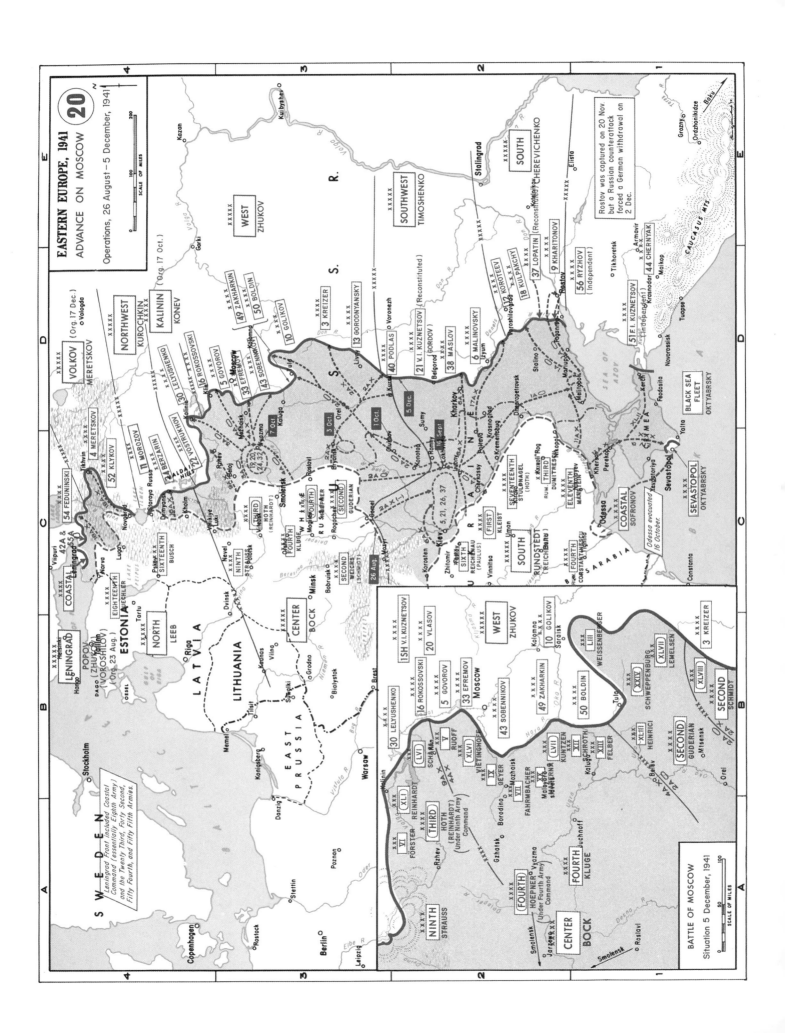

EASTERN EUROPE, 1941
20
ADVANCE ON MOSCOW
Operations, 26 August – 5 December, 1941

Leningrad Front included Coastal
Command (essentially Eighth Army)
and the Twenty Third, Forty Second,
Fifty Fourth, and Fifty Fifth Armies.

Rostov was captured on 20 Nov.
but a Russian counterattack
forced a German withdrawal on
2 Dec.

Odessa evacuated
16 October.

BATTLE OF MOSCOW
Situation 5 December, 1941

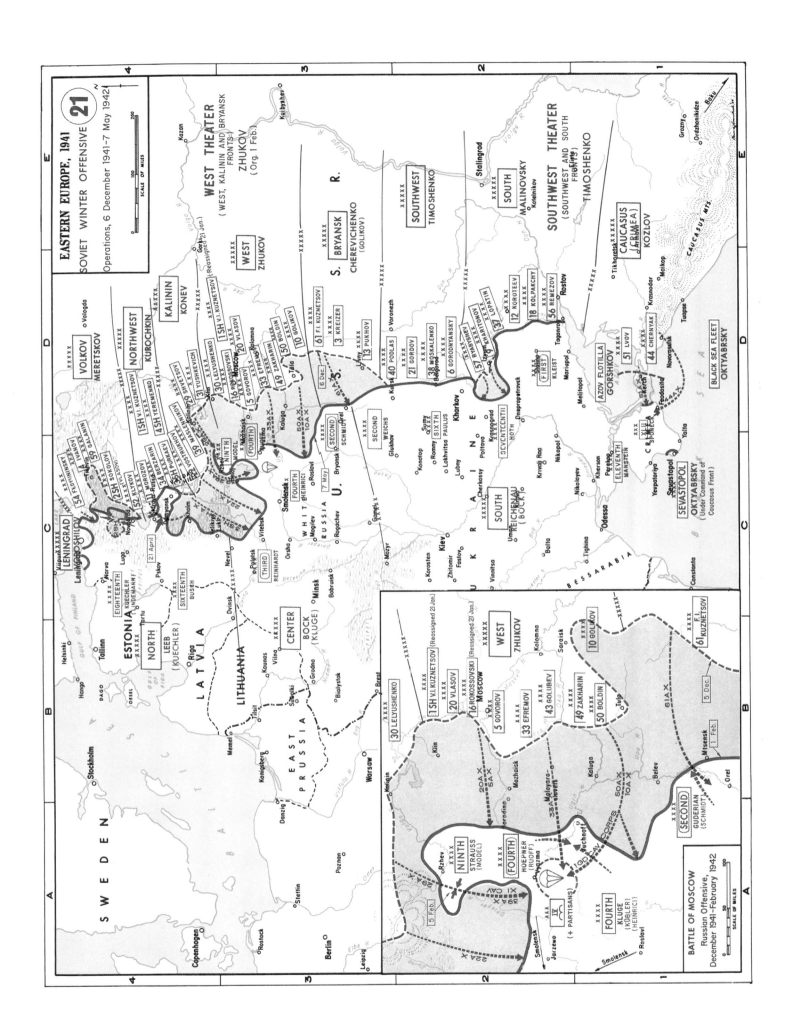

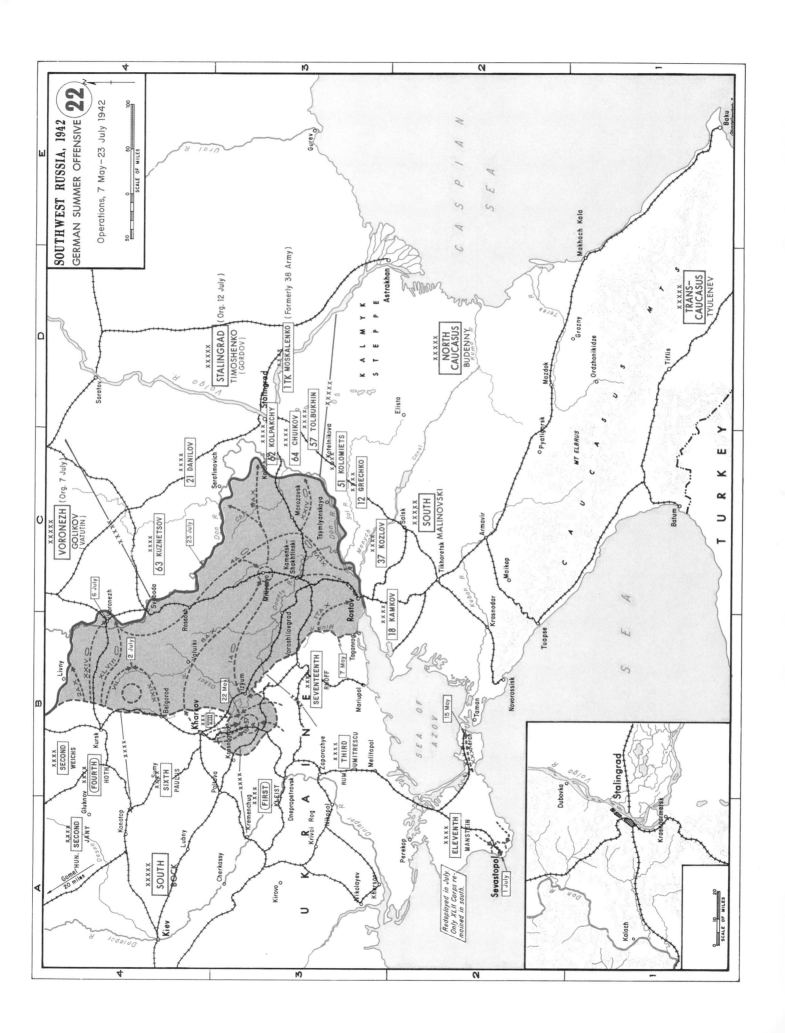

SOUTHWEST RUSSIA, 1942
22
GERMAN SUMMER OFFENSIVE

Operations, 7 May – 23 July 1942

SCALE OF MILES
50   0   50   100

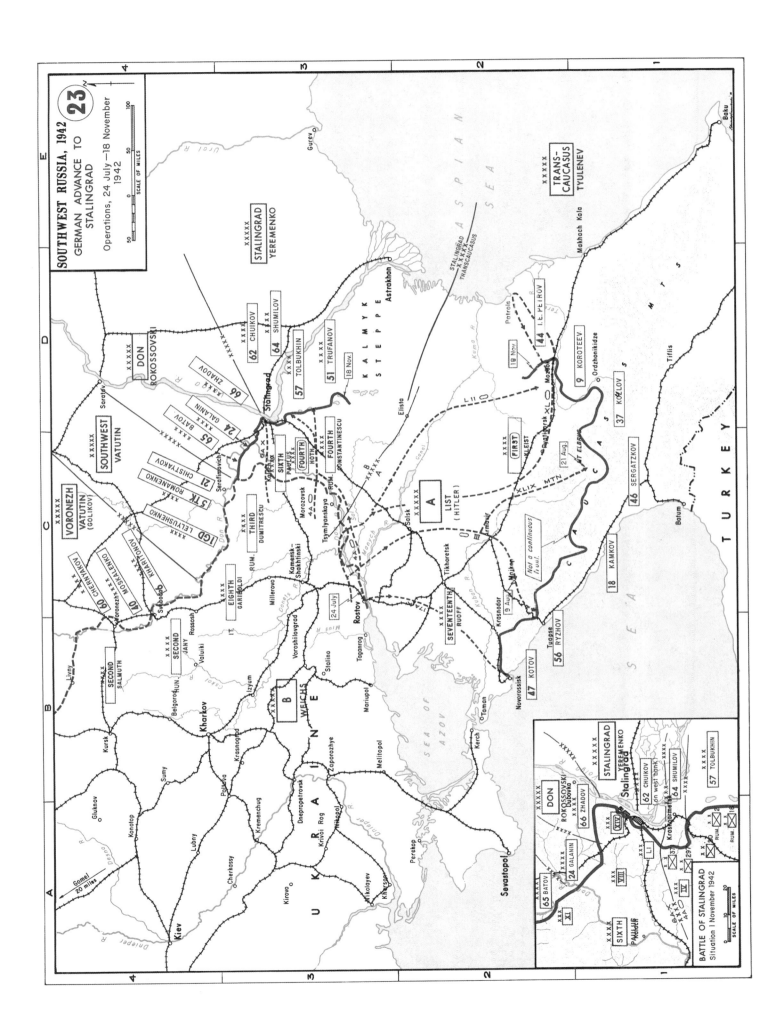

SOUTHWEST RUSSIA, 1942
23
GERMAN ADVANCE TO STALINGRAD
Operations, 24 July–18 November 1942

SCALE OF MILES
50   0   50   100

BATTLE OF STALINGRAD
Situation 1 November 1942
SCALE OF MILES
20   10   0   20

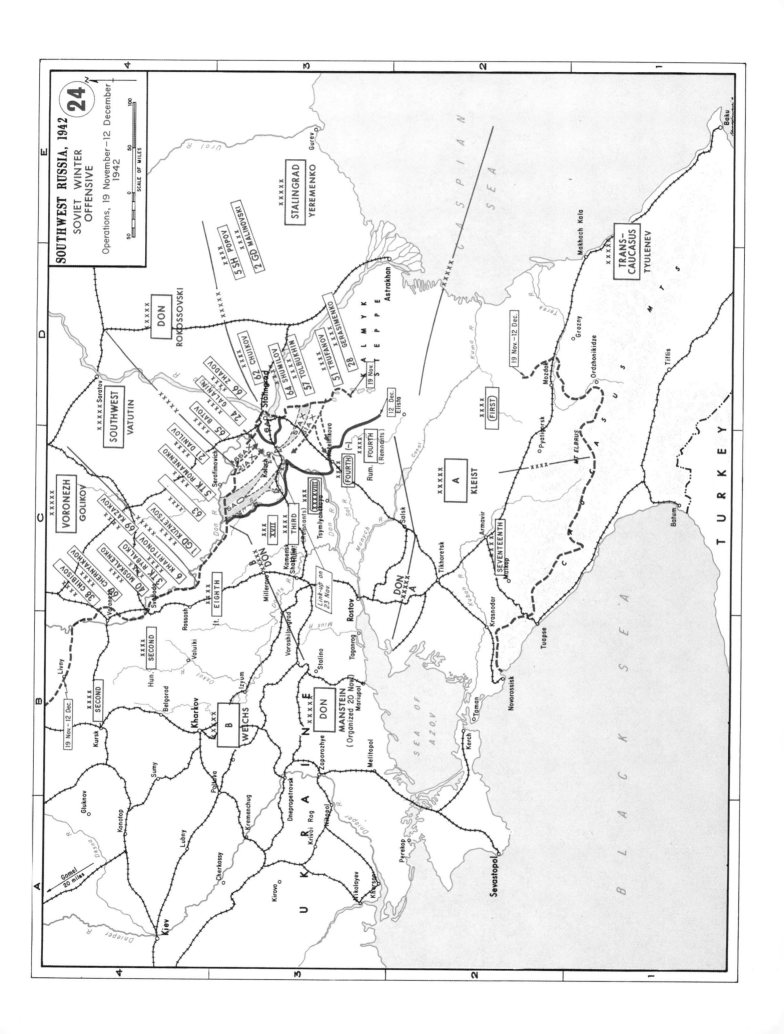

SOUTHWEST RUSSIA, 1942

24

SOVIET WINTER OFFENSIVE

Operations, 19 November–12 December 1942

SCALE OF MILES

STALINGRAD
YEREMENKO

DON
ROKOSSOVSKI

SOUTHWEST
VATUTIN

VORONEZH
GOLIKOV

5 SH POPOV
2 GD MALINOVSKI

66 ZHADOV
24 GALANIN
65 BATOV
21 DANILOV
5 TK ROMANENKO
63
69 KUZNETSOV
I GD KHARITONOV
6
3 TK RYBALKO
40 MOSKALENKO
60 CHERNYAKHOV
38 CHIBISOV

62 CHUIKOV
64 SHUMILOV
57 TOLBUKHIN
51 TRUFANOV
28 GERASIMENKO

19 Nov.

12 Dec.
Elista

FOURTH
Rum. FOURTH (Remnants)

FOURTH (–)

THIRD
Tsymlyanskaya

XVII

EIGHTH
It.

SECOND
Hun.

DON
A

KLEIST
A
FIRST

19 Nov–12 Dec.

SEVENTEENTH

DON
MANSTEIN
(Organized 20 Nov)

WEICHS
B

SECOND

19 Nov–12 Dec.

TRANS-
CAUCASUS
TYULENEV

19 Nov–12 Dec.

Link-up on
23 Nov.

Kamensk
Shakhty

Link-up 20 Nov

UKRAINE

Gomel
20 miles

Baku

Makhach Kala

Astrakhan
Gurev

Mozdok
Grozny
Ordzhonikidze
Pyatigorsk
MT ELBRUS
Tiflis

Armavir
Matkop
Tikhoretsk
Krasnodar
Tuapse
Novorossisk
Tamari
Taman
Kerch
Sevastopol
Perekop

Salsk
Rostov
Taganrog
Stalino
Mariupol
Melitopol
Zaporozhye
Nikopol
Krivoi Rog
Dnepropetrovsk
Kremenchug
Cherkassy
Kirovo
Nikolayev
Kherson
Kiev

Lubny
Poltava
Sumy
Glukhov
Konotop

Kursk
Belgorod
Kharkov
Izyum
Valuiki
Rossosh
Svoboda
Voronezh
Livny

Saratov
Stalingrad
Serafimovich
Kalach
Millerovo
Voroshilovgrad

Elista

TURKEY

CASPIAN SEA

BLACK SEA

SEA OF AZOV

KALMYK STEPPE

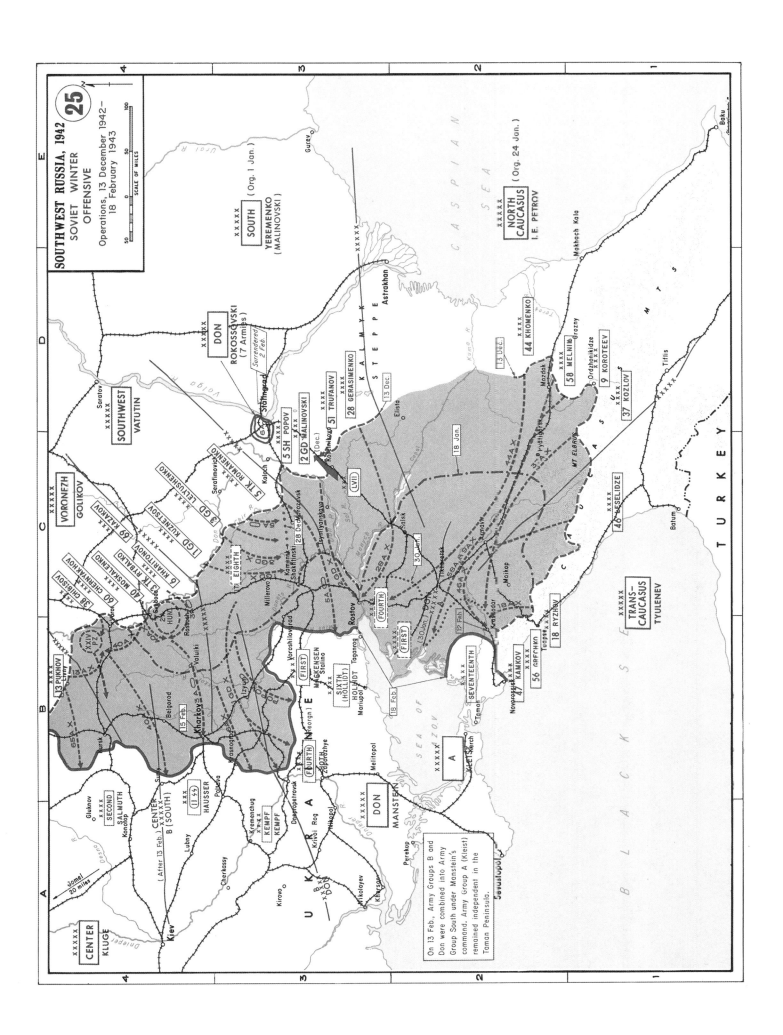

SOUTHWEST RUSSIA, 1942
25
SOVIET WINTER
OFFENSIVE

Operations, 13 December 1942–
18 February 1943

SCALE OF MILES

On 13 Feb, Army Groups B and
Don were combined into Army
Group South under Manstein's
command. Army Group A (Kleist)
remained independent in the
Taman Peninsula.

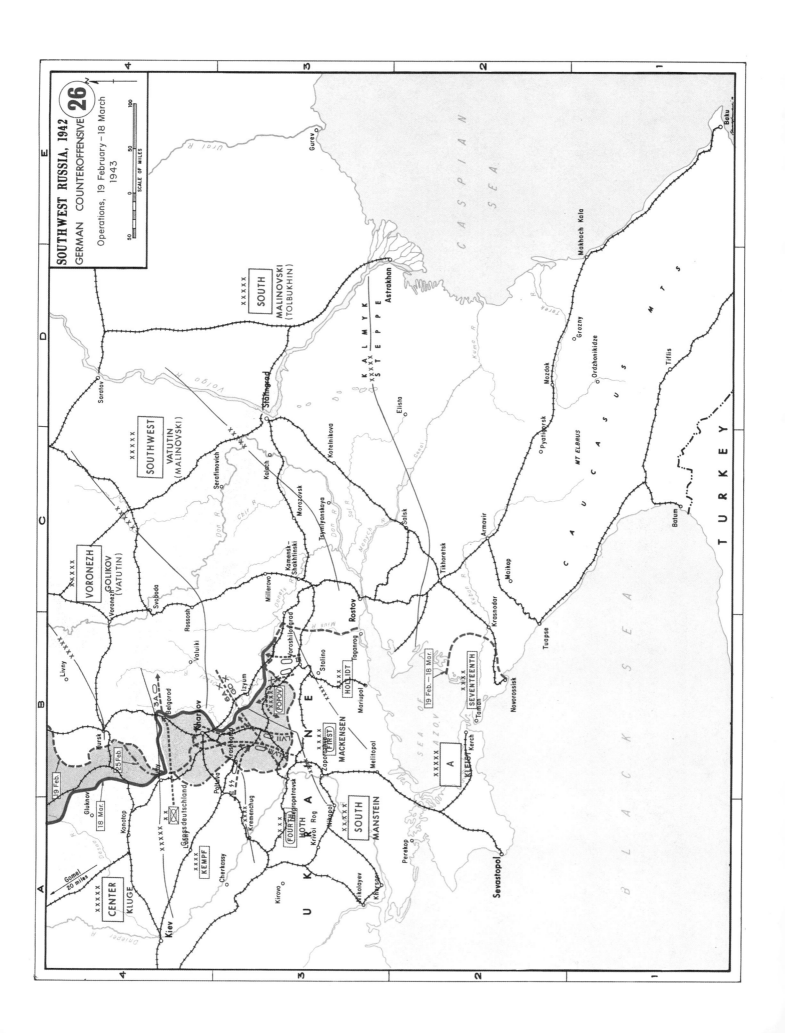

SOUTHWEST RUSSIA, 1942

26

GERMAN COUNTEROFFENSIVE

Operations, 19 February – 18 March
1943

SCALE OF MILES

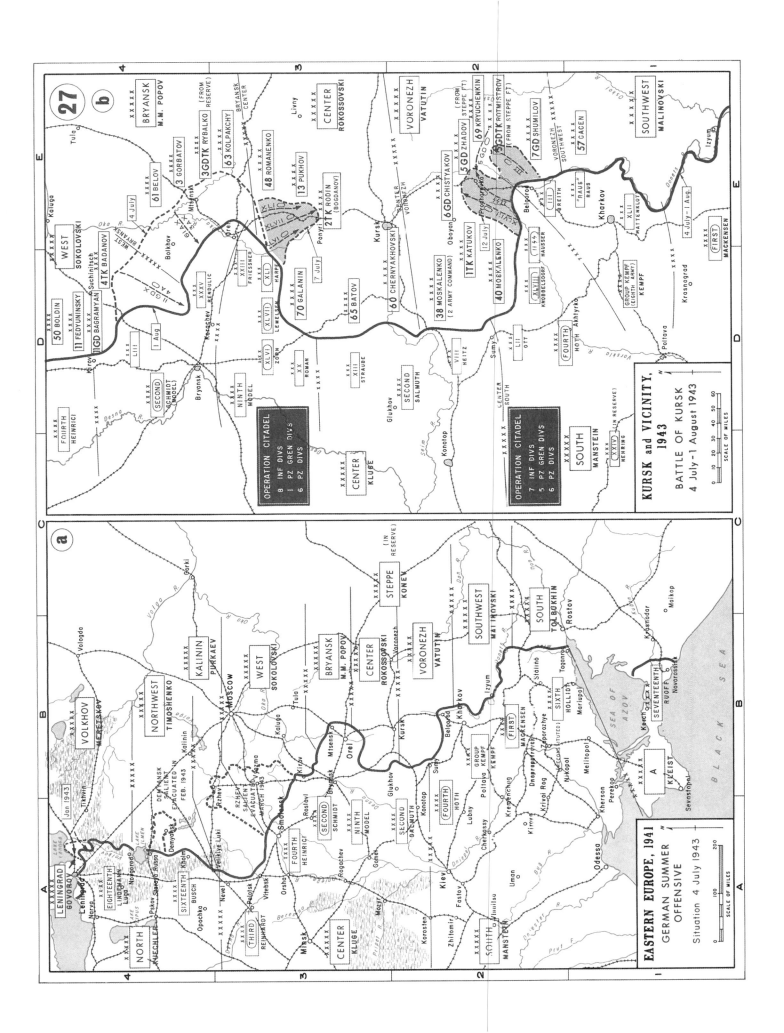

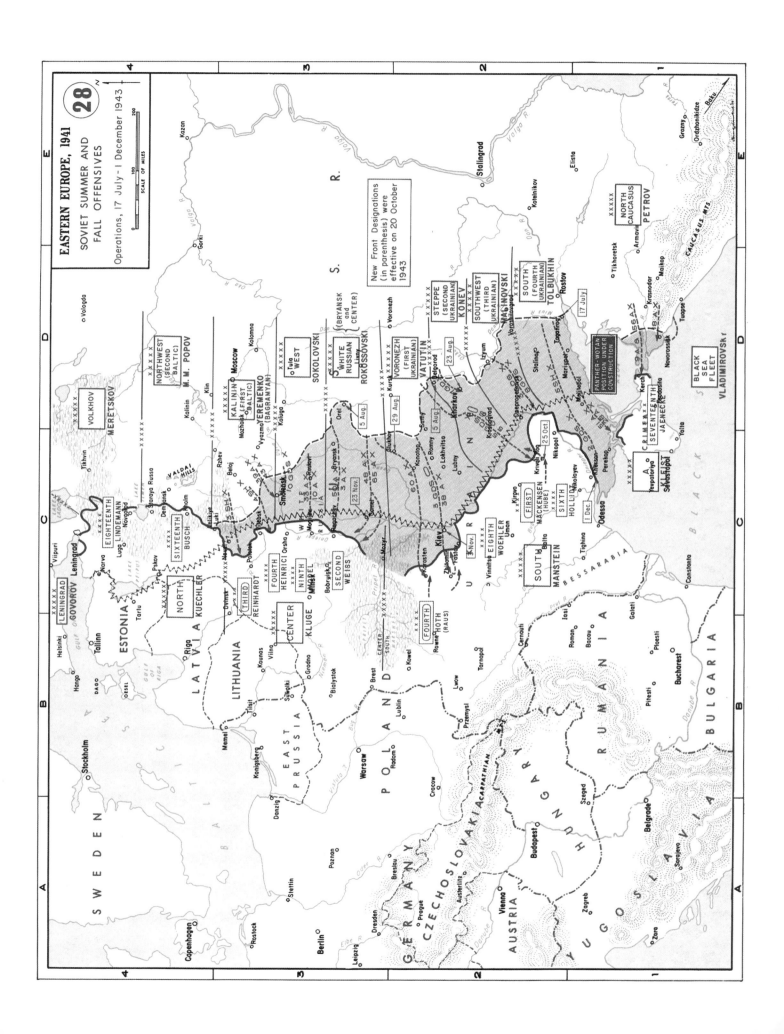

EASTERN EUROPE, 1941

28

SOVIET SUMMER AND FALL OFFENSIVES

Operations, 17 July–1 December 1943

SCALE OF MILES

New Front Designations
(in parenthesis) were
effective on 20 October
1943

PANTHER–WOTAN
POSITION UNDER
CONSTRUCTION

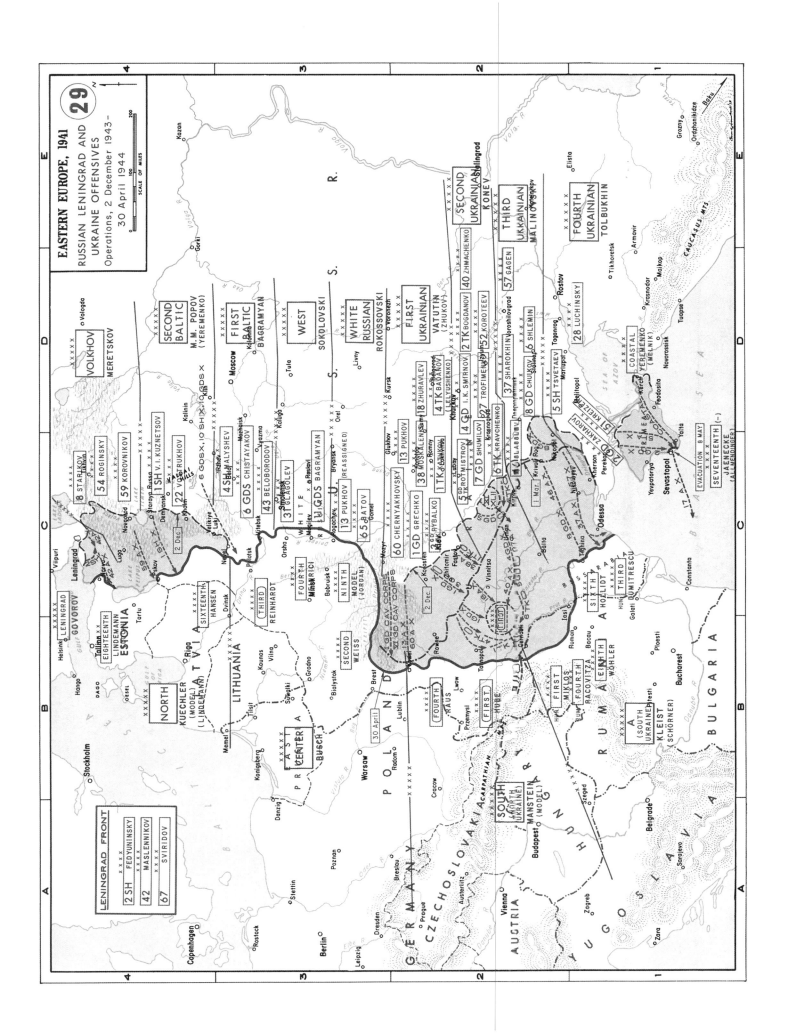

EASTERN EUROPE, 1941

29

RUSSIAN LENINGRAD AND
UKRAINE OFFENSIVES
Operations, 2 December 1943–
30 April 1944

SCALE OF MILES
0   100   200

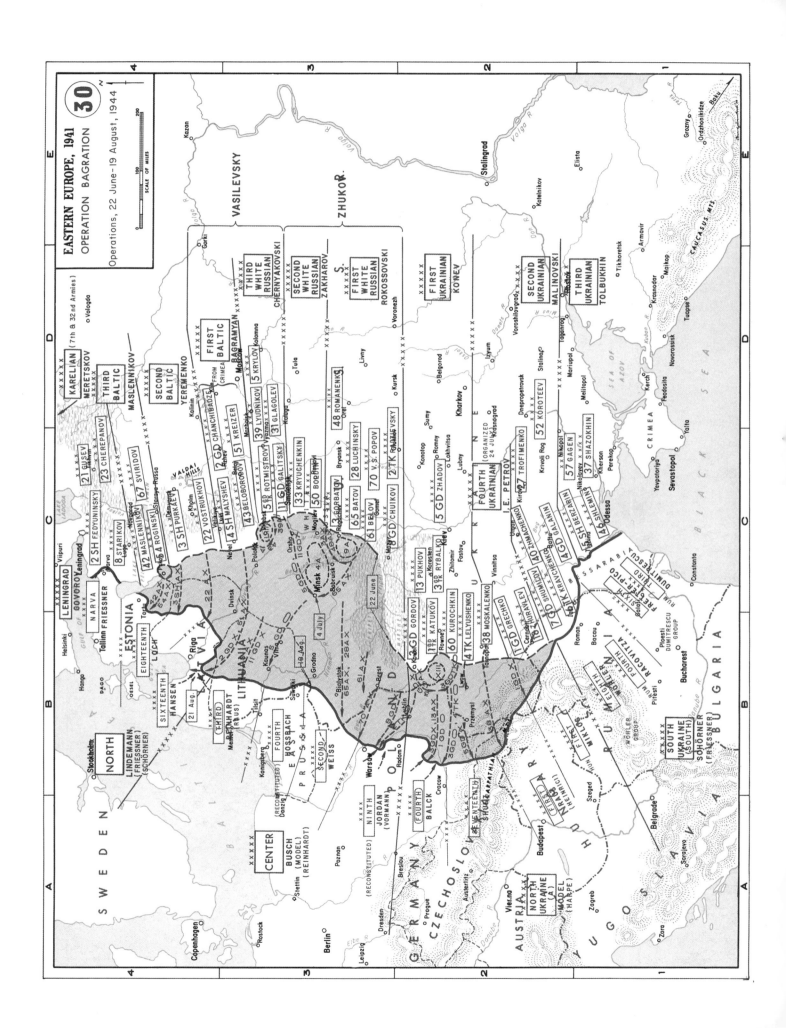

EASTERN EUROPE, 1941
30
OPERATION BAGRATION
Operations, 22 June–19 August, 1944

SCALE OF MILES

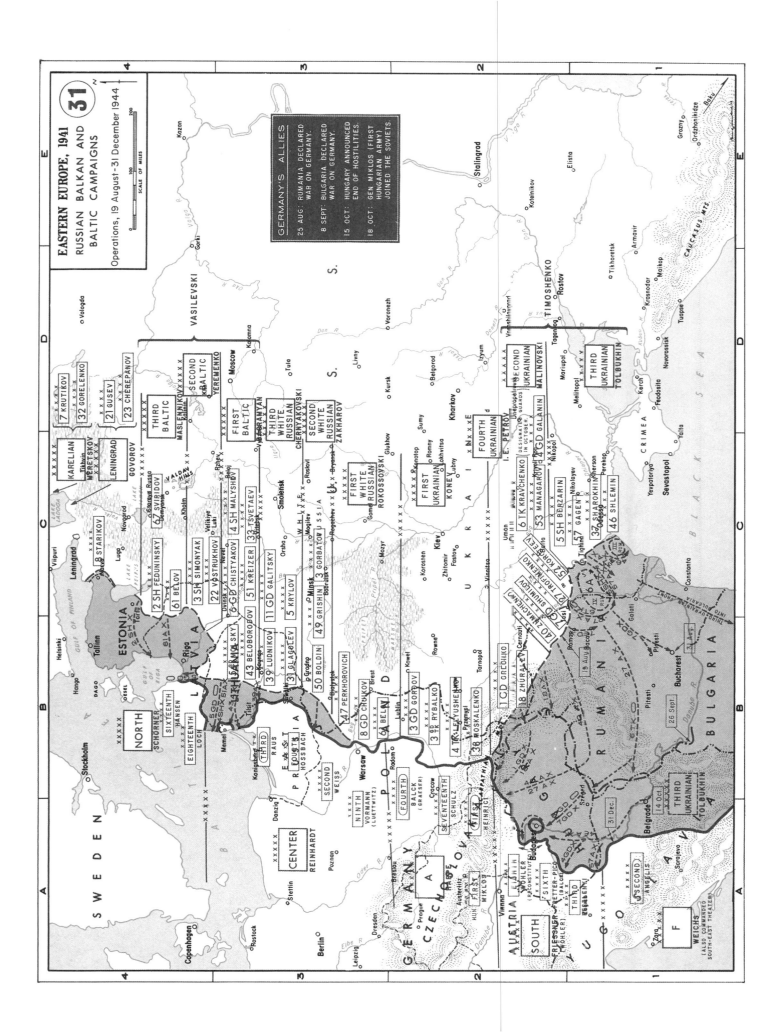

EASTERN EUROPE, 1941
RUSSIAN BALKAN AND
BALTIC CAMPAIGNS

31

Operations, 19 August–31 December 1944

SCALE OF MILES
0   100   200

GERMANY'S ALLIES

25 AUG: RUMANIA DECLARED
WAR ON GERMANY.

8 SEPT: BULGARIA DECLARED
WAR ON GERMANY.

15 OCT: HUNGARY ANNOUNCED
END OF HOSTILITIES.

18 OCT: GEN MIKLOS (FIRST
HUNGARIAN ARMY)
JOINED THE SOVIETS.

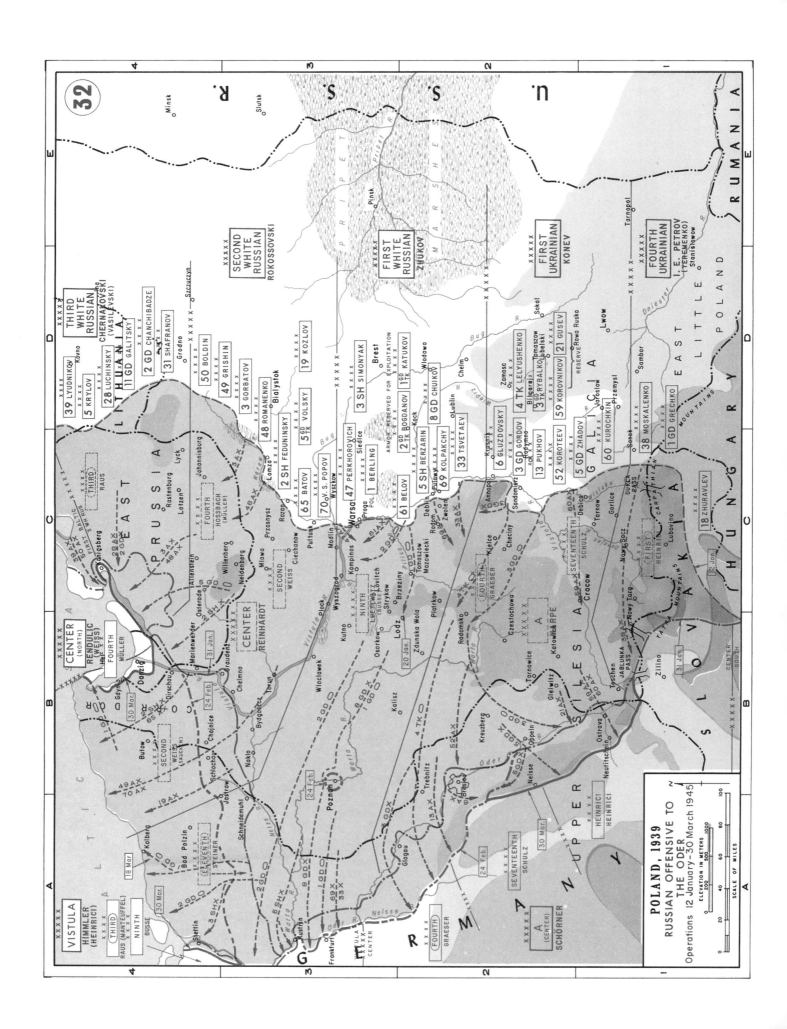

POLAND, 1939
RUSSIAN OFFENSIVE TO
THE ODER
Operations 12 January–30 March 1945

32

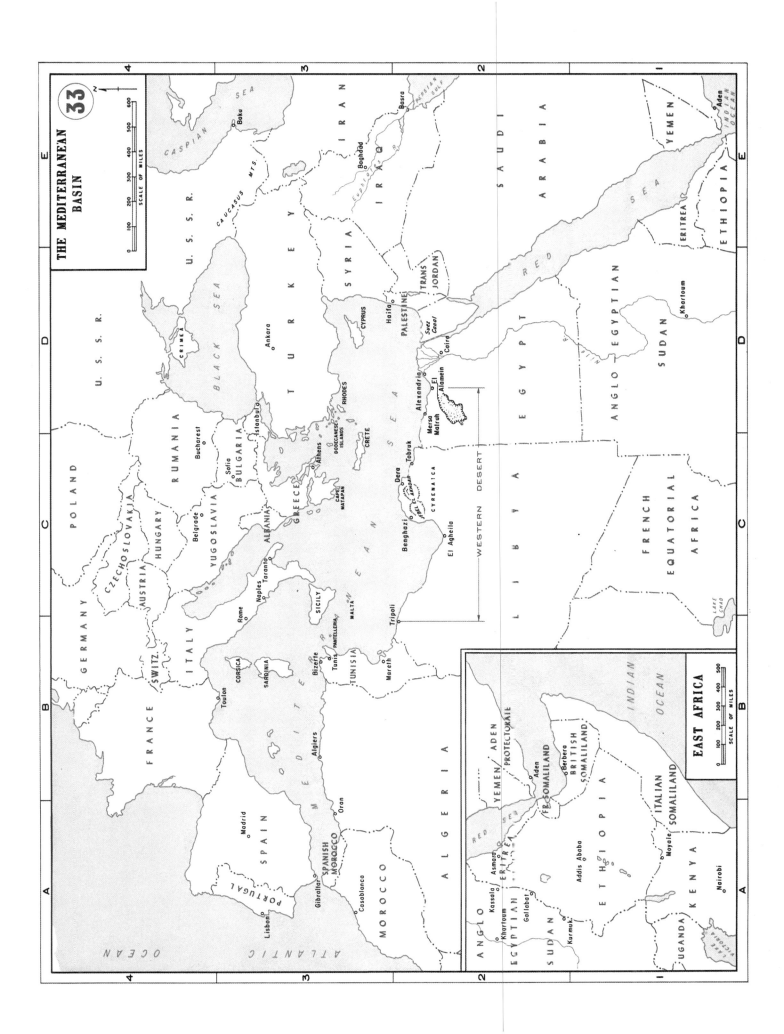

THE MEDITERRANEAN BASIN

33

SCALE OF MILES
0 100 200 300 400 500 600

EAST AFRICA

SCALE OF MILES
0 100 200 300 400 500

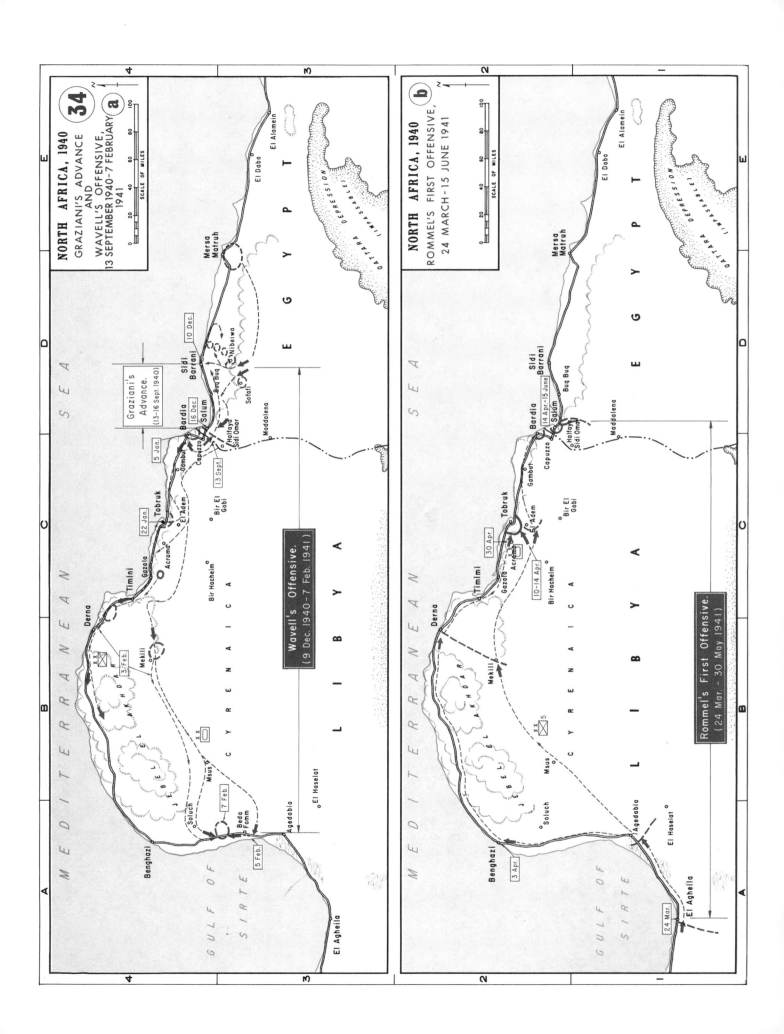

NORTH AFRICA, 1940
GRAZIANI'S ADVANCE
AND
WAVELL'S OFFENSIVE,
13 SEPTEMBER 1940–7 FEBRUARY 1941

34 a

SCALE OF MILES
0   20   40   60   80   100

MEDITERRANEAN   SEA

Derna
Timimi
Gazala
Tobruk
Acroma
El Adem
Bir El Gobi
Bir Hacheim
Benghazi
Soluch
Msus
Beda Fomm
Agedabia
El Haselat
El Agheila

GULF OF SIRTE

C Y R E N A I C A

L I B Y A

J E B E L   A K H D A R

Mekili
XX [ ] 3 Feb.
[ ] 7 Feb.
5 Feb.
22 Jan.
5 Jan.
13 Sept.
16 Dec.
10 Dec.

Bardia
Salum
Capuzzo
Sollum
Halfaya
Sidi Omar
Maddalena
Sidi Barrani
Nibeiwa
Buq Buq
Sofafi

Graziani's Advance.
(13–16 Sept. 1940)

Mersa Matruh
El Daba
El Alamein

E G Y P T

QATTARA DEPRESSION
(IMPASSABLE)

Wavell's Offensive.
(9 Dec. 1940 – 7 Feb. 1941)

NORTH AFRICA, 1940
ROMMEL'S FIRST OFFENSIVE,
24 MARCH–15 JUNE 1941

34 b

SCALE OF MILES
0   20   40   60   80   100

MEDITERRANEAN   SEA

Derna
Timimi
Gazala
Tobruk
Acroma
El Adem
Bir El Gobi
Bir Hacheim
Benghazi
Soluch
Msus
Agedabia
El Haselat
El Agheila

GULF OF SIRTE

C Y R E N A I C A

L I B Y A

J E B E L   A K H D A R

Mekili
XX 5
30 Apr.
10–14 Apr.
3 Apr.
24 Mar.

Bardia
Salum
Capuzzo
Halfaya
Sidi Omar
Maddalena
Sidi Barrani
Buq Buq
Gambut
14 Apr.–15 June
Bir El Gobi

Mersa Matruh
El Daba
El Alamein

E G Y P T

QATTARA DEPRESSION
(IMPASSABLE)

Rommel's First Offensive.
(24 Mar. – 30 May 1941)

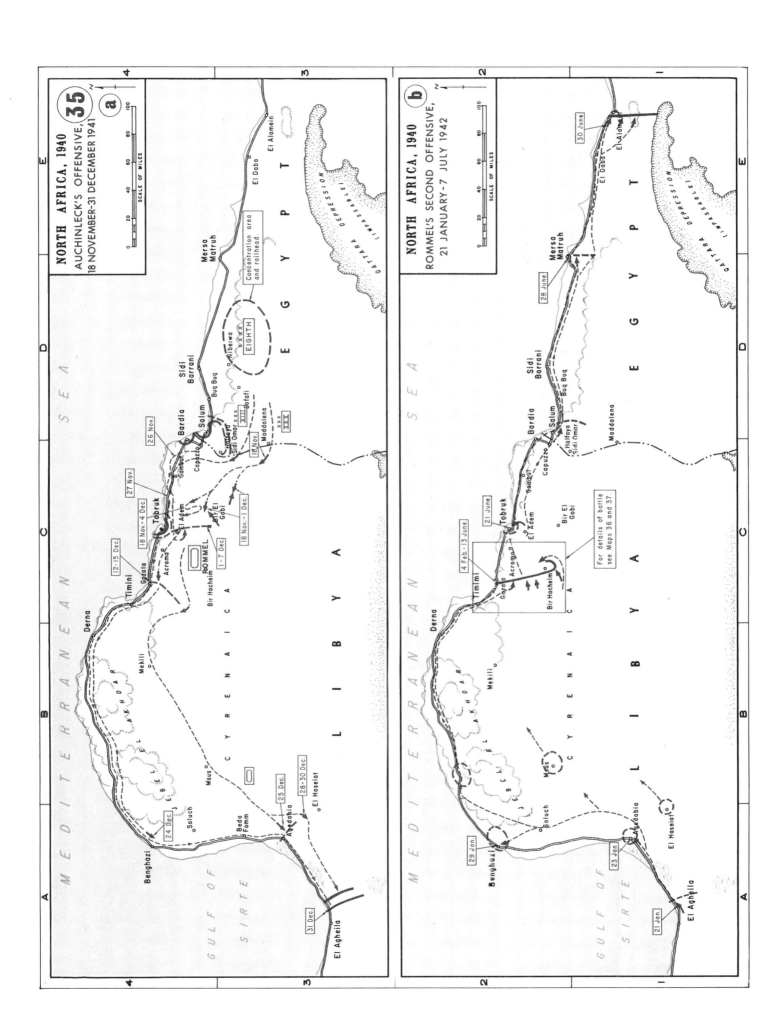

NORTH AFRICA, 1940

35

a

AUCHINLECK'S OFFENSIVE, 18 NOVEMBER-31 DECEMBER 1941

SCALE OF MILES

NORTH AFRICA, 1940

b

ROMMEL'S SECOND OFFENSIVE, 21 JANUARY-7 JULY 1942

SCALE OF MILES

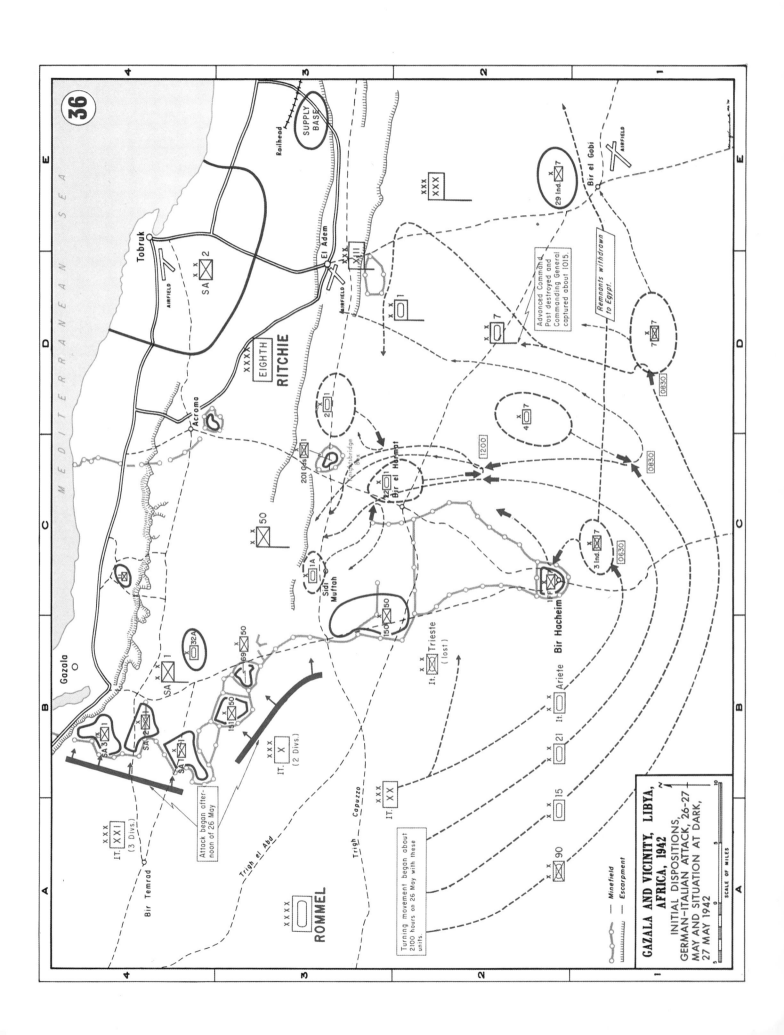

GAZALA AND VICINITY, LIBYA,
AFRICA, 1942

INITIAL DISPOSITIONS,
GERMAN-ITALIAN ATTACK, 26-27
MAY AND SITUATION AT DARK,
27 MAY 1942

— Minefield
— — Escarpment

SCALE OF MILES

36

MEDITERRANEAN SEA

Tobruk

SUPPLY BASE

Railhead

El Adem

AIRFIELD

Acroma

RITCHIE

EIGHTH

SA 2

AIRFIELD

29 Ind 7

Bir el Gobi

AIRFIELD

Remnants withdrawn
to Egypt.

Advanced Command
Post destroyed and
Commanding General
captured about 1015.

7

7

0830

7

4

1200

0830

201 Gds

Kingsbridge
Box

Bir el Harmat

50

1A

Sid
Muftah

3 Ind 7

0630

150 50

150 50

90 Lt

Bir Hacheim

It. Trieste
(lost)

It. Ariete

21

15

90

Gazala

32A

SA 1

169 50

151 50

SA3 1

SA2 1

SA1 1

Bir Temrad

IT. XXI
(3 Divs.)

Attack began after-
noon of 26 May

Trigh el Abd

Trigh Capuzzo

IT. X
(2 Divs.)

Turning movement began about
2100 hours on 26 May with these
units.

ROMMEL

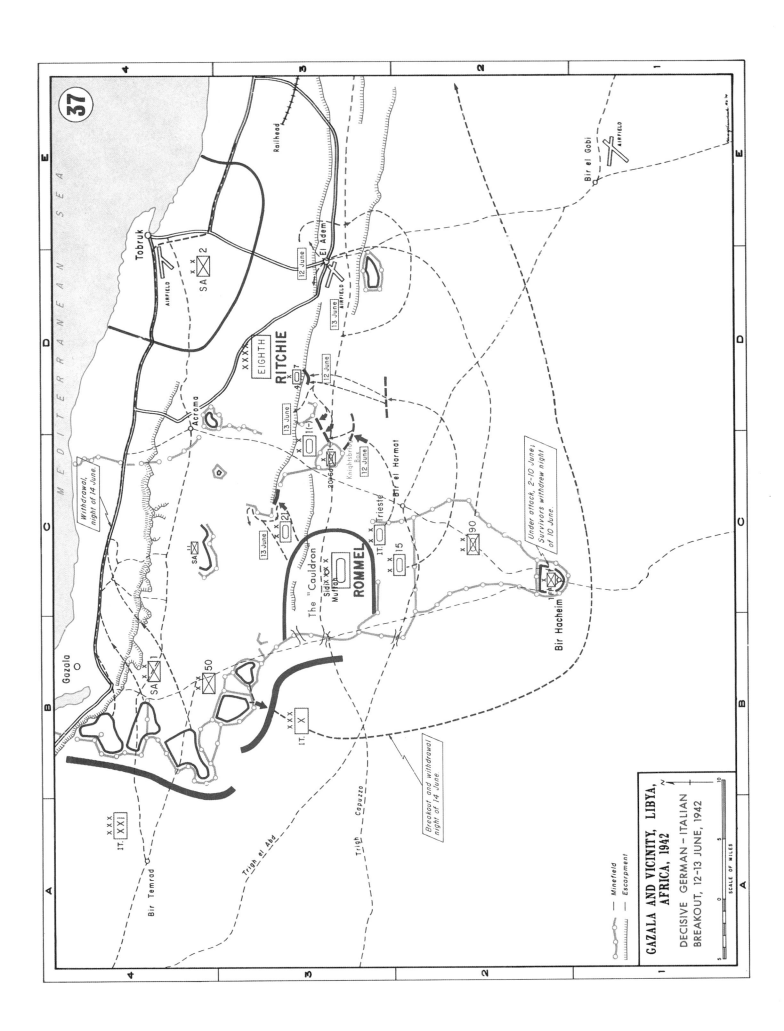

GAZALA AND VICINITY, LIBYA,
AFRICA, 1942

DECISIVE GERMAN – ITALIAN
BREAKOUT, 12–13 JUNE, 1942

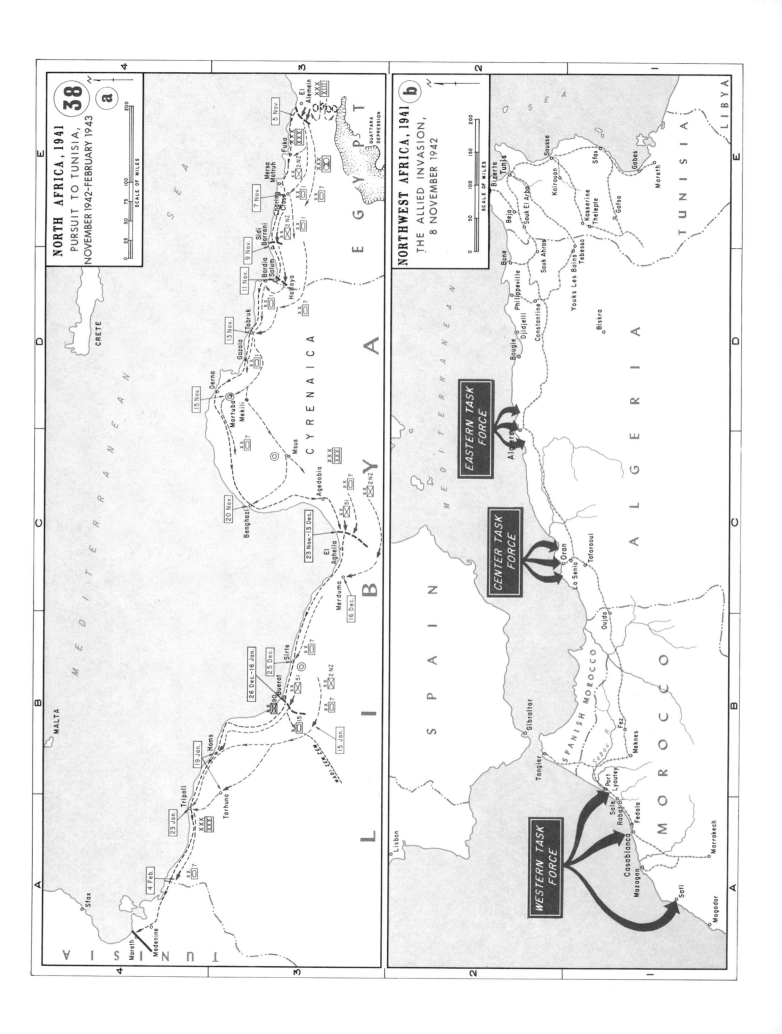

NORTH AFRICA, 1941

38 **a**

PURSUIT TO TUNISIA,
NOVEMBER 1942—FEBRUARY 1943

SCALE OF MILES
0   25   50   75   100   200

NORTHWEST AFRICA, 1941

38 **b**

THE ALLIED INVASION,
8 NOVEMBER 1942

SCALE OF MILES
0   50   100   150   200

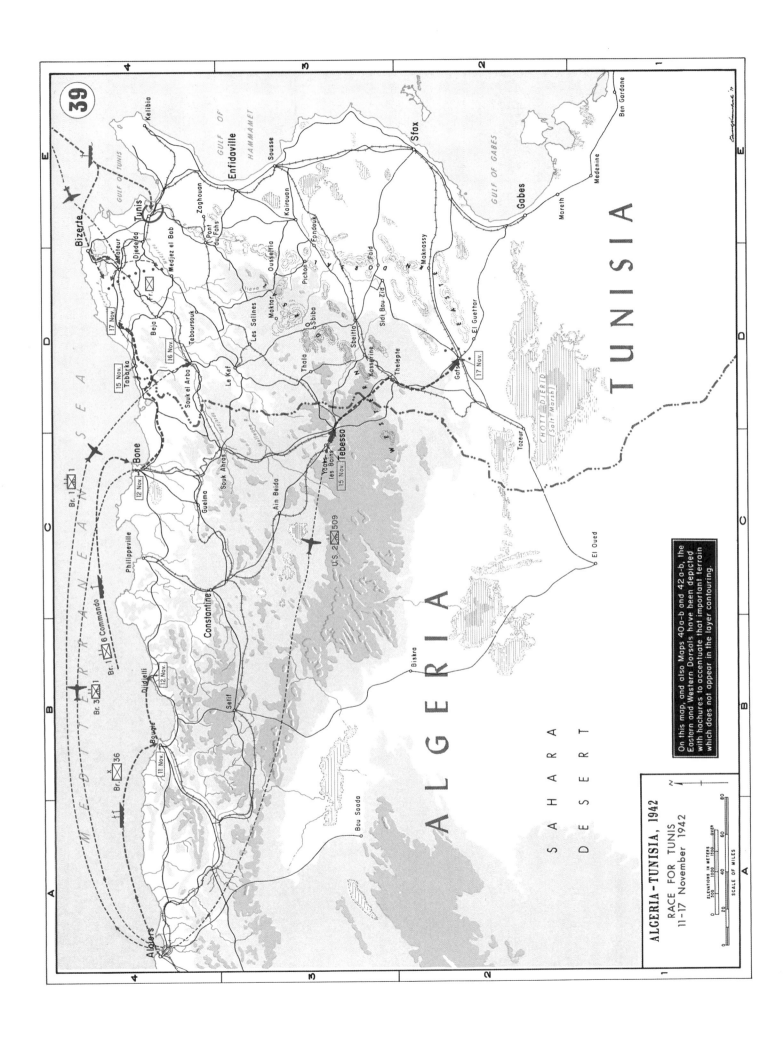

ALGERIA-TUNISIA, 1942

RACE FOR TUNIS
11-17 November 1942

On this map, and also Maps 40a-b and 42a-b, the
Eastern and Western Dorsals have been depicted
with hachures to accentuate that important terrain
which does not appear in the layer contouring.

ELEVATIONS IN METERS

SCALE OF MILES

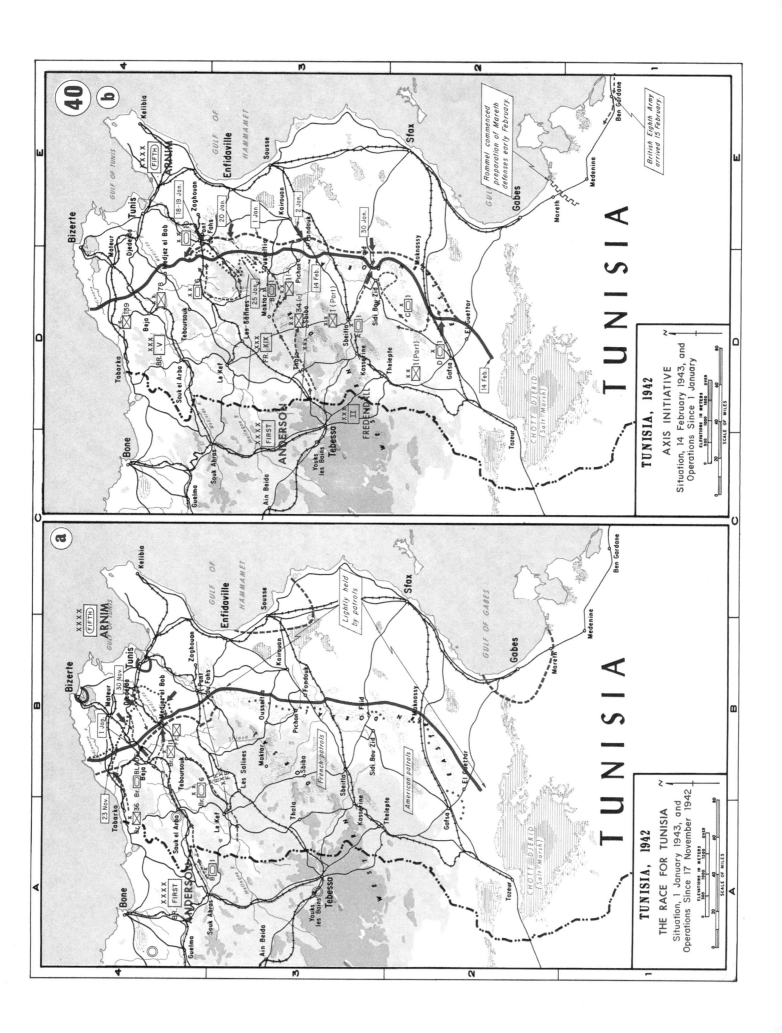

TUNISIA, 1942

THE RACE FOR TUNISIA

Situation, 1 January 1943, and
Operations Since 17 November 1942

French patrols

American patrols

Lightly held by patrols

TUNISIA, 1942

AXIS INITIATIVE

Situation, 14 February 1943, and
Operations Since 1 January

Rommel commenced preparation of Mareth defenses early February.

British Eighth Army arrived 15 February

TUNISIA

TUNISIA

40

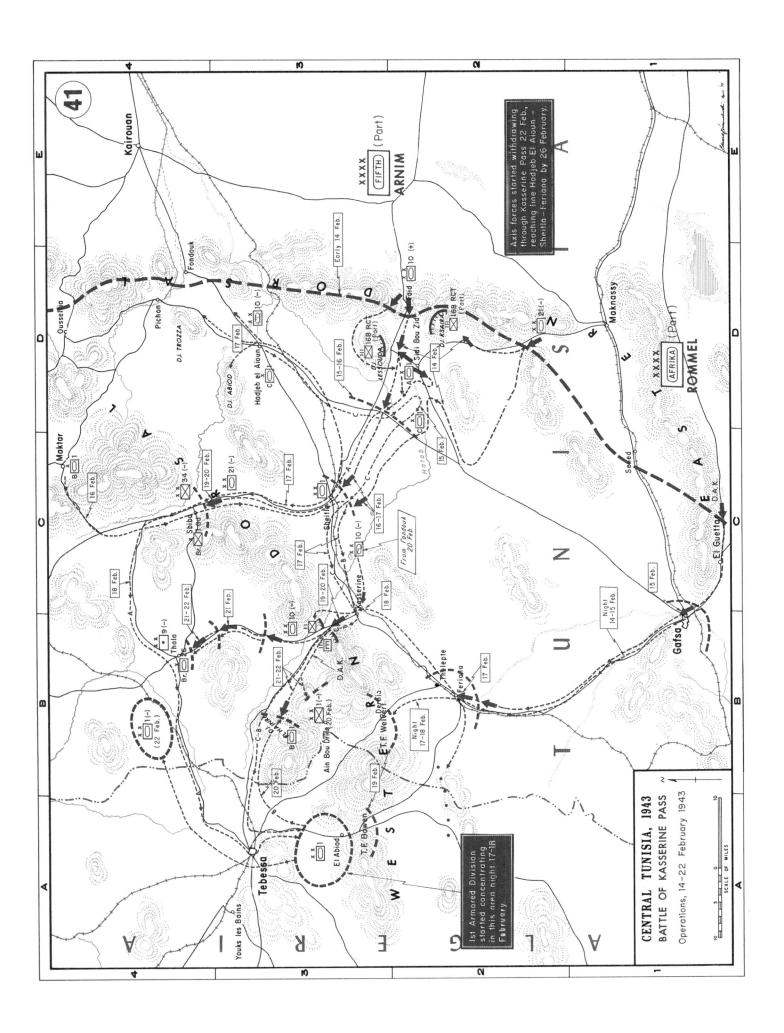

41

Axis forces started withdrawing through Kasserine Pass 22 Feb, reaching line Hadjeb El Aioun – Sbeitla –Feriana by 26 February

1st Armored Division started concentrating in this area night 17-18 February.

CENTRAL TUNISIA, 1943
BATTLE OF KASSERINE PASS

Operations, 14–22 February 1943

SCALE OF MILES

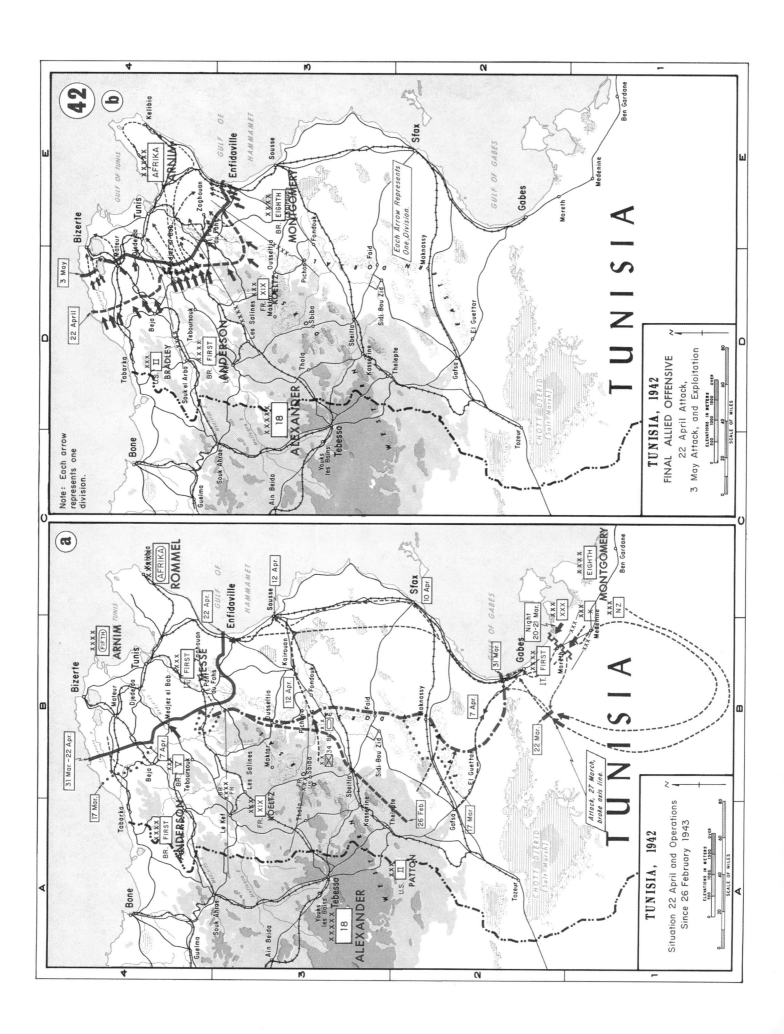

b

42

Note: Each arrow represents one division.

Bizerte

GULF OF TUNIS

Kelibia

X X X X X AFRIKA
ARNIM

3 May

22 April

Tunis

Mateur

Oued Zarga

Djebel Achour

Zaghouan

GULF OF HAMMAMET

Enfidaville

Sousse

Medjez el Bab

du Fahs

MONTGOMERY
BR. XXXX EIGHTH

Bone

Tabarka

Beja

Teboursouk

Souk el Arba

U.S. XXX II
BRADLEY

BR. XXXX FIRST
ANDERSON

Les Salines

Maktar

KOELTZ
FR. XXX XIX

Ousseltia

Pichon

Fondouk

Sfax

GULF OF GABES

Guelma

Souk Ahras

Ain Beida

Youks les Bains

Tebessa

XXXXX 18
ALEXANDER

Thala

Sbiba

Sbeitla

Kasserine

Feriana

Thelepte

Faid

Sidi Bou Zid

Each Arrow Represents
One Division.

Maknassy

El Guettar

Gafsa

Gabes

Mareth

Medenine

Ben Gardane

GULF OF GABES

CHOTT DJERID
(Salt Marsh)

Tozeur

TUNISIA

TUNISIA, 1942

FINAL ALLIED OFFENSIVE

22 April Attack,
3 May Attack, and Exploitation

ELEVATIONS IN METERS
SCALE OF MILES

N

---

a

Bizerte

GULF OF TUNIS

ARNIM
XXXX FIFTH

TUNIS

ROMMEL
X X X AFRIKA

Tunis

Mateur

Djedeida

Medjez el Bab

MESSE
XXXX FIRST

Zaghouan
du Fahs

GULF OF HAMMAMET

Enfidaville

22 Apr.

Sousse

12 Apr.

31 Mar.-22 Apr.

17 Mar.

Bone

Tabarka

Beja

Teboursouk

BR. XXX V

Le Kef

KOELTZ
FR. XXX XIX

Les Salines

Maktar

Thala

FR
XXX

Ousseltia

Pichon

12 Apr.

Fondouk

Kairouan

Sfax

10 Apr.

Guelma

Souk Ahras

Ain Beida

Youks les Bains

Tebessa

XXXXX 18
ALEXANDER

U.S. XXX II
PATTON

Sbiba

Sbeitla

34 Bo

Kasserine

26 Feb.

Thelepte

Feriana

Gafsa

17 Mar.

Sidi Bou Zid

Faid

7 Apr.

Maknassy

El Guettar

7 Apr.

22 Mar.

31 Mar.

Gabes

IT. FIRST
XXXX

Mareth

Night
20-21 Mar.

Medenine

XXX
XXX

XXX
NZ

MONTGOMERY
XXXX EIGHTH

Ben Gardane

Attack, 27 March,
broke axis line.

CHOTT DJERID
(Salt Marsh)

Tozeur

TUNISIA

TUNISIA, 1942

Situation 22 April and Operations
Since 26 February 1943

ELEVATIONS IN METERS
SCALE OF MILES

N

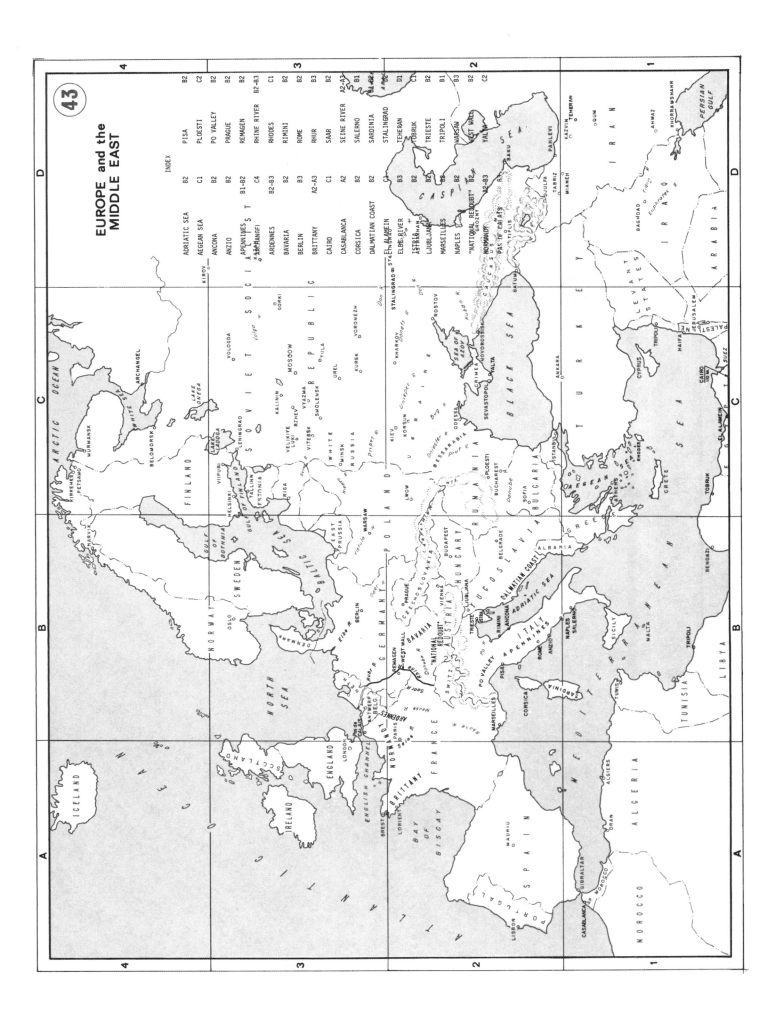

EUROPE and the MIDDLE EAST

43

INDEX

ADRIATIC SEA	B2	PISA	B2
AEGEAN SEA	C1	PLOESTI	C1
ANCONA	B2	PO VALLEY	B2
ANZIO	B2	PRAGUE	B2
APENNINES	B1-B2	REMAGEN	B2-B3
ARKHANGEL	C4	RHINE RIVER	C1
ARDENNES	B2-B3	RHODES	C1
BAVARIA	B2	RIMINI	B2
BERLIN	B3	ROME	B3
BRITTANY	A2-A3	RHUR	B2
CAIRO	C1	SAAR	B2
CASABLANCA	A2	SEINE RIVER	A2-A3
CORSICA	B2	SALERNO	B1
DALMATIAN COAST	B2	SARDINIA	B1-B2
EL ALAMEIN	C1	STALINGRAD	A2-A3
ELBE RIVER	B3	TEHERAN	D1
ASTRAKHAN	B2	TOBRUK	B2
LJUBLJANA	B2	TRIESTE	B1
MARSEILLES	B2	TRIPOLI	B3
NAPLES	B2	WARSAW	B2
"NATIONAL REDOUBT"	A2-M	WEST WALL	C2
NORMANDY	A2-M	YALTA	

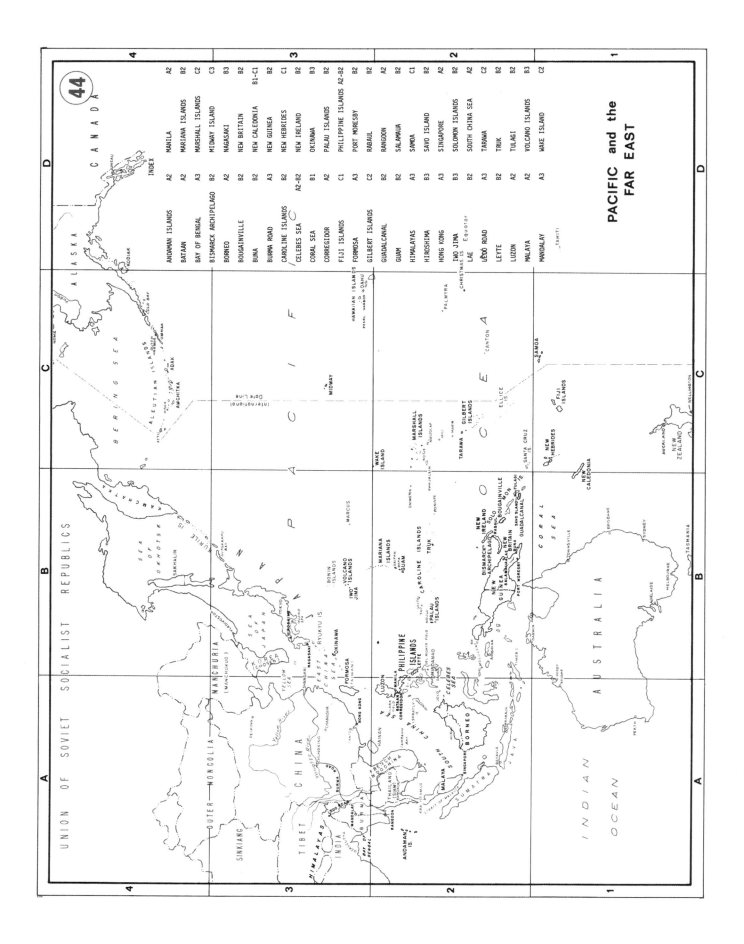

PACIFIC and the FAR EAST

44

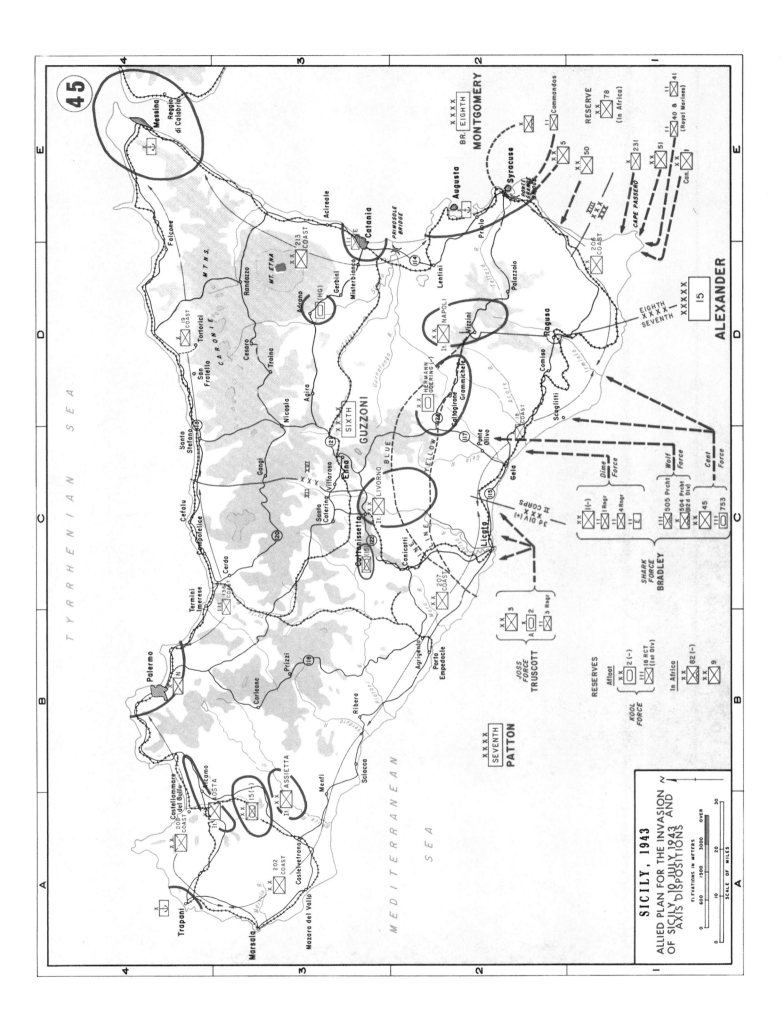

SICILY, 1943

ALLIED PLAN FOR THE INVASION
OF SICILY, 10 JULY 1943 AND
AXIS DISPOSITIONS

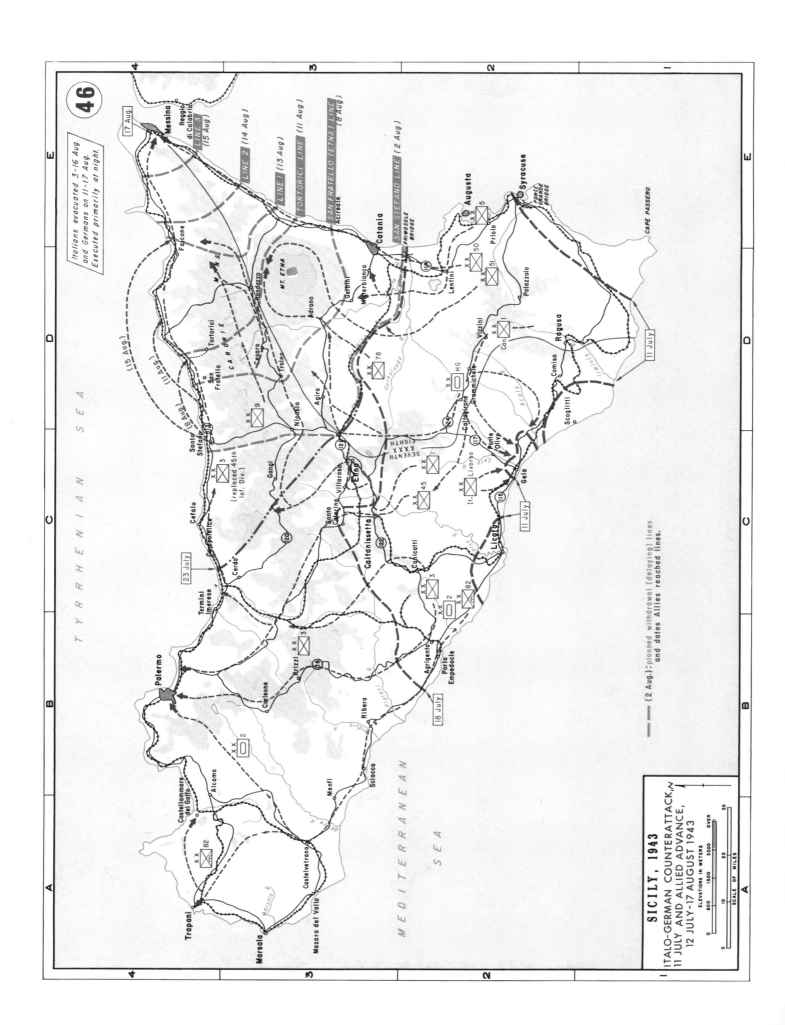

SICILY, 1943

ITALO-GERMAN COUNTERATTACK,
11 JULY AND ALLIED ADVANCE,
12 JULY–17 AUGUST 1943

46

Italians evacuated 3–16 Aug.
and Germans on 11–17 Aug.
Executed primarily at night.

(2 Aug.)–planned withdrawal (delaying) lines
and dates Allies reached lines.

LINE 3 (15 Aug.)
LINE 2 (14 Aug.)
LINE 1 (13 Aug.)
TORTORICI LINE (11 Aug.)
SAN FRATELLO (ETNA) LINE (8 Aug.)
SAN STEFANO LINE (2 Aug.)

TYRRHENIAN SEA

MEDITERRANEAN SEA

ELEVATIONS IN METERS
600   1500   3000   OVER
SCALE OF MILES
0   10   20   30

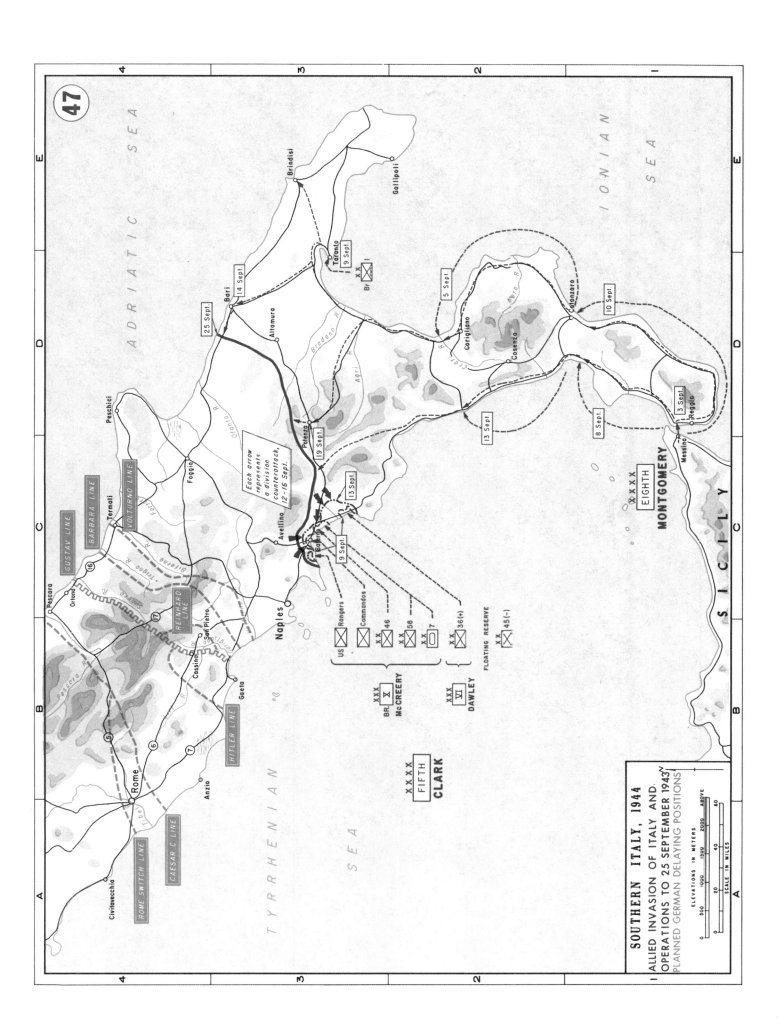

SOUTHERN ITALY, 1944

ALLIED INVASION OF ITALY AND OPERATIONS TO 25 SEPTEMBER 1943 (PLANNED GERMAN DELAYING POSITIONS)

ELEVATIONS IN METERS

SCALE IN MILES

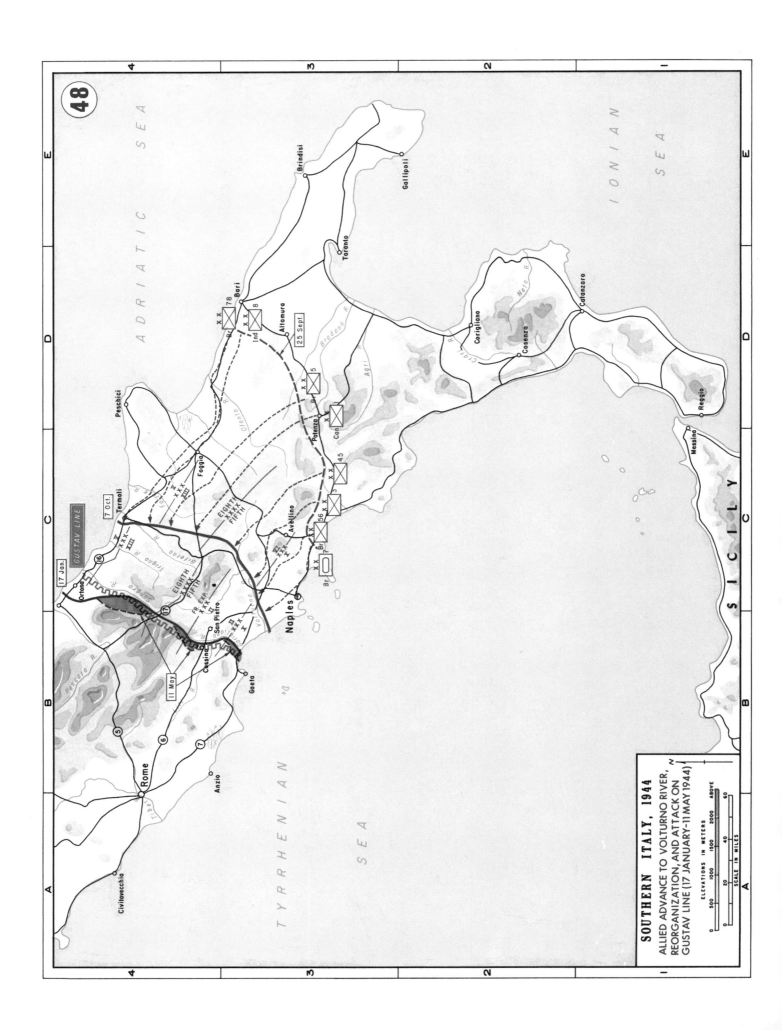

SOUTHERN ITALY, 1944

ALLIED ADVANCE TO VOLTURNO RIVER,
REORGANIZATION, AND ATTACK ON
GUSTAV LINE (17 JANUARY–11 MAY 1944)

ELEVATIONS IN METERS

500	1000	1500	2000	ABOVE
0	20	40	60	

SCALE IN MILES

48

GUSTAV LINE

7 Oct.

17 Jan.

11 May

25 Sept.

ADRIATIC SEA

TYRRHENIAN SEA

IONIAN SEA

SICILY

Rome
Civitavecchia
Anzio
Gaeta
Cassino
San Pietro
Naples
Avellino
Foggia
Termoli
Peschici
Ortona
Potenza
Altamura
Bari
Brindisi
Taranto
Gallipoli
Corigliano
Cosenza
Catanzaro
Reggio
Messina

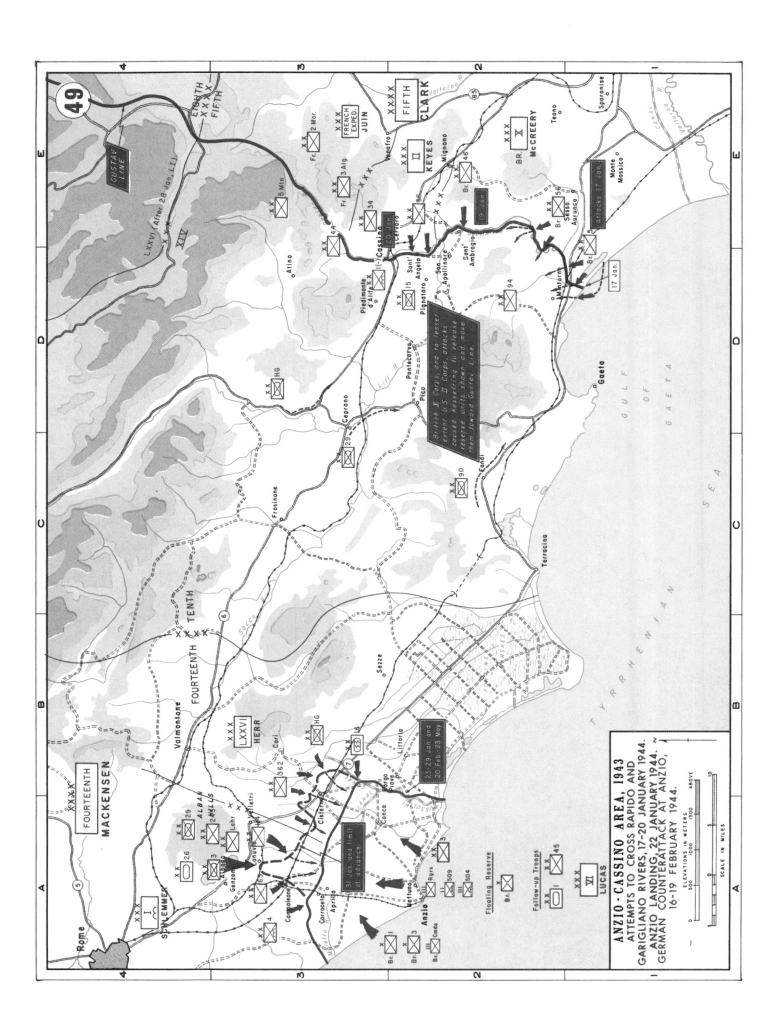

ANZIO-CASSINO AREA, 1943

ATTEMPTS TO CROSS RAPIDO AND
GARIGLIANO RIVERS, 17-20 JANUARY 1944.
ANZIO LANDING, 22 JANUARY 1944.
GERMAN COUNTERATTACK AT ANZIO,
16-19 FEBRUARY 1944.

49

GUSTAV LINE

FOURTEENTH
MACKENSEN

TENTH

FOURTEENTH

EIGHTH
FIFTH

Rome

Frosinone

Terracina

TYRRHENIAN SEA

GULF OF GAETA

Gaeta

ELEVATIONS IN METERS

500   1000   1500   ABOVE

SCALE IN MILES

British X Corps, and to lesser
extent U.S. II Corps, attacks
caused Kesselring to release
reserve units shown and move
them toward Gustav Line

FIFTH
CLARK

FRENCH EXPED.
JUIN

II
KEYES

Br. X
McCREERY

Attacks 17 Jan.

17 Jan.

19 Jan.

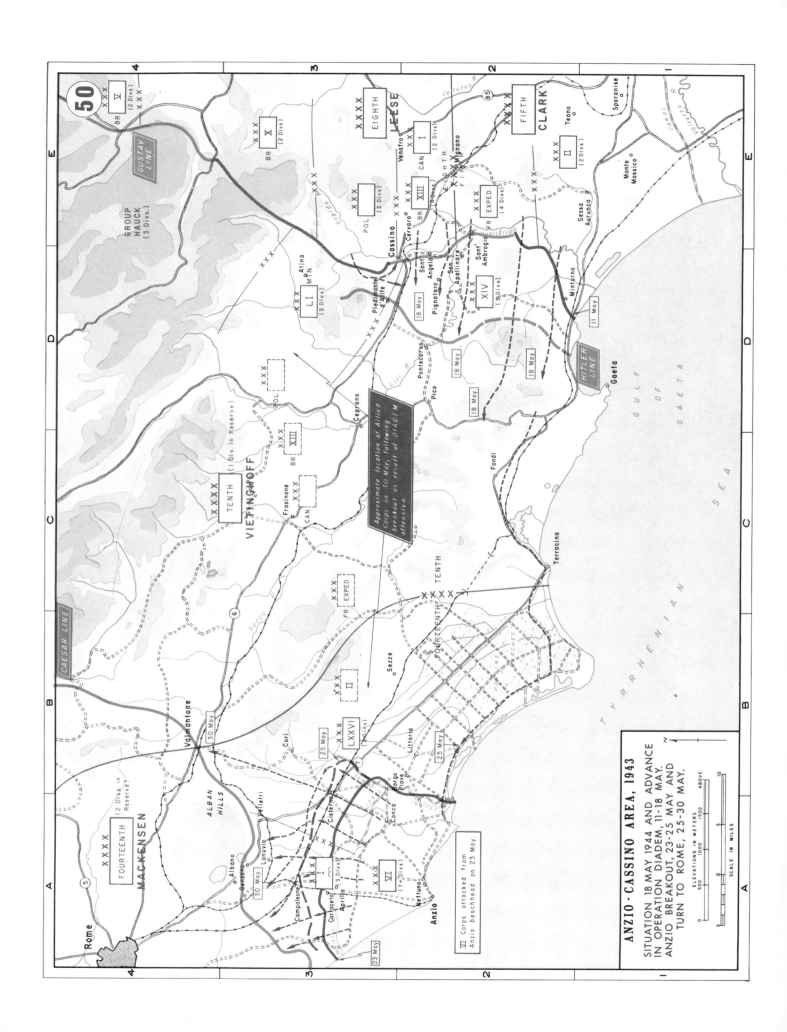

ANZIO - CASSINO AREA, 1943

SITUATION 18 MAY 1944 AND ADVANCE
IN OPERATION DIADEM, 11-18 MAY.
ANZIO BREAKOUT, 23-25 MAY AND
TURN TO ROME, 25-30 MAY.

ELEVATIONS IN METERS

| 500 | 1000 | 1500 | ABOVE |

SCALE IN MILES

VI Corps attacked from
Anzio beachhead on 23 May.

Approximate location of Allied
Corps on 30 May, following
breakout as result of DIADEM
offensive.

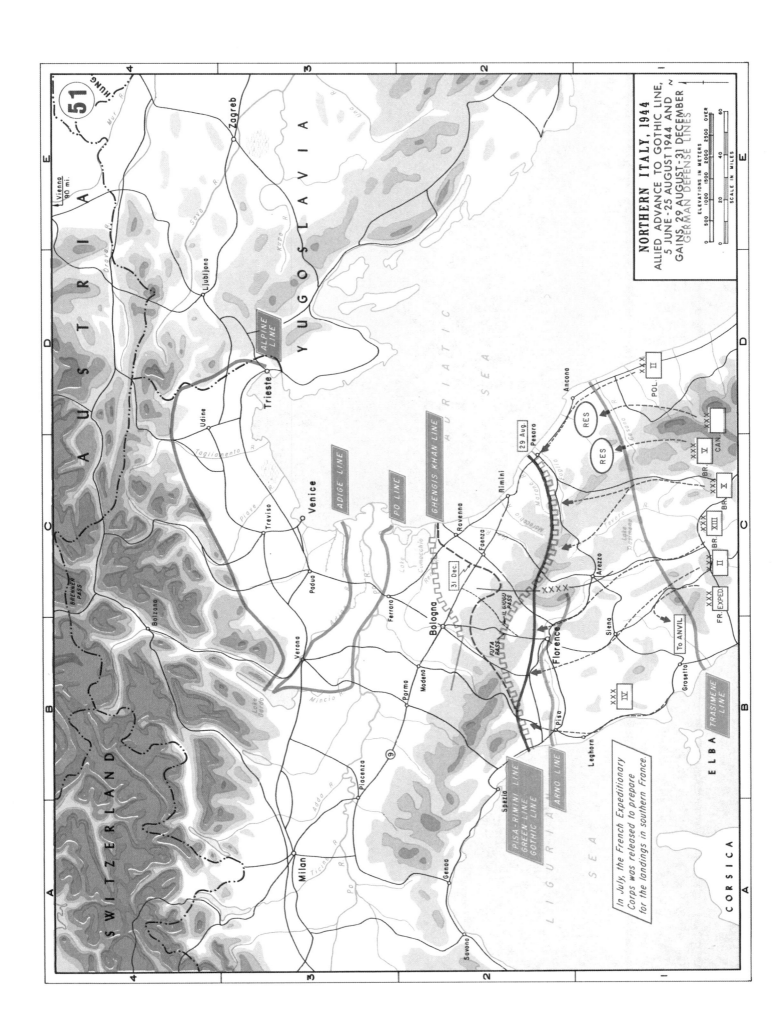

NORTHERN ITALY, 1944
ALLIED ADVANCE TO GOTHIC LINE,
5 JUNE - 25 AUGUST 1944 AND
GAINS, 29 AUGUST-31 DECEMBER
GERMAN DEFENSE LINES

ELEVATIONS IN METERS
500 1000 1500 2000 2500 OVER

SCALE IN MILES

In July, the French Expeditionary
Corps was released to prepare
for the landings in southern France.

ALPINE LINE

ADIGE LINE

PO LINE

GHENGIS KHAN LINE

PISA-RIMINI LINE
GREEN LINE
GOTHIC LINE

LIGURIAN ARNO LINE

TRASIMENE LINE

SWITZERLAND

AUSTRIA

Vienna 90 mi.

YUGOSLAVIA

Zagreb

Ljubljana

Trieste

Udine

Venice

Treviso

Padua

Verona

Brenner Pass

Bolzano

Milan

Piacenza

Parma

Modena

Bologna

Ferrara

Ravenna

Faenza

Rimini

Pesaro

29 Aug.

Ancona

31 Dec.

FUTA PASS

IL GIOGO PASS

Florence

Arezzo

Siena

Pisa

Leghorn

Spezia

Genoa

Savona

Grosseto

To ANVIL

ADRIATIC SEA

LIGURIAN SEA

CORSICA

ELBA

RES

RES

XXX POL. II

XXXX

XXX BR. V CAN.

XXX BR. X

XXX BR. XIII

XXX II

XXX FR. EXPED

XXX IV

51

HUNG.

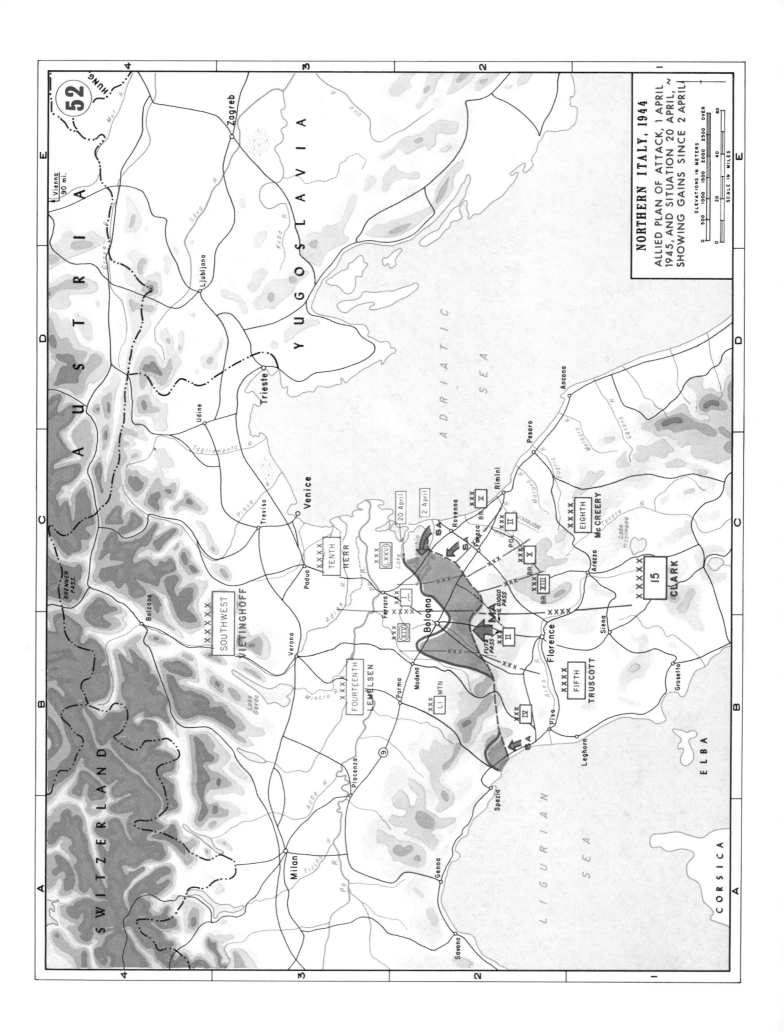

NORTHERN ITALY, 1944

ALLIED PLAN OF ATTACK, 1 APRIL 1945, AND SITUATION 20 APRIL, SHOWING GAINS SINCE 2 APRIL

ELEVATIONS IN METERS

0   500 1000 1500 2000 2500 OVER

SCALE IN MILES

0   20   40   60

52

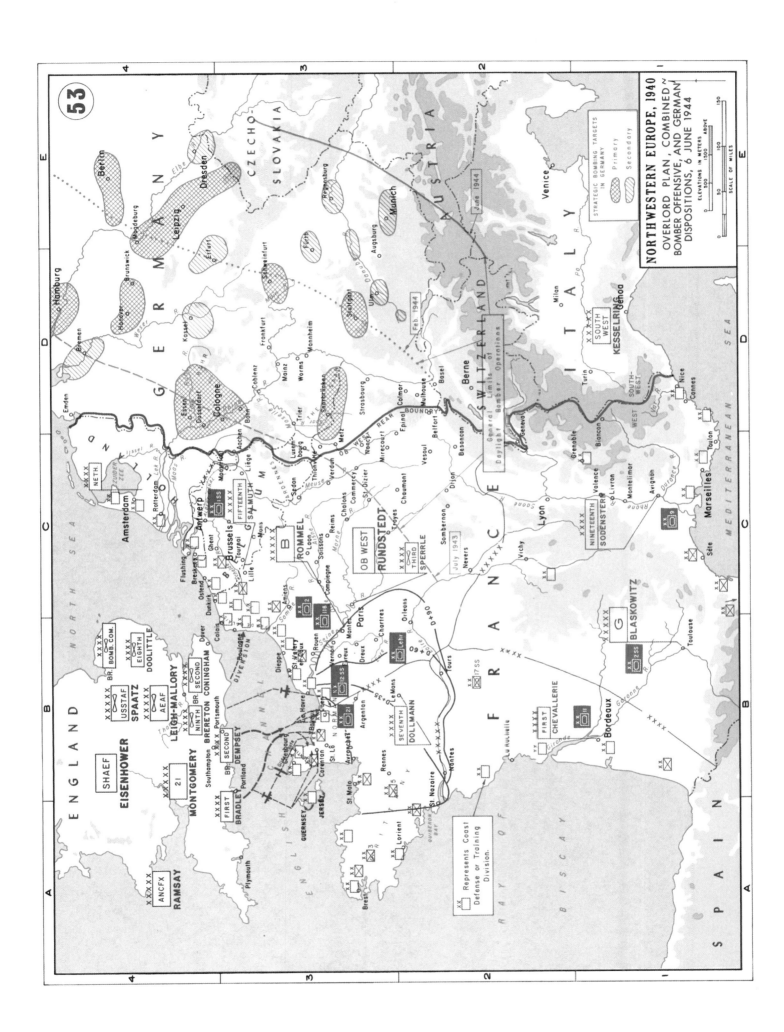

NORTHWESTERN EUROPE, 1940
OVERLORD PLAN, COMBINED
BOMBER OFFENSIVE, AND GERMAN
DISPOSITIONS, 6 JUNE 1944

STRATEGIC BOMBING TARGETS
IN GERMANY
Primary
Secondary

ELEVATIONS IN METERS
0   500   1500   ABOVE
         100   150
SCALE OF MILES

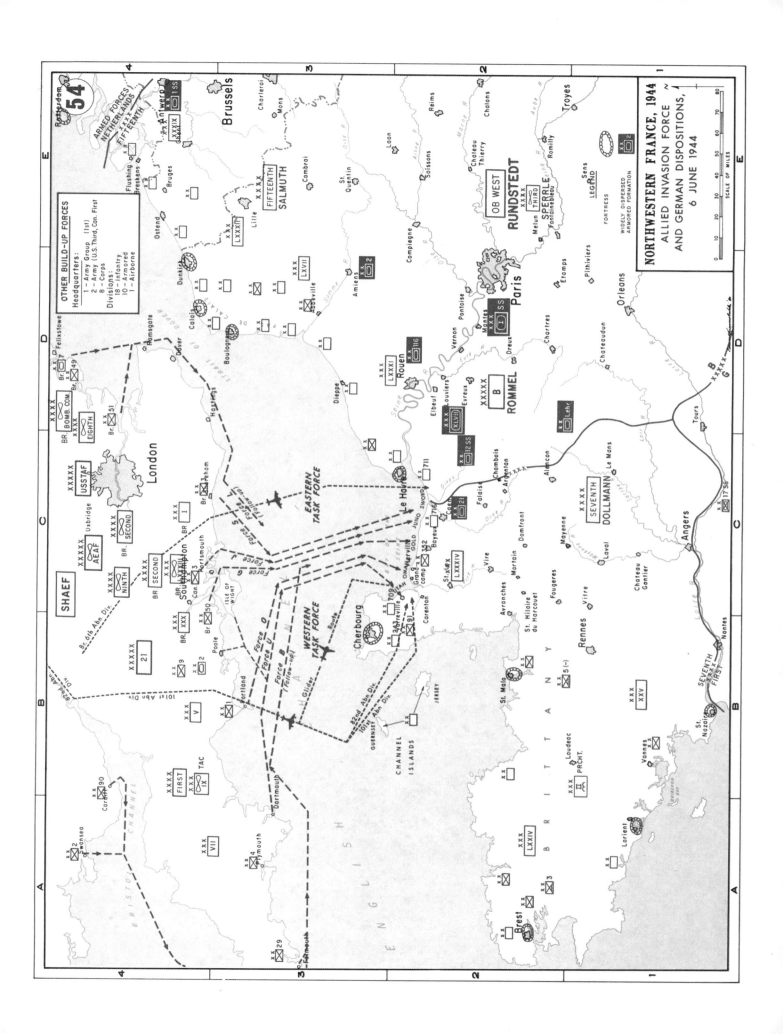

NORTHWESTERN FRANCE, 1944
ALLIED INVASION FORCE
AND GERMAN DISPOSITIONS,
6 JUNE 1944

SCALE OF MILES

LEGEND

FORTRESS

WIDELY DISPERSED
ARMORED FORMATION

OTHER BUILD-UP FORCES

Headquarters:
1 — Army Group (1st)
2 — Army (U.S.Third, Can. First)
8 — Corps
Divisions:
18 — Infantry
10 — Armored
1 — Airborne

54

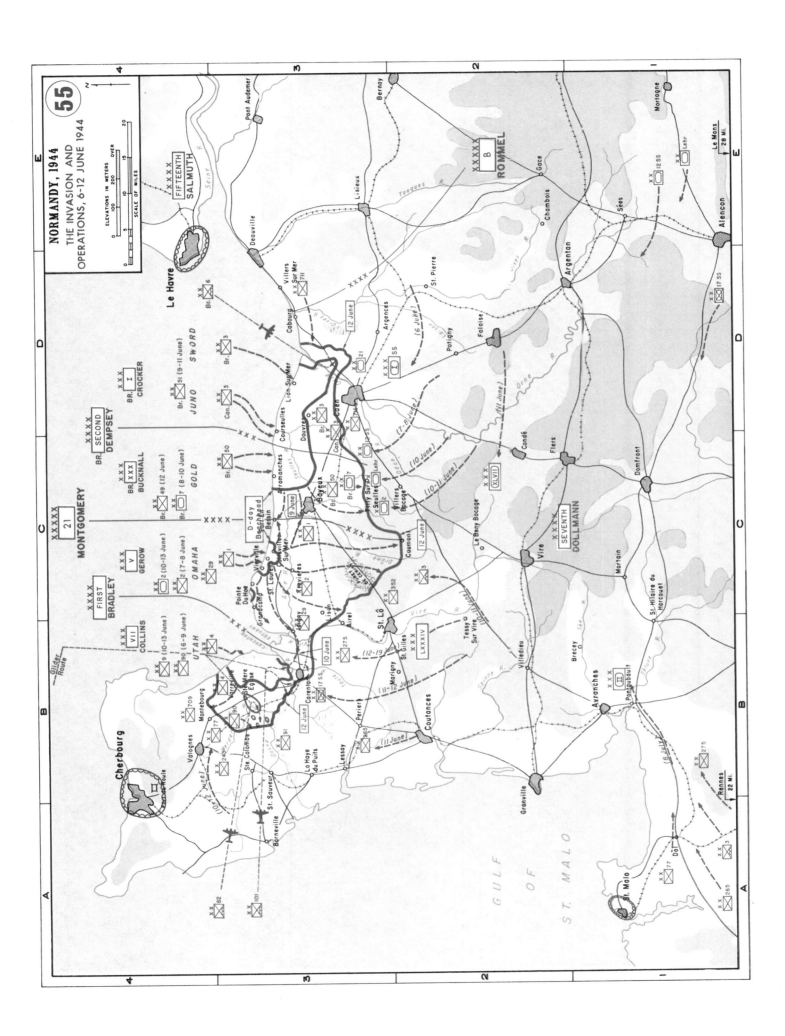

NORMANDY, 1944
THE INVASION AND
OPERATIONS, 6-12 JUNE 1944

55

ELEVATIONS IN METERS
SCALE OF MILES

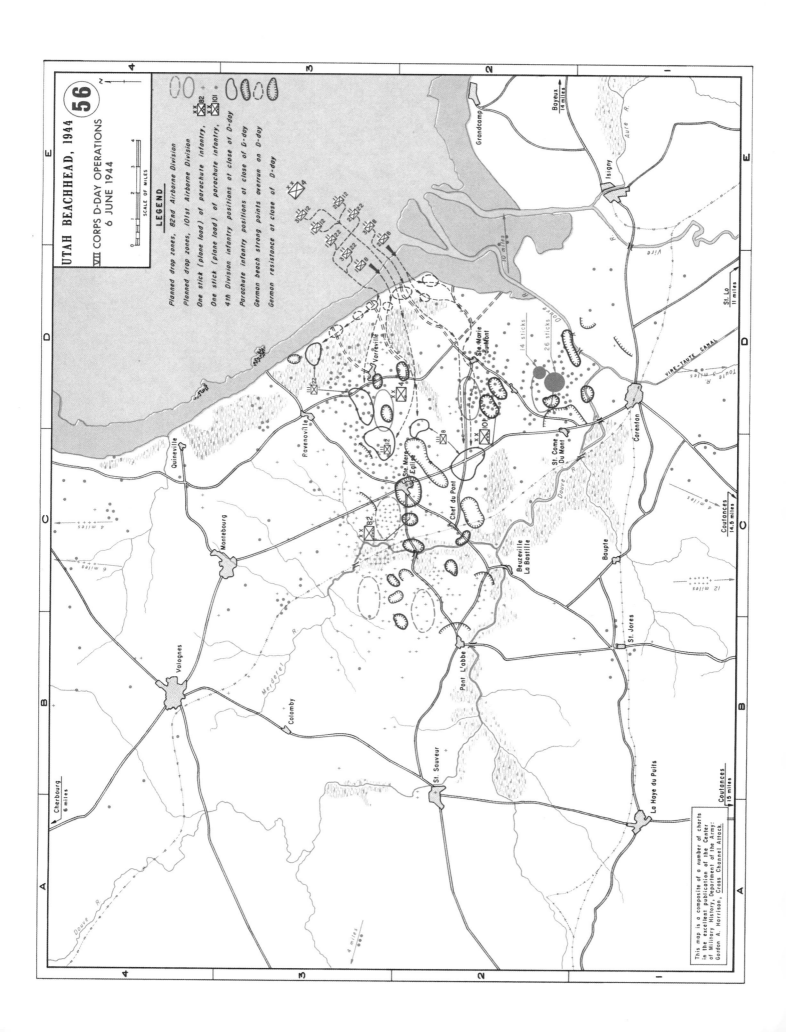

UTAH BEACHHEAD, 1944

56

VII CORPS D-DAY OPERATIONS
6 JUNE 1944

LEGEND

Planned drop zones, 82nd Airborne Division

Planned drop zones, 101st Airborne Division

One stick (plane load) of parachute infantry,

One stick (plane load) of parachute infantry,

4th Division infantry positions at close of D-day

Parachute infantry positions at close of D-day

German beach strong points overrun on D-day

German resistance at close of D-day

SCALE OF MILES

0   1   2   3   4

This map is a composite of a number of charts in the excellent publication of the Center of Military History, Department of the Army: Gordon A. Harrison, *Cross Channel Attack.*

Cherbourg 6 miles

Valognes

Montebourg

Quineville

Colomby

St. Sauveur

Pont L'abbe

La Haye du Puits

Coutances 15 miles

St. Jores

Boupte

Beuzeville La Bastille

Coutances 14.5 miles

Ravenoville

Varenoville

Ste. Mere Eglise

Chef du Pont

St. Come Du Mont

Corentan

Ste. Marie DuMont

14 sticks

26 sticks

VIRE-TAUTE CANAL

Taute R.

Douve R.

Merderet R.

Douve R.

Vire R.

Aure R.

Grandcamp

Boyeux 14 miles

Isigny

St. Lo 11 miles

St. Lo 11 miles

Coutances 4 miles

4 miles

6 miles

4 miles

12 miles

10 miles

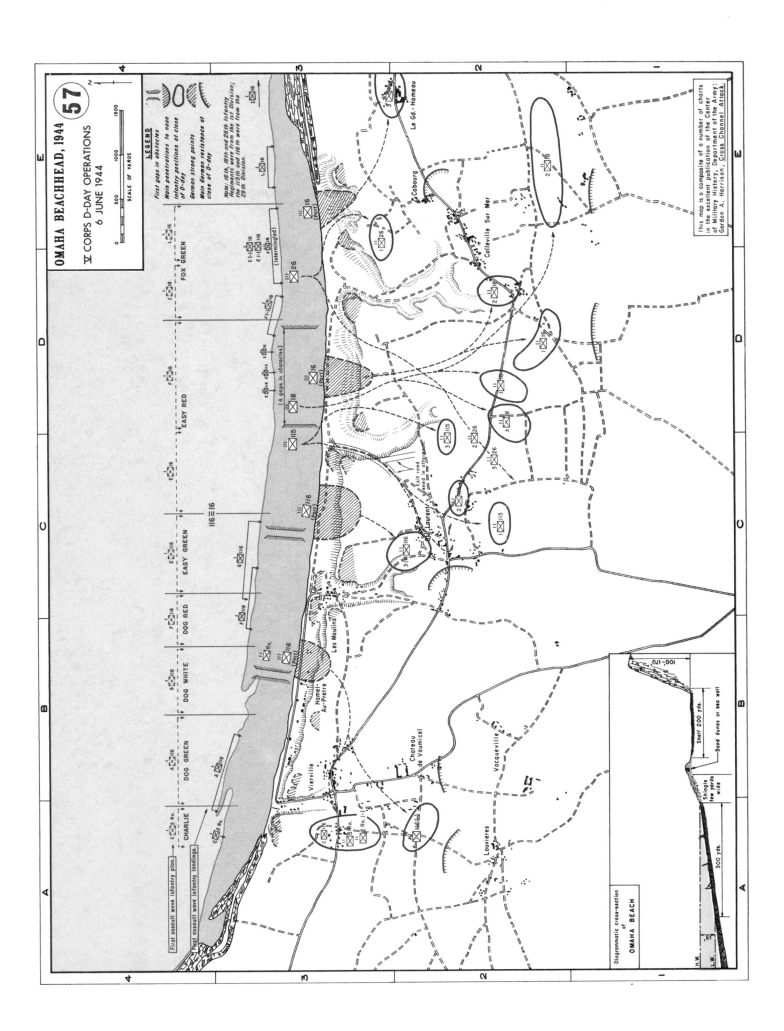

OMAHA BEACHHEAD, 1944

V CORPS D-DAY OPERATIONS
6 JUNE 1944

57

N

LEGEND

First gaps in obstacles

Main penetrations to noon of D-day

Infantry positions at close of D-day

German strong points

Main German resistance at close of D-day

Note: 16th, 18th and 26th Infantry Regiments were from the 1st Division; the 115th and 116th were from the 29th Division.

SCALE OF YARDS

0   500   1000   1500

This map is a composite of a number of charts in the excellent publication of the Center of Military History, Department of the Army: Gordon A. Harrison, Cross Channel Attack.

Diagrammatic cross-section of OMAHA BEACH

H.W.
L.W.

300 yds.

Shingle few yards wide

Sand dunes or sea wall

Shelf 200 yds.

100-170

First assault wave infantry landings.

First assault wave infantry plan.

CHARLIE   DOG GREEN   DOG WHITE   DOG RED   EASY GREEN   EASY RED   FOX GREEN

Vierville   Hamel-Au-Pretre   Les Moulins   St Laurent   Colleville Sur Mer   Cabourg   Le Gd.-Hameau

Chateau de Vaumicel   Vacqueville   Louvieres   Louvieres

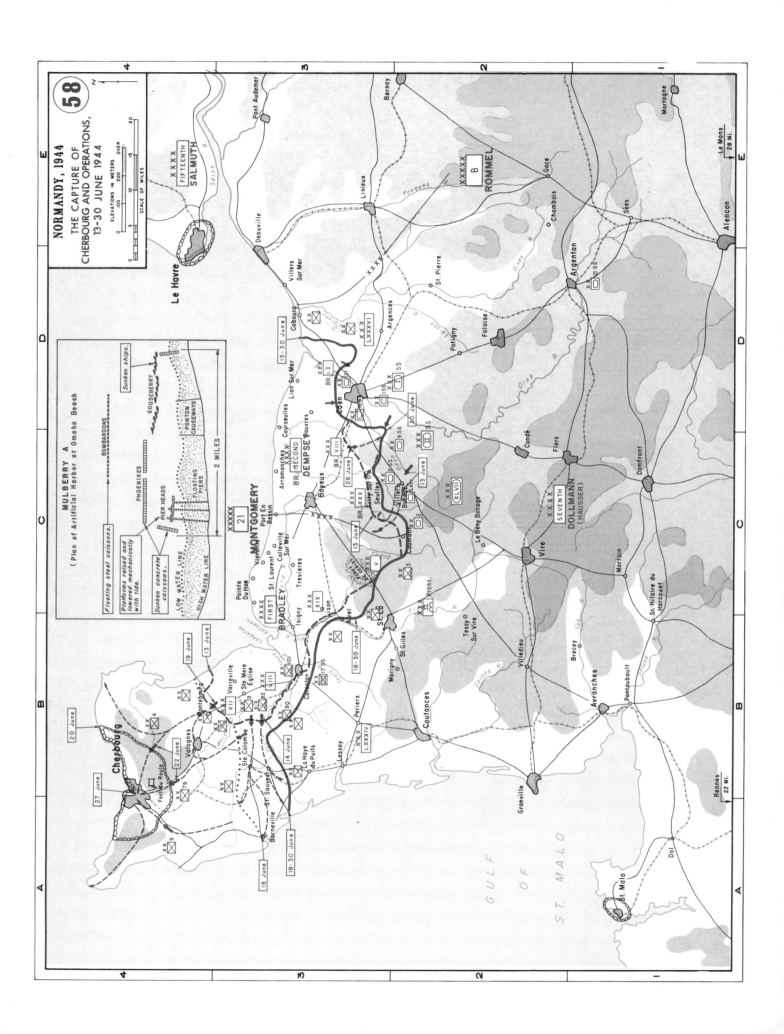

NORMANDY, 1944

58

THE CAPTURE OF
CHERBOURG AND OPERATIONS,
13-30 JUNE 1944

ELEVATIONS IN METERS
100   200   OVER
SCALE OF MILES

MULBERRY A
(Plan of Artificial Harbor at Omaha Beach)

Floating steel caissons.
Platforms raised and
lowered mechanically
with tide.
Sunken concrete caissons.
LOW WATER LINE
HIGH WATER LINE
PIER HEADS
FLOATING
PIERS
PONTON
CAUSEWAYS
PHOENIXES
GOOSEBERRY
Sunken ships.
BOMBARDONS
2 MILES

Le Havre
FIFTEENTH
SALMUTH
Seine R.
Pont Audemer
Berney
Mortagne
Le Mans
28 Mi.
ROMMEL
B
Gace
Chambois
Sées
Alencon
Lisieux
Touques R.
St. Pierre
Argentan
Goss
Villers
Sur Mer
Deauville
Cabourg
13-30 June
LXXXVI
Argences
Potigny
Falaise
Dives R.
Orne R.
Condé
Flers
Domfront
Lion Sur Mer
Courseulles
Caen
BR. I
30 June
I SS
9 SS
II SS
13 June
Arromanches
Bayeux
DEMPSE
BR. SECOND
BR. VIII
26 June
Odon R.
Seulles
Villers
Bocage
XLVII
SEVENTH
DOLLMANN
(HAUSSER)
Vire
Le Bény Bocage
Port En
Bessin
MONTGOMERY
21
Pouvres
Tilly Sur
Seulles
BR. XXX
Coumont
13 June
Mortain
St. Hilaire du
Harcouet
Pointe
Du Hoe
St. Laurent
Colleville
Sur Mer
Trevieres
Isigny
BRADLEY
FIRST
XIX
St. Lo
VIRE R.
Rcht.
Tessy
Sur Vire
Villedieu
Brecey
Sée R.
Avranches
Pontaubault
Carteret
ESTUARY
18-30 June
St. Gilles
Marigny
Coutances
Granville
GULF
OF
ST. MALO
19 June
13 June
Montebourg
Ste. Mere
Eglise
Vorrgville
VII
XII
90
Carentan
17 SS
18-30 June
Periers
Lessay
LXXXIV
Rennes
22 Mi.
Cherbourg
20 June
22 June
27 June
Fort du Roule
79
Valognes
Ste. Colombe
St. Sauveur
La Haye
du Puits
Barneville
14 June
18-30 June
18 June
9
St. Malo
Dol

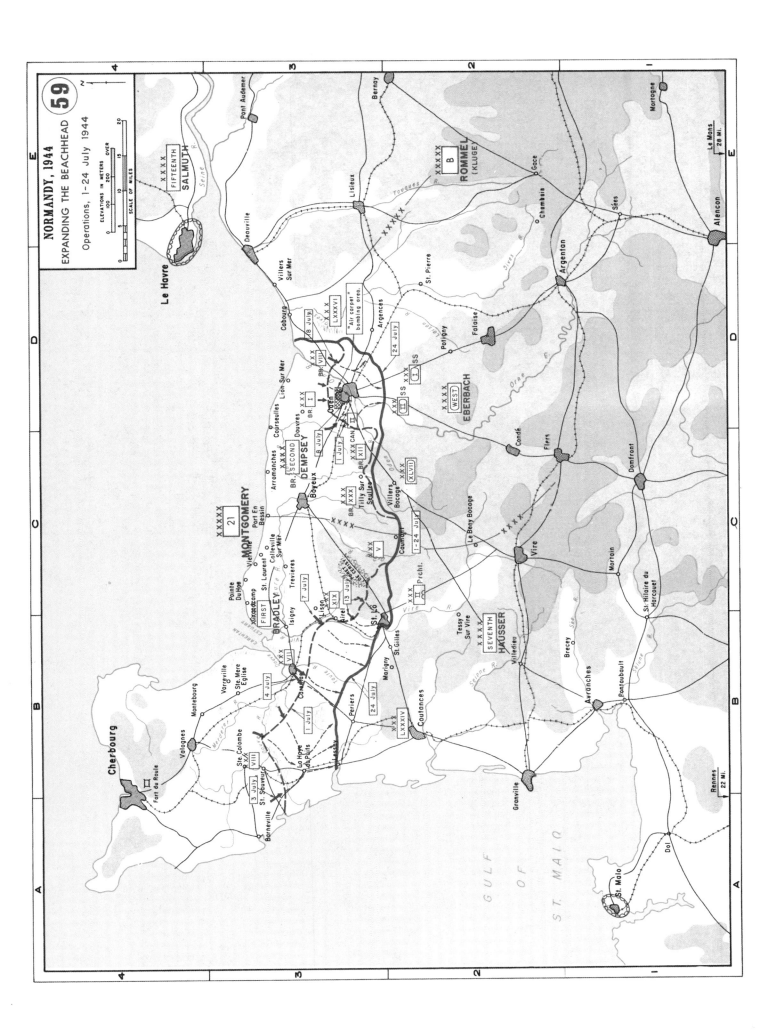

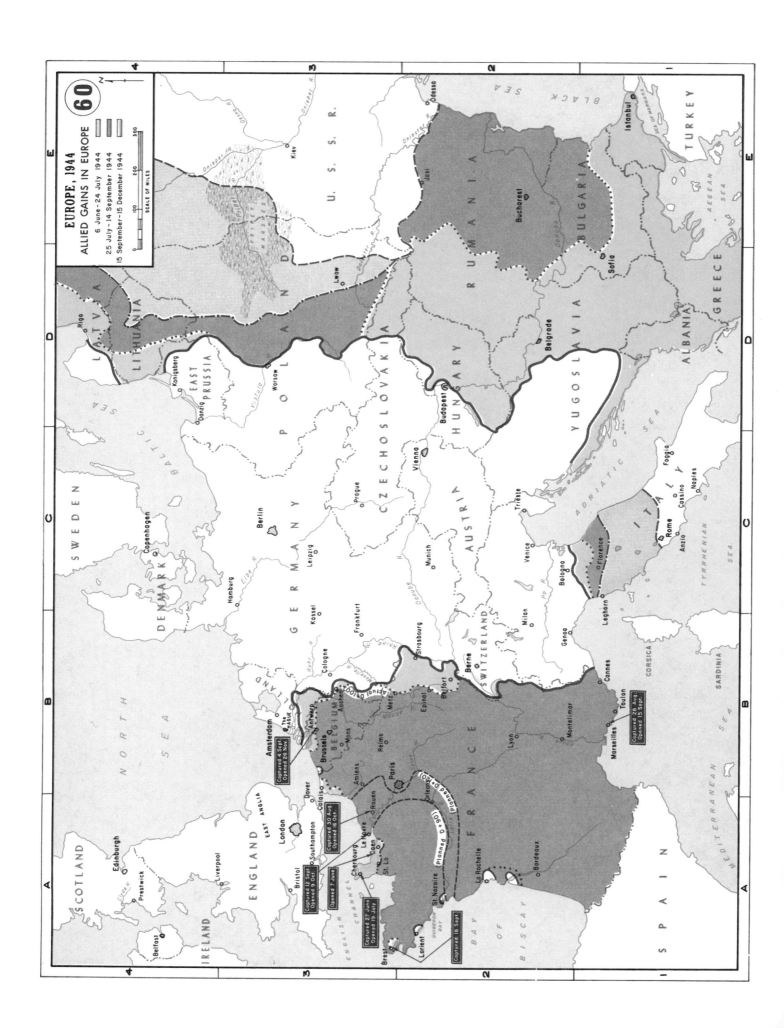

EUROPE, 1944
ALLIED GAINS IN EUROPE

6 June–24 July 1944
25 July–14 September 1944
15 September–15 December 1944

SCALE OF MILES

60

N

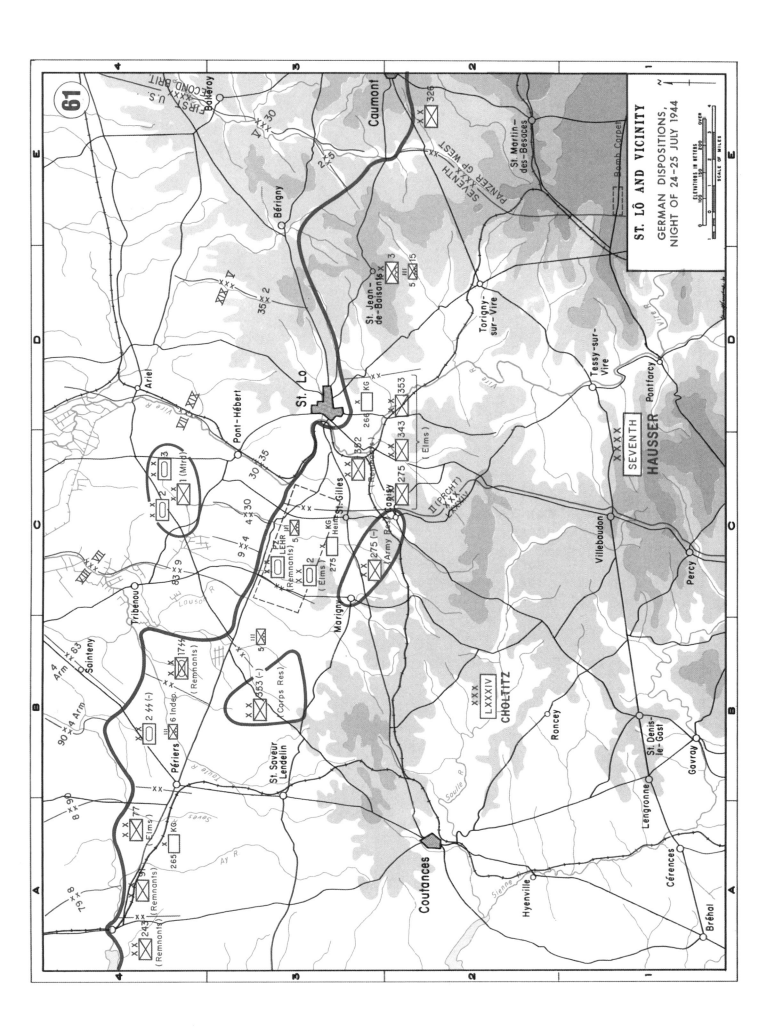

ST. LÔ AND VICINITY

GERMAN DISPOSITIONS,
NIGHT OF 24–25 JULY 1944

61

ST. LÔ AND VICINITY

THE *COBRA* OPERATION,
25–29 JULY 1944

62

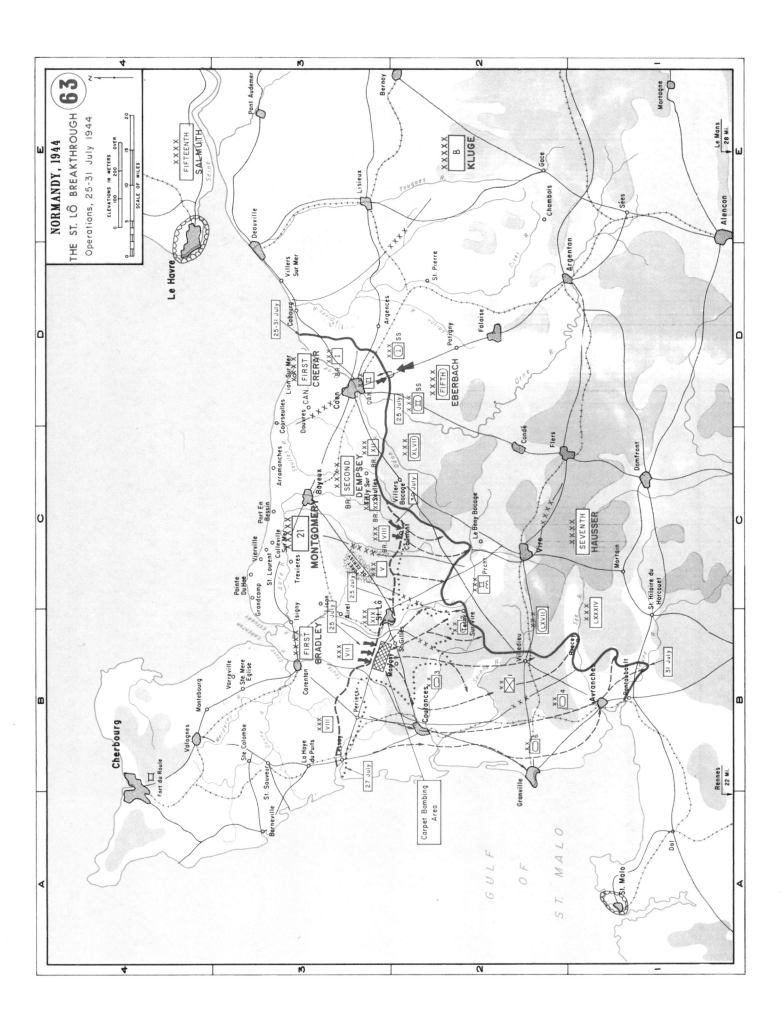

NORMANDY, 1944

63

THE ST. LÔ BREAKTHROUGH

Operations, 25-31 July 1944

ELEVATIONS IN METERS

0   100   200   OVER

SCALE OF MILES

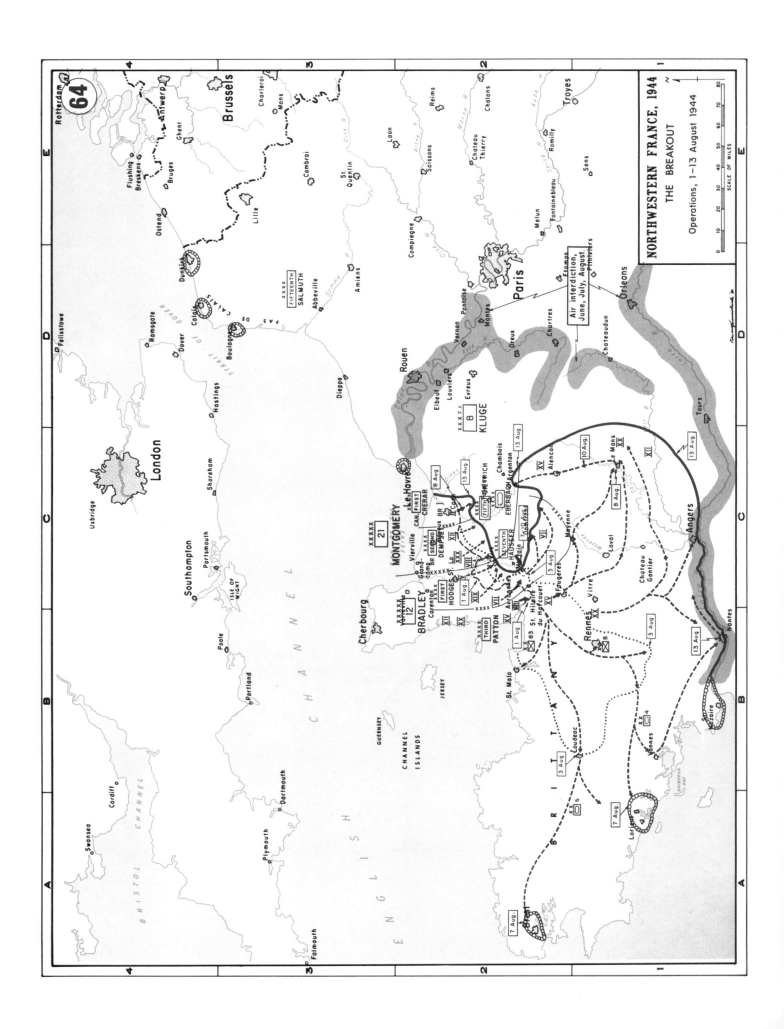

NORTHWESTERN FRANCE, 1944
THE BREAKOUT
Operations, 1–13 August 1944

SCALE OF MILES

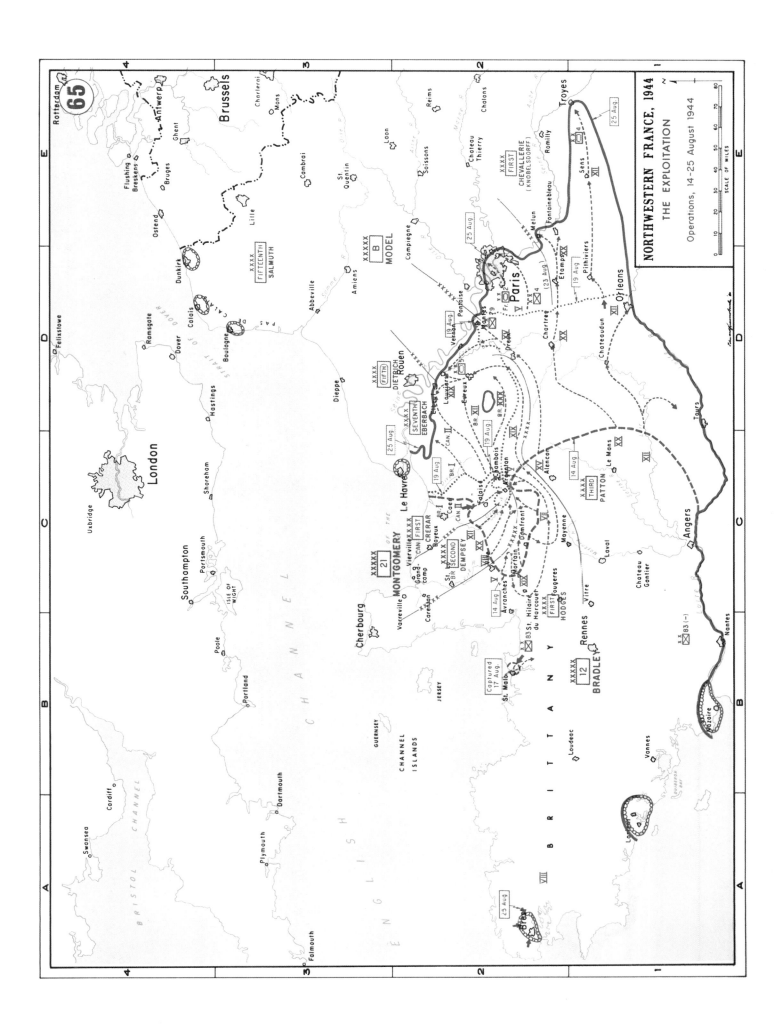

NORTHWESTERN FRANCE, 1944
THE EXPLOITATION
Operations, 14–25 August 1944

SCALE OF MILES

65

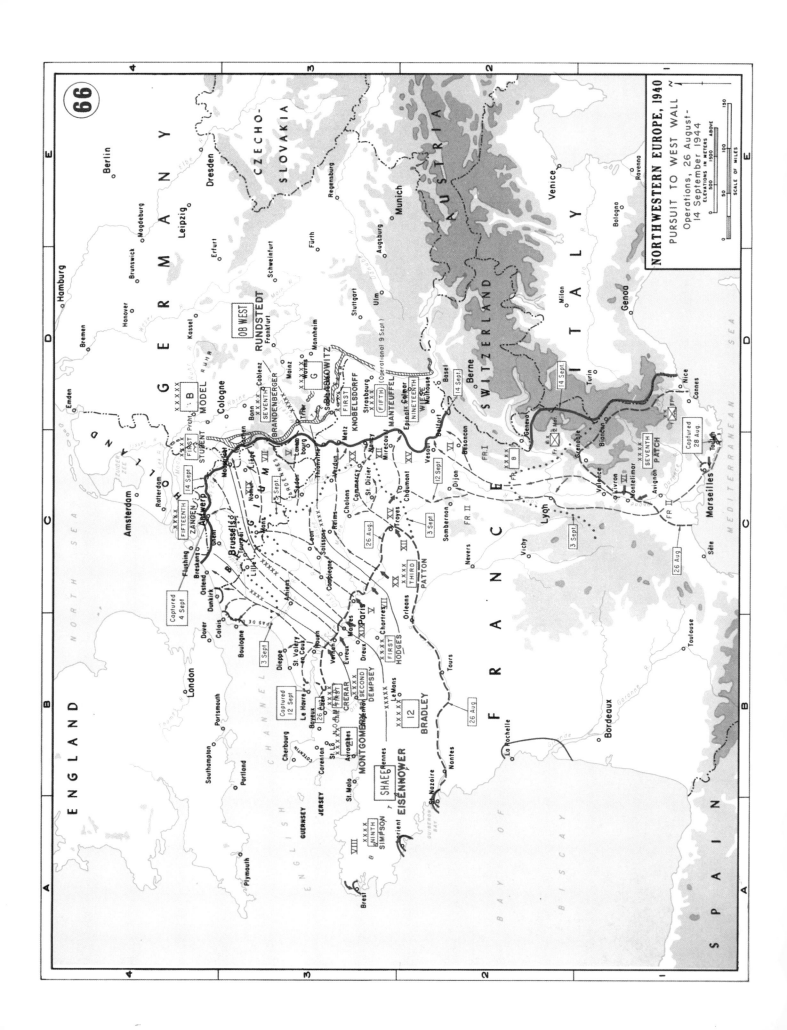

NORTHWESTERN EUROPE, 1940
PURSUIT TO WEST WALL
Operations, 26 August–
14 September 1944
ELEVATIONS IN METERS ABOVE
SCALE OF MILES

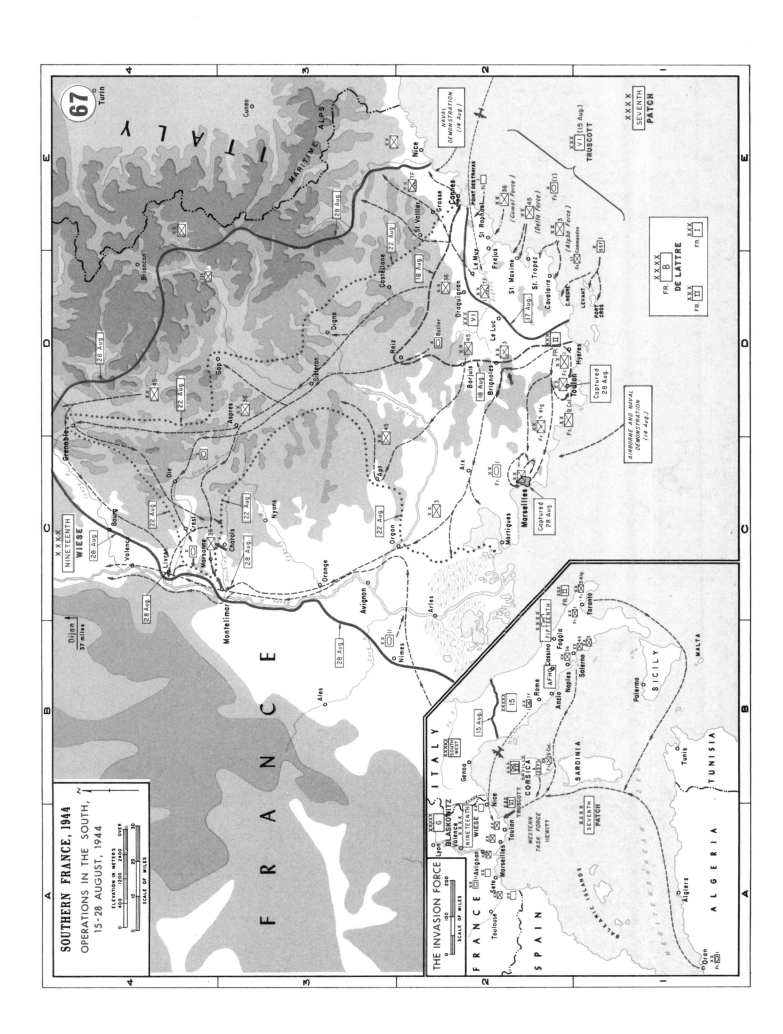

SOUTHERN FRANCE, 1944

OPERATIONS IN THE SOUTH,
15-28 AUGUST, 1944

ELEVATION IN METERS
400 1200 2400 OVER

SCALE OF MILES
0   10   20   30

THE INVASION FORCE

SCALE OF MILES
0   100   200

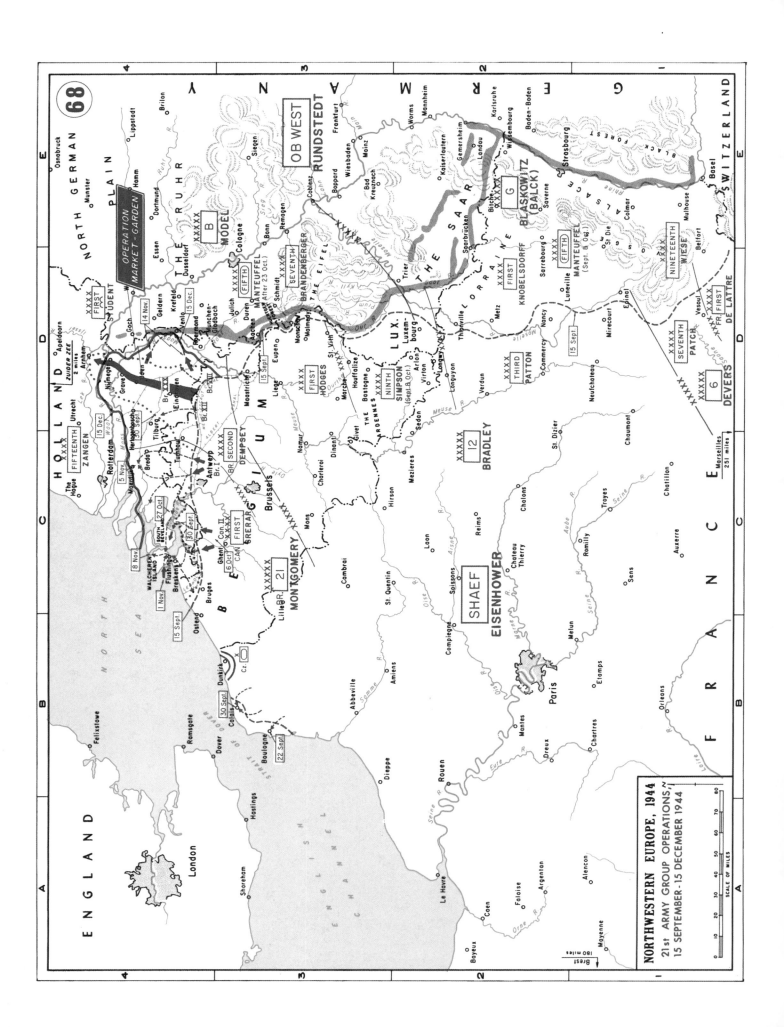

NORTHWESTERN EUROPE, 1944
21st ARMY GROUP OPERATIONS
15 SEPTEMBER-15 DECEMBER 1944

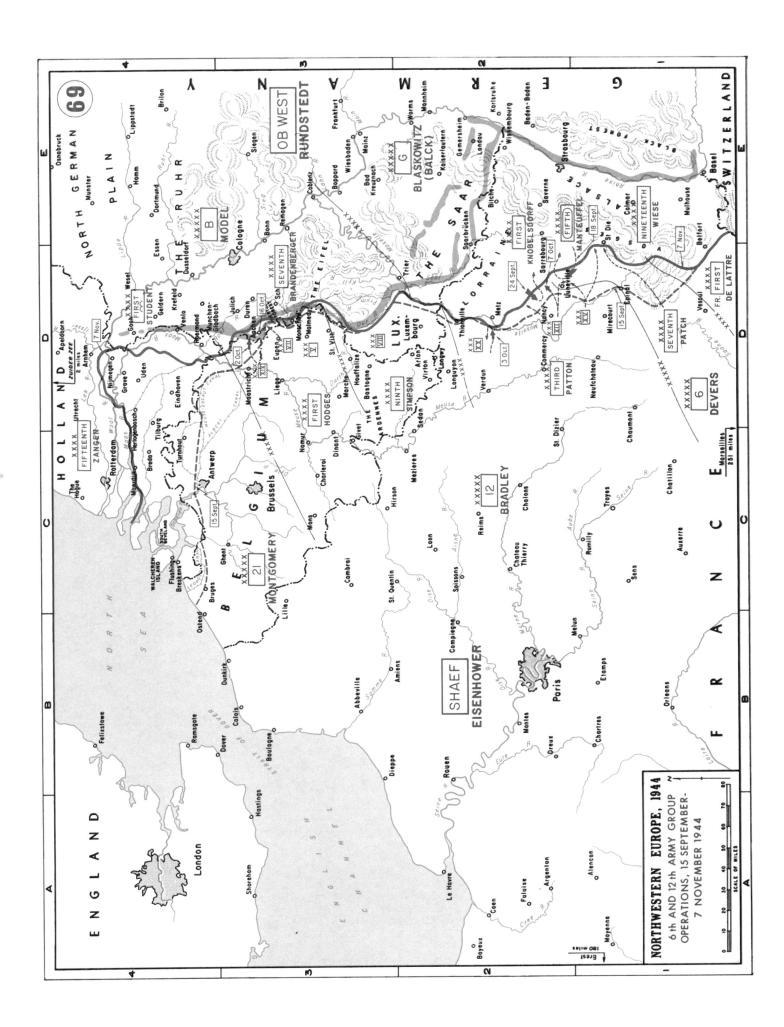

NORTHWESTERN EUROPE, 1944
6th AND 12th ARMY GROUP
OPERATIONS, 15 SEPTEMBER-
7 NOVEMBER 1944

SCALE OF MILES

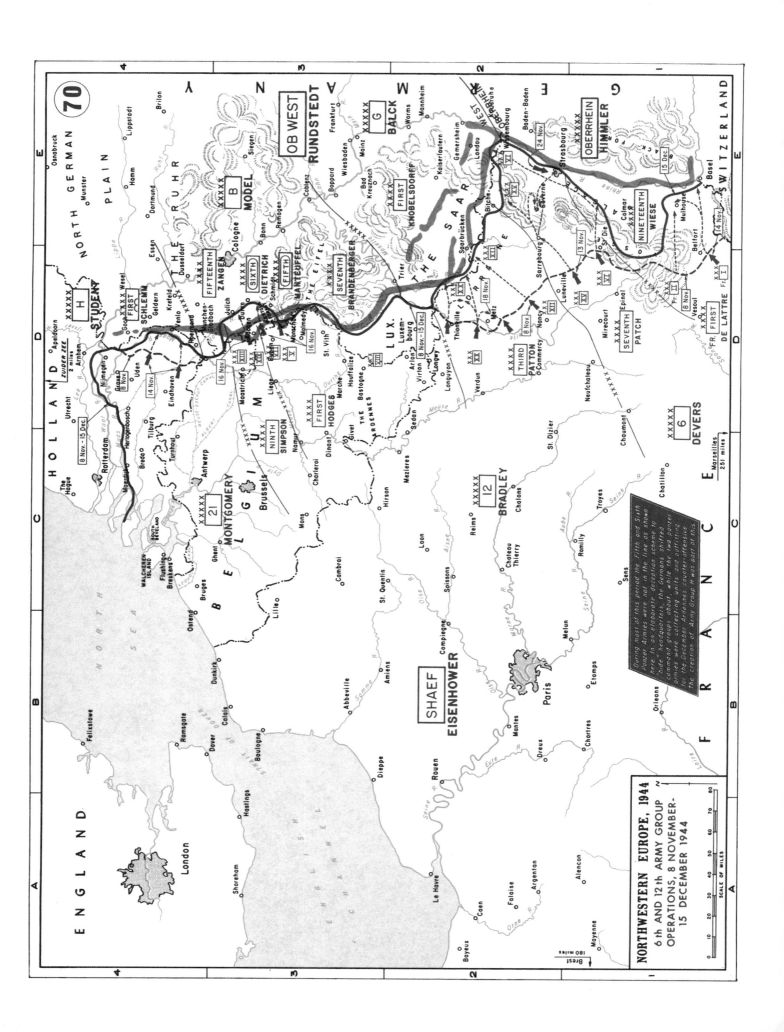

NORTHWESTERN EUROPE, 1944
6th AND 12th ARMY GROUP
OPERATIONS, 8 NOVEMBER-
15 DECEMBER 1944

During most of this period the Fifth and Sixth
Panzer Armies were not in the line as shown
here in an elaborate deception scheme to
hide headquarters, the Germans shifted
command groups about, while the two panzer
armies were collecting units and outfitting
for the December Ardennes counter-offensive.
The creation of Army Group H was part of this.

70

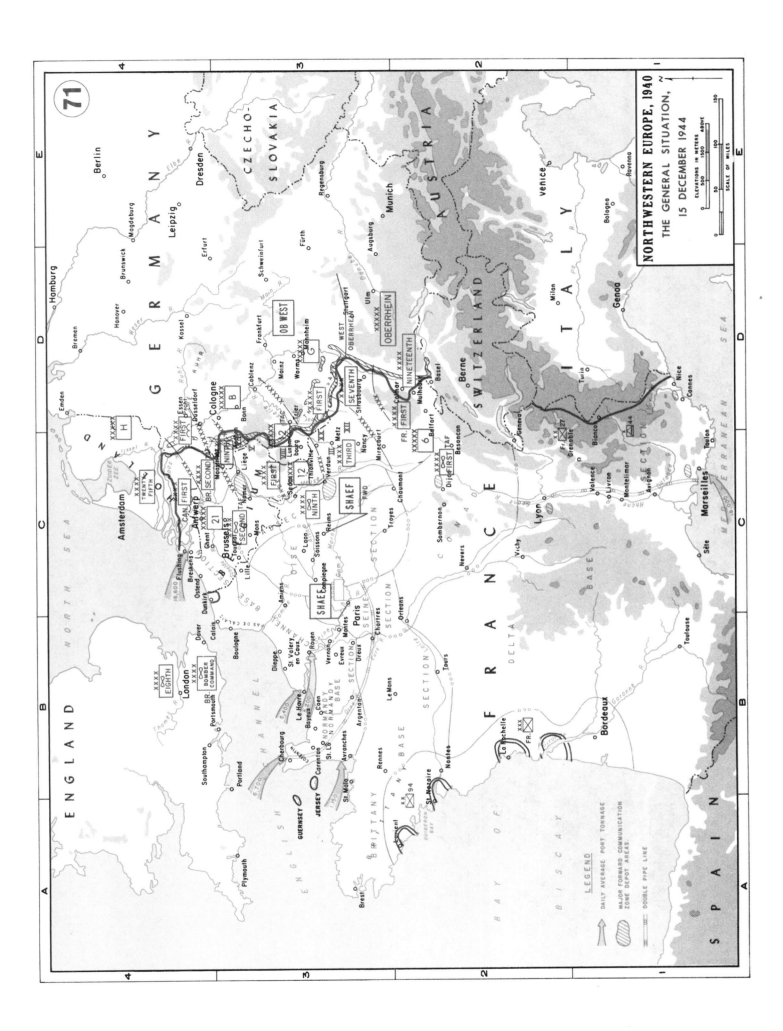

NORTHWESTERN EUROPE, 1940
THE GENERAL SITUATION,
15 DECEMBER 1944

ELEVATIONS IN METERS
500 1500 ABOVE

SCALE OF MILES

LEGEND

DAILY AVERAGE PORT TONNAGE

MAJOR FORWARD COMMUNICATION
ZONE DEPOT AREAS

DOUBLE PIPE LINE

71

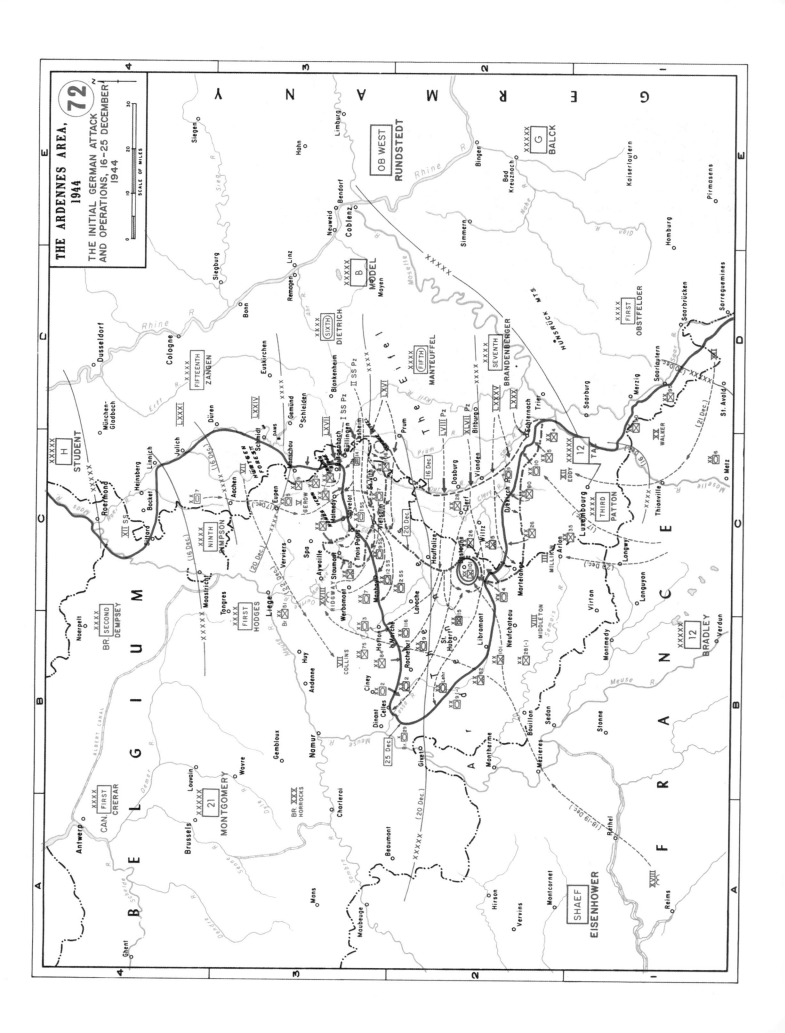

THE ARDENNES AREA, 1944

72

THE INITIAL GERMAN ATTACK
AND OPERATIONS, 16-25 DECEMBER
1944

SCALE OF MILES

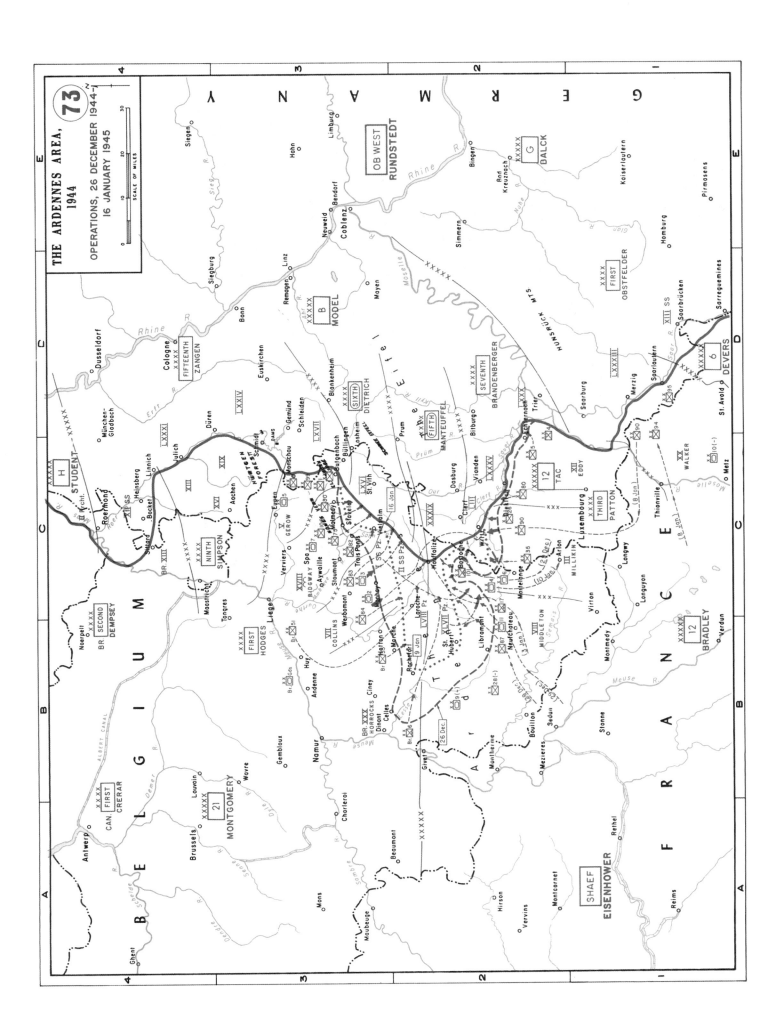

THE ARDENNES AREA, 1944

73

OPERATIONS, 26 DECEMBER 1944–
16 JANUARY 1945

SCALE OF MILES

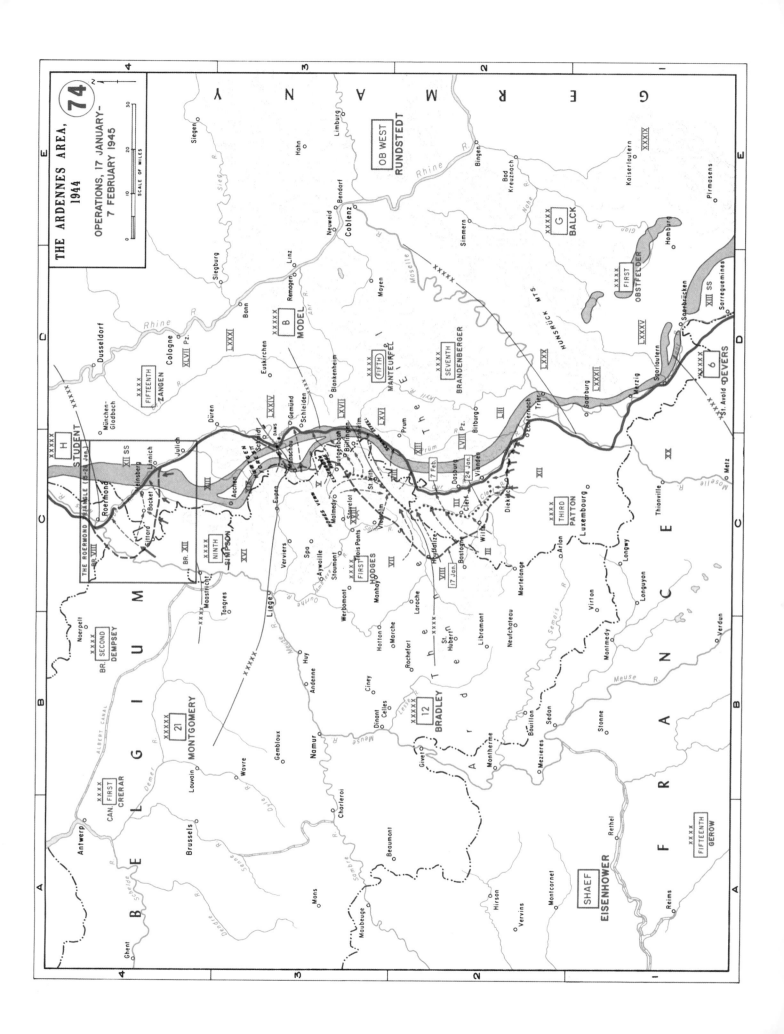

THE ARDENNES AREA,
1944

74

OPERATIONS, 17 JANUARY–
7 FEBRUARY 1945

SCALE OF MILES

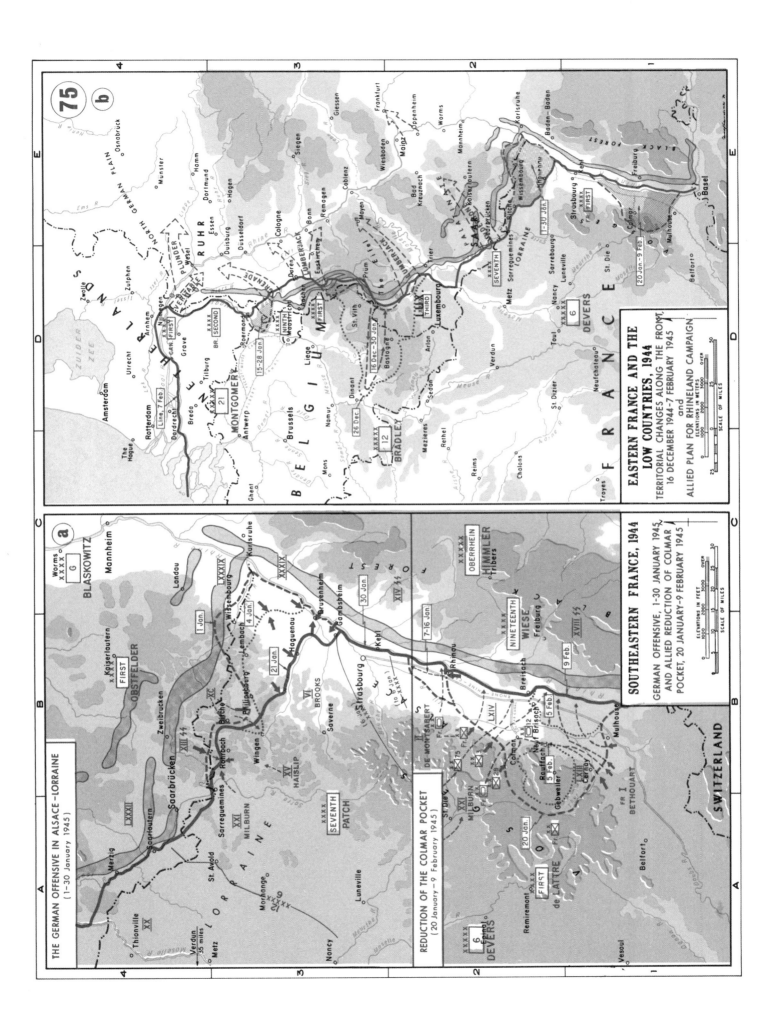

THE GERMAN OFFENSIVE IN ALSACE-LORRAINE
(1–30 January 1945)

REDUCTION OF THE COLMAR POCKET
(20 January–9 February 1945)

SOUTHEASTERN FRANCE, 1944
GERMAN OFFENSIVE, 1–30 JANUARY 1945,
AND ALLIED REDUCTION OF COLMAR
POCKET, 20 JANUARY–9 FEBRUARY 1945

ELEVATIONS IN FEET
1000   2000   3000   OVER
SCALE OF MILES

EASTERN FRANCE AND THE
LOW COUNTRIES, 1944
TERRITORIAL CHANGES ALONG THE FRONT,
16 DECEMBER 1944–7 FEBRUARY 1945
and
ALLIED PLAN FOR RHINELAND CAMPAIGN

ELEVATIONS IN METERS
1000   2000   3000   OVER
SCALE OF MILES

75

a

b

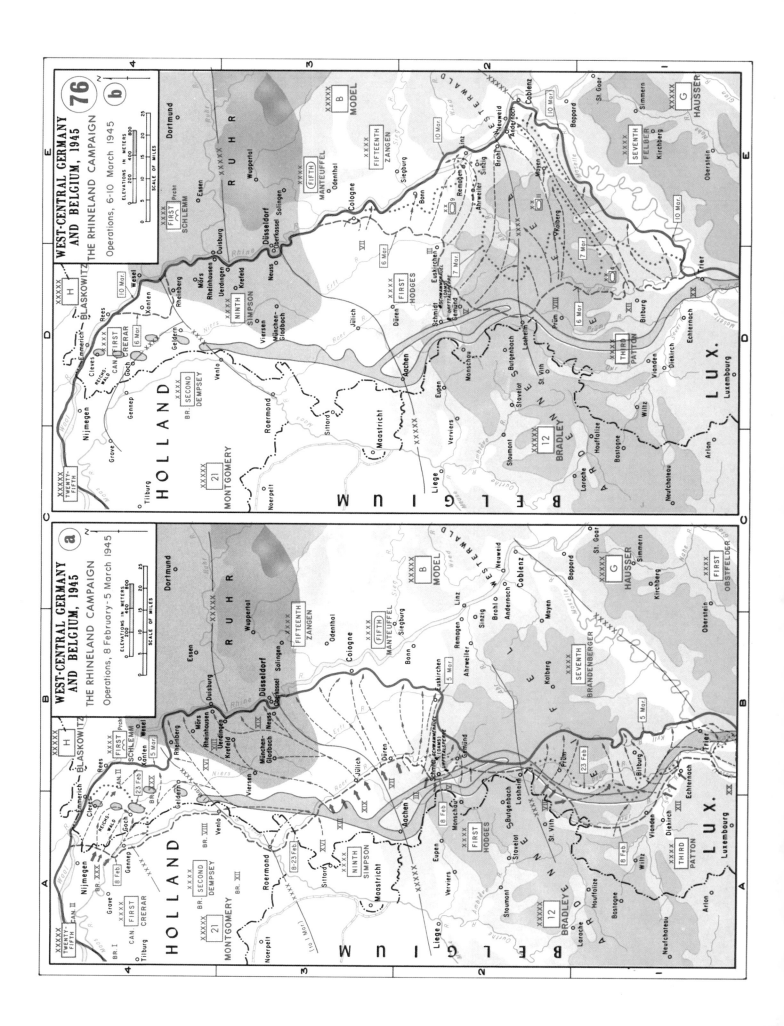

WEST-CENTRAL GERMANY
AND BELGIUM, 1945
THE RHINELAND CAMPAIGN
Operations, 6-10 March 1945

76
b

WEST-CENTRAL GERMANY
AND BELGIUM, 1945
THE RHINELAND CAMPAIGN
Operations, 8 February-5 March 1945

a

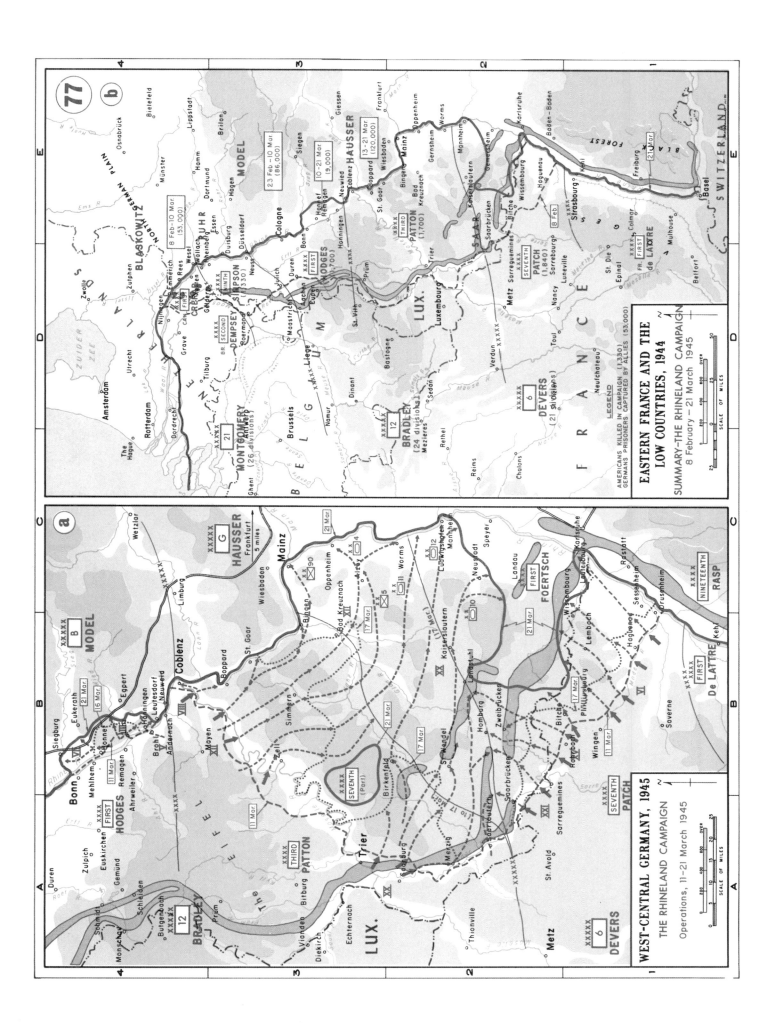

WEST-CENTRAL GERMANY, 1945

THE RHINELAND CAMPAIGN

Operations, 11–21 March 1945

SCALE OF MILES

EASTERN FRANCE AND THE LOW COUNTRIES, 1944

SUMMARY—THE RHINELAND CAMPAIGN

8 February – 21 March 1945

LEGEND

AMERICANS KILLED IN CAMPAIGN (1,330)
GERMANS PRISONERS CAPTURED BY ALLIES (53,000)

SCALE OF MILES

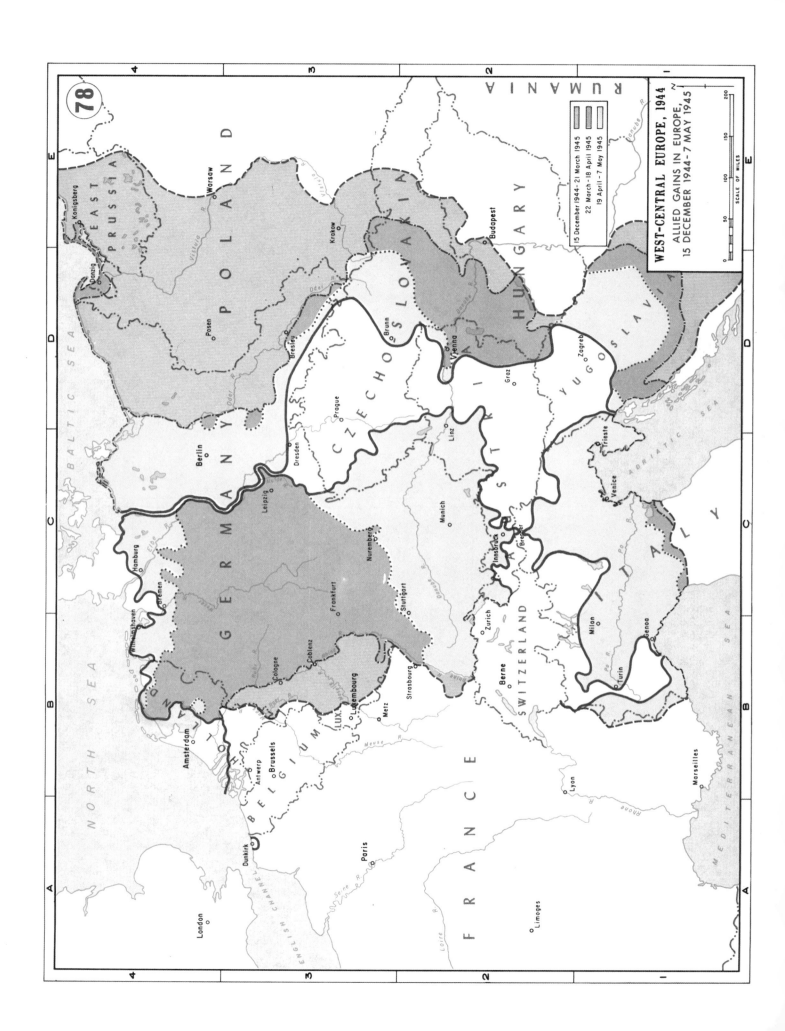

WEST-CENTRAL EUROPE, 1944

ALLIED GAINS IN EUROPE,
15 DECEMBER 1944-7 MAY 1945

15 December 1944-21 March 1945
22 March-18 April 1945
19 April-7 May 1945

SCALE OF MILES
0   50   100   150   200

78

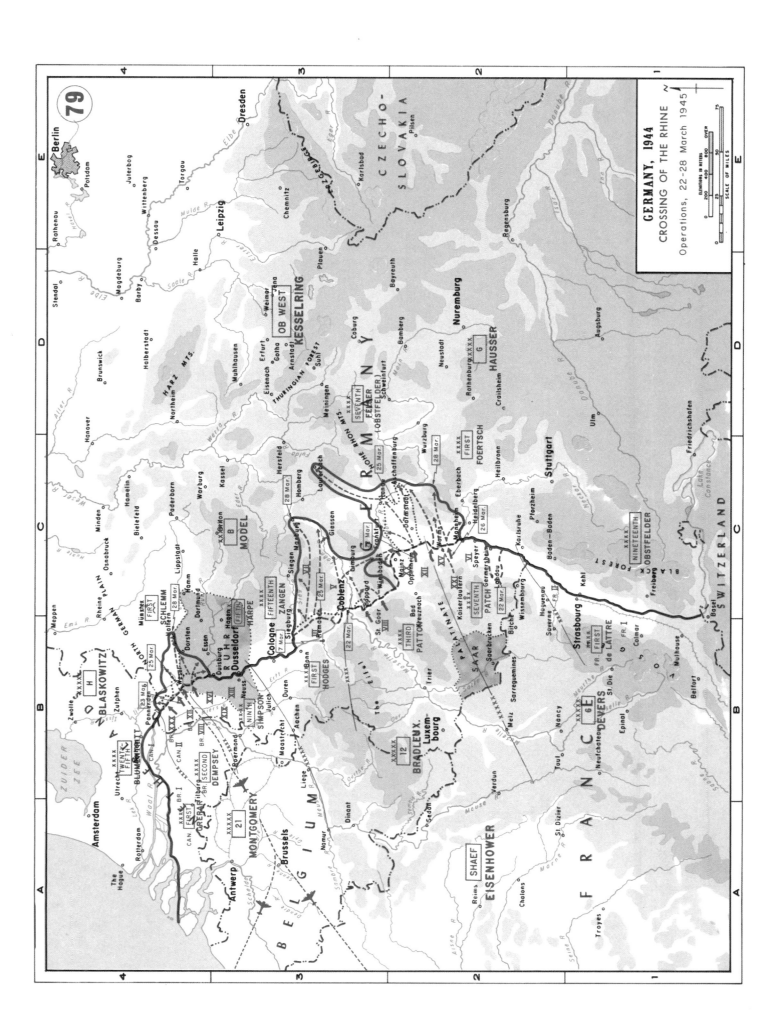

GERMANY, 1944
CROSSING OF THE RHINE
Operations, 22–28 March 1945

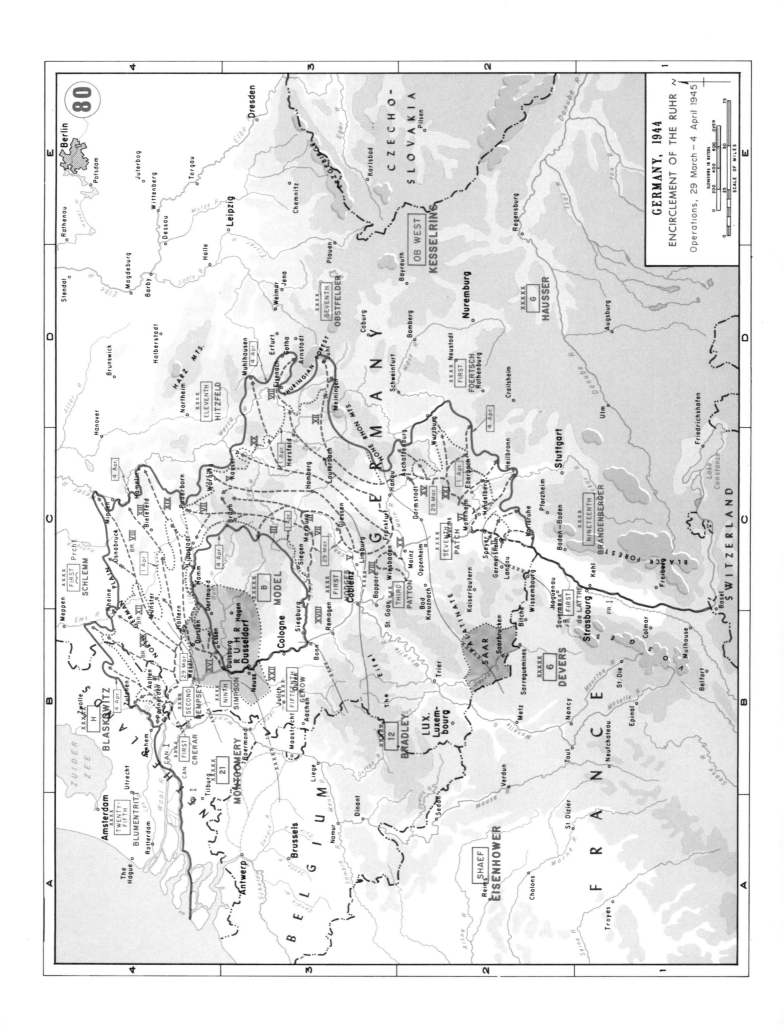

GERMANY, 1944
ENCIRCLEMENT OF THE RUHR
Operations, 29 March – 4 April 1945

ELEVATIONS IN METERS
SCALE OF MILES

80

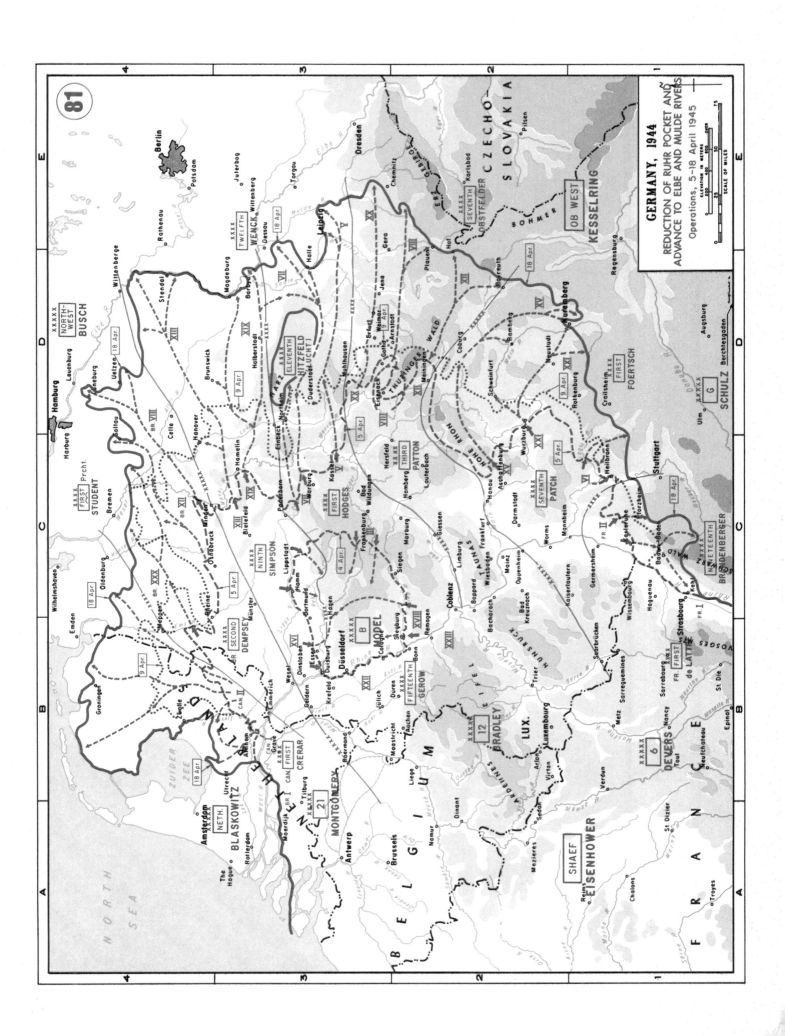

GERMANY, 1944

REDUCTION OF RUHR POCKET AND
ADVANCE TO ELBE AND MULDE RIVERS

Operations, 5–18 April 1945

SCALE OF MILES

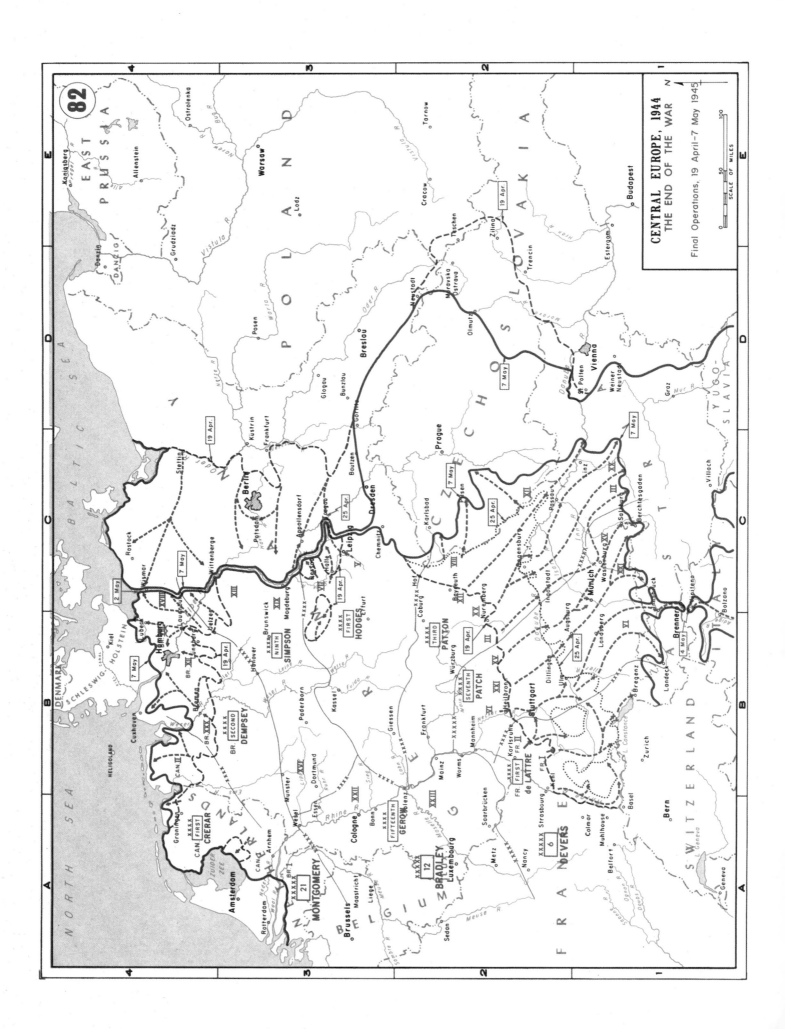

CENTRAL EUROPE, 1944
THE END OF THE WAR

Final Operations, 19 April–7 May 1945

SCALE OF MILES

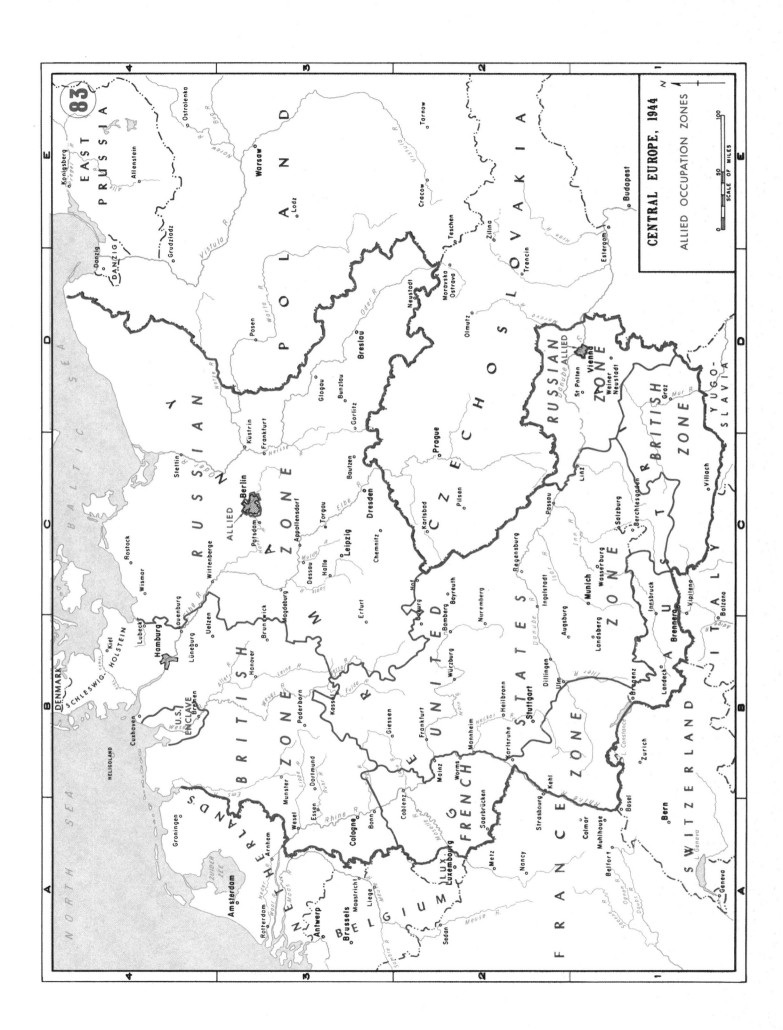

CENTRAL EUROPE, 1944

ALLIED OCCUPATION ZONES

SCALE OF MILES

83

Part Two
Campaign Atlas
to
Asia and the Pacific

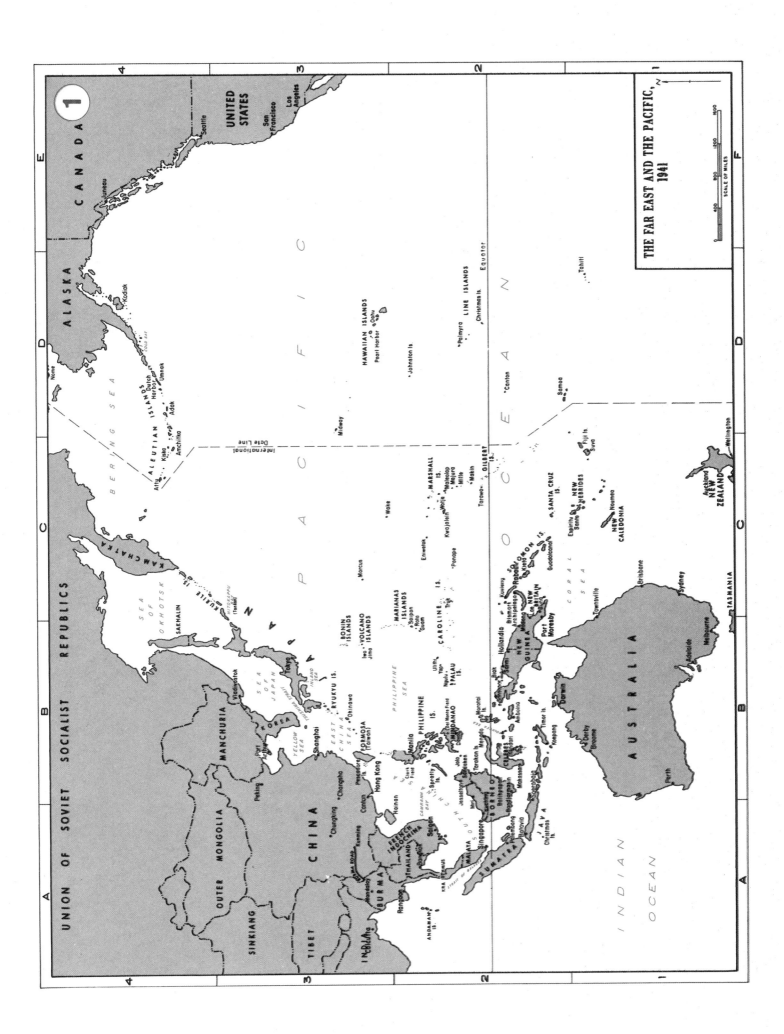

THE FAR EAST AND THE PACIFIC, 1941

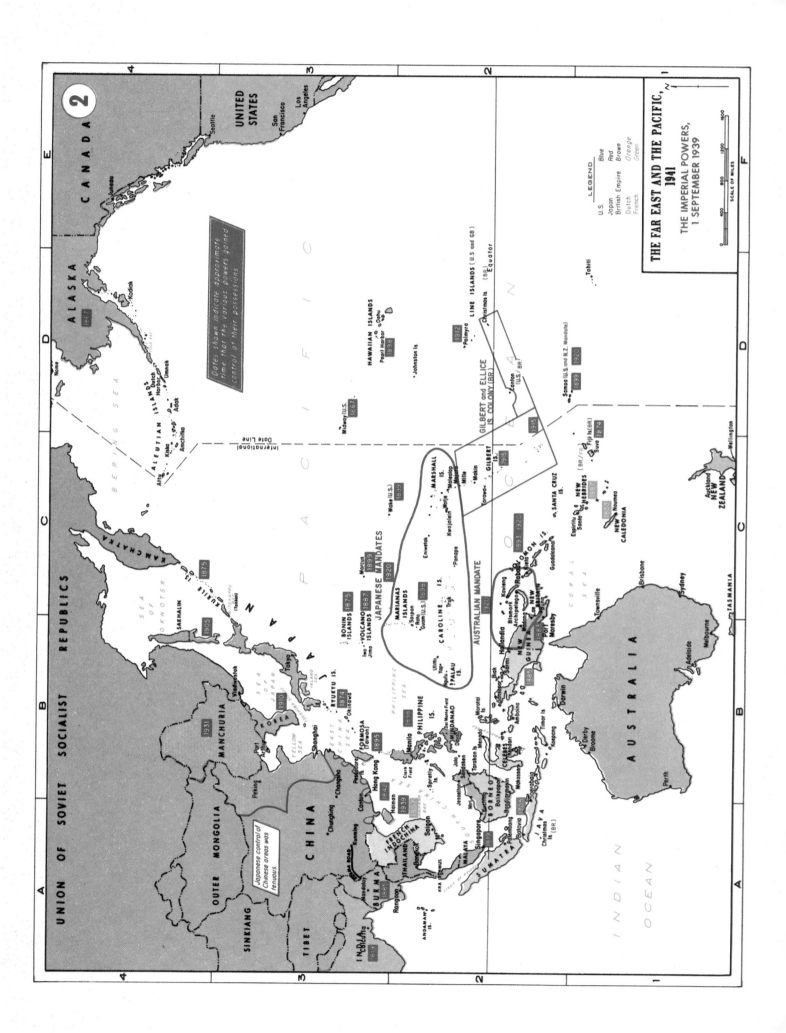

THE FAR EAST AND THE PACIFIC,
1941

THE IMPERIAL POWERS, 1 SEPTEMBER 1939

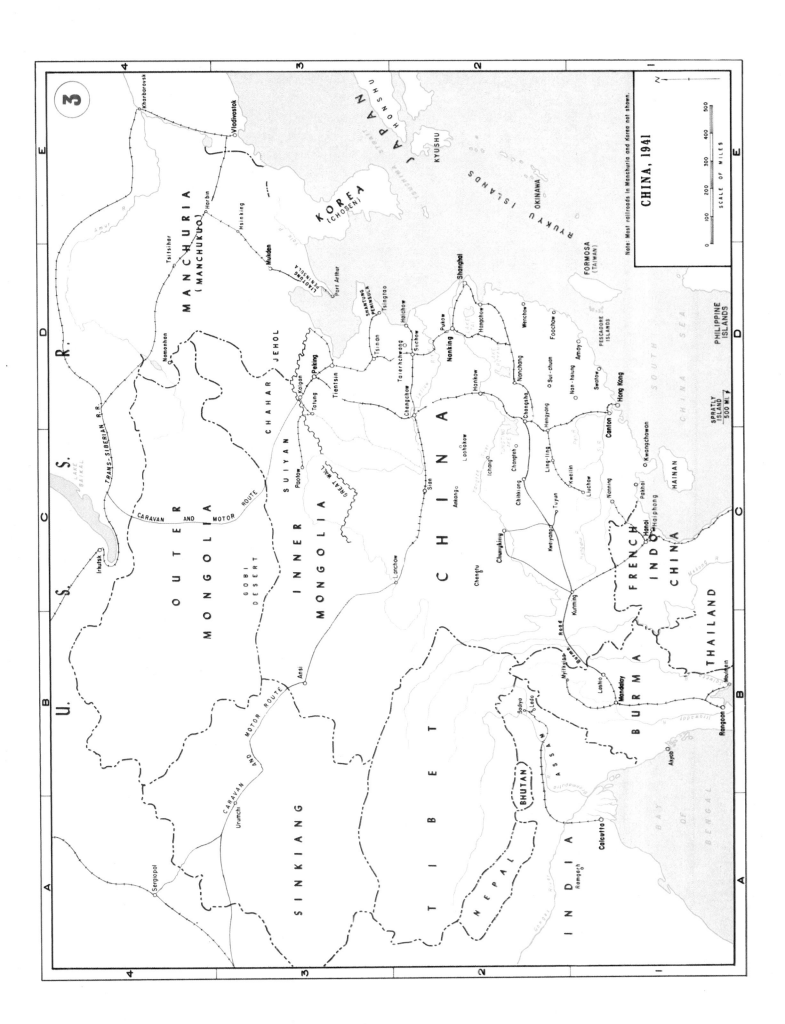

CHINA, 1941

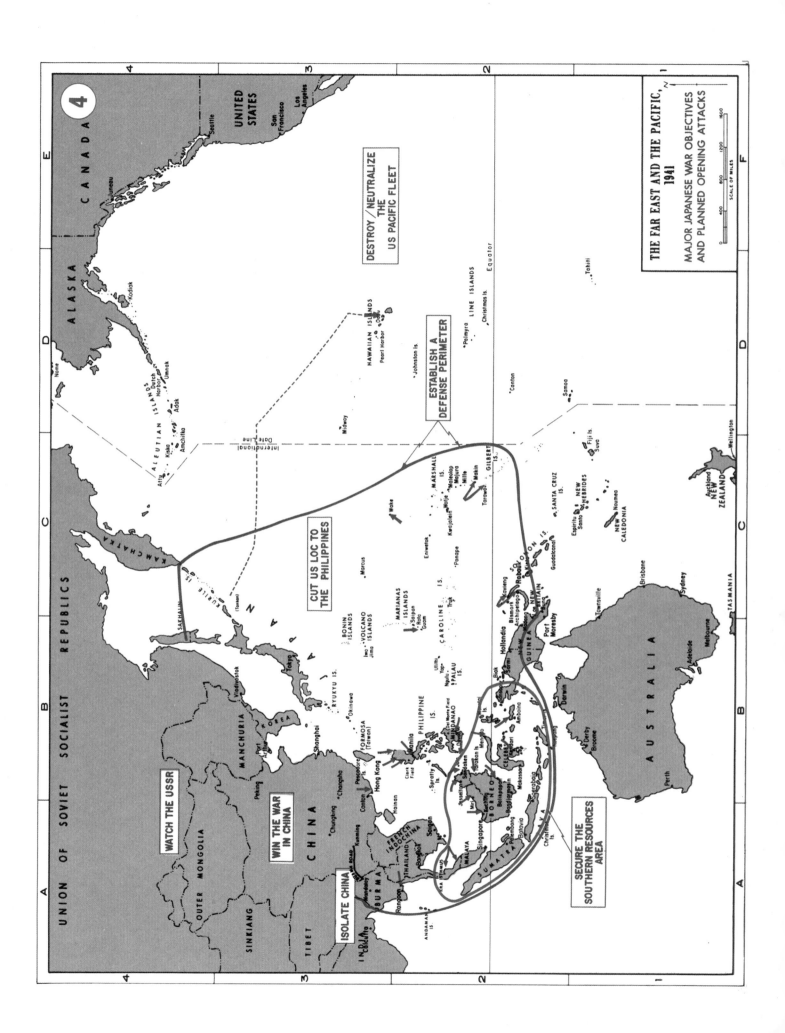

THE FAR EAST AND THE PACIFIC, 1941

MAJOR JAPANESE WAR OBJECTIVES AND PLANNED OPENING ATTACKS

SCALE OF MILES
0   400   800   1200   1600

DESTROY/NEUTRALIZE THE US PACIFIC FLEET

ESTABLISH A DEFENSE PERIMETER

CUT US LOC TO THE PHILIPPINES

WATCH THE USSR

WIN THE WAR IN CHINA

ISOLATE CHINA

SECURE THE SOUTHERN RESOURCES AREA

UNION OF SOVIET SOCIALIST REPUBLICS

OUTER MONGOLIA

SINKIANG

TIBET

INDIA

CHINA

MANCHURIA

KOREA

BURMA

THAILAND

FRENCH INDOCHINA

MALAYA

SUMATRA

BORNEO

CELEBES

JAVA

PHILIPPINE IS.

MINDANAO

FORMOSA (Taiwan)

RYUKYU IS.

JAPAN

KAMCHATKA

SAKHALIN

KURILE IS.

AUSTRALIA

TASMANIA

NEW ZEALAND

NEW GUINEA

NEW BRITAIN

SOLOMON IS.

NEW HEBRIDES

NEW CALEDONIA

SANTA CRUZ IS.

FIJI IS.

GILBERT IS.

MARSHALL IS.

CAROLINE IS.

MARIANAS ISLANDS

VOLCANO ISLANDS

BONIN ISLANDS

PALAU IS.

HAWAIIAN ISLANDS

LINE ISLANDS

ALEUTIAN ISLANDS

ALASKA

CANADA

UNITED STATES

International Date Line

Equator

CANADA

UNITED STATES

Seattle
San Francisco
Los Angeles
Juneau
Nome
Kodiak
Dutch Harbor
Umnak
Adak
Amchitka
Kiska
Attu
Midway
Pearl Harbor
Oahu
Johnston Is.
Palmyra
Christmas Is.
Canton
Samoa
Tahiti
Wellington
Auckland
Noumea
Suva
Espiritu Santo
Guadalcanal
Rabaul
Kavieng
Bismarck Archipelago
Port Moresby
Hollandia
Biak
Sorol
Ambon
Darwin
Derby
Broome
Perth
Adelaide
Melbourne
Sydney
Brisbane
Townsville
Tarawa
Makin
Mili
Maloelap
Wotje
Kwajalein
Enewetok
Wake
Marcus
Ponape
Truk
Ulithi
Yap
Ngulu
Saipan
Rota
Guam
Iwo Jima
Chichi Jima
Okinawa
Shanghai
Peking
Port Arthur
Vladivostok
Tokyo
Chungking
Changsha
Canton
Nanning
Kunming
Hong Kong
Hainan
Hanoi
Saigon
Bangkok
Mandalay
Rangoon
Singapore
Penang
Batavia
Palembang
Banjermasin
Balikpapan
Tarakan
Sandakan
Jesselton
Miri
Kuching
Makassar
Menado
Morotai
Halmahera
Ambon
Kendari
Surabaya
Christmas Is.
ANDAMAN IS.
Spratly Is.
Clark Field
Manila
Davao
SABANG
BURMA ROAD
Equator

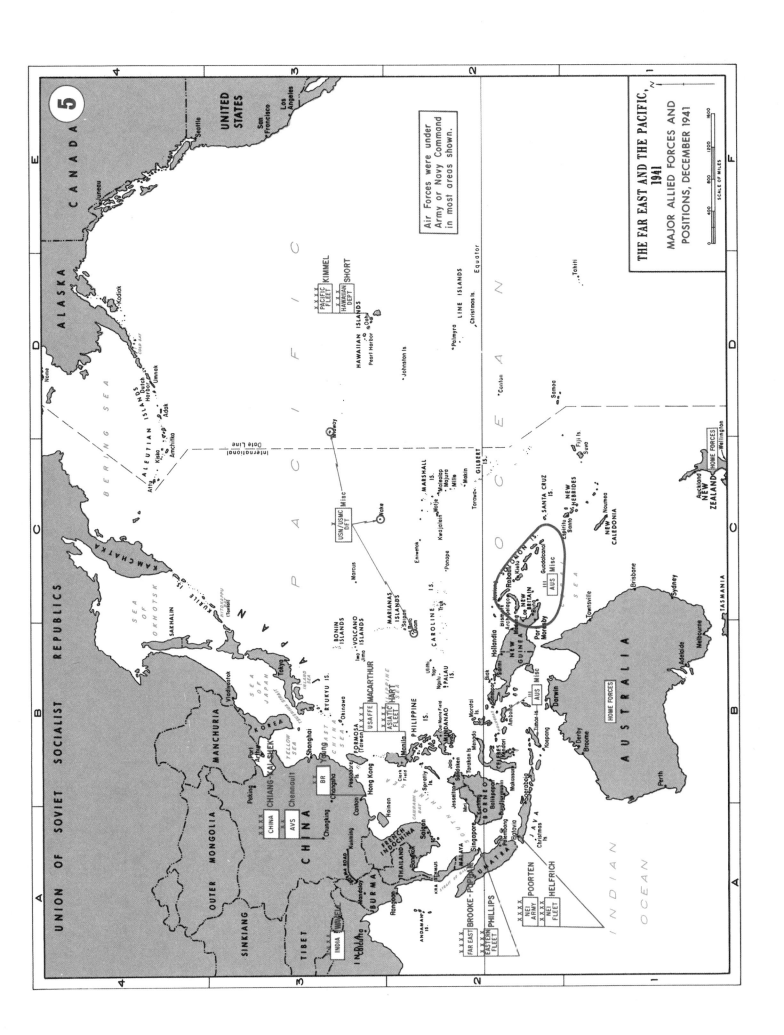

THE FAR EAST AND THE PACIFIC,
1941

MAJOR ALLIED FORCES AND
POSITIONS, DECEMBER 1941

SCALE OF MILES
0   400   800   1200   1600

Air Forces were under
Army or Navy Command
in most areas shown.

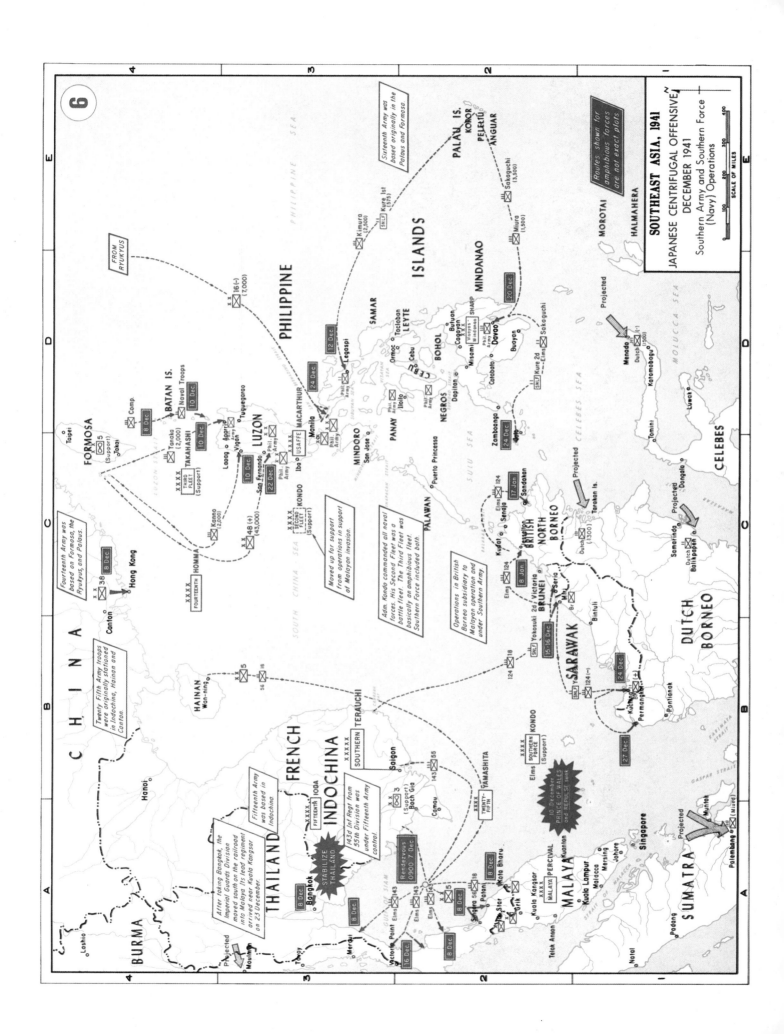

SOUTHEAST ASIA, 1941
JAPANESE CENTRIFUGAL OFFENSIVE
DECEMBER 1941
Southern Army and Southern Force
(Navy) Operations

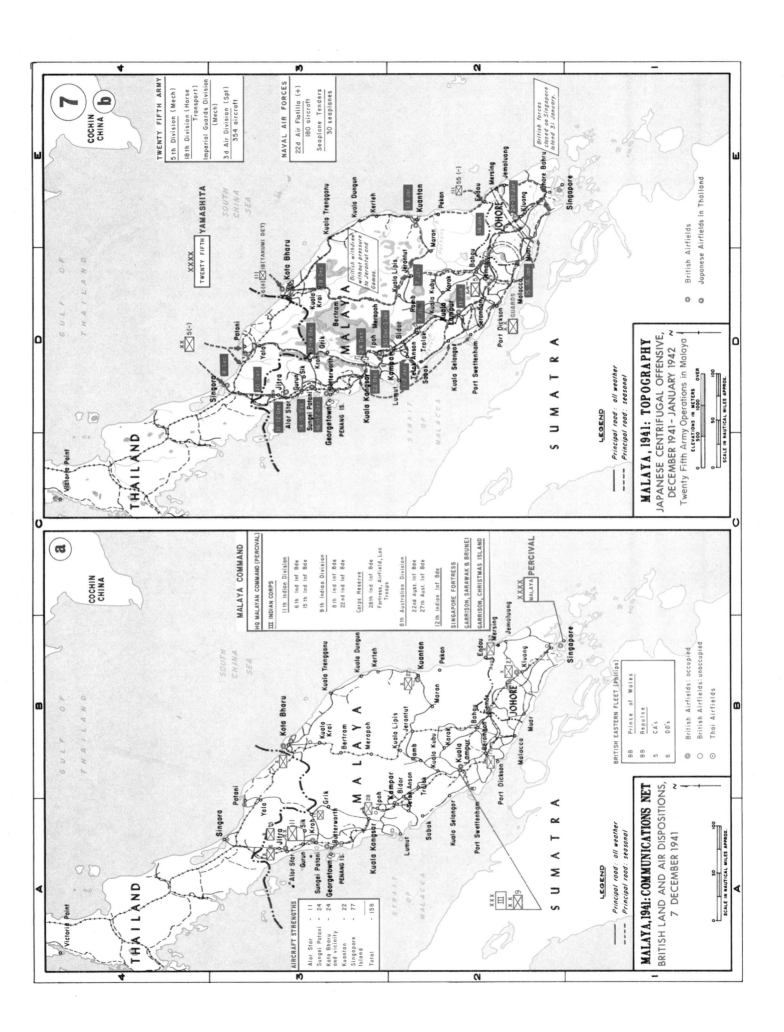

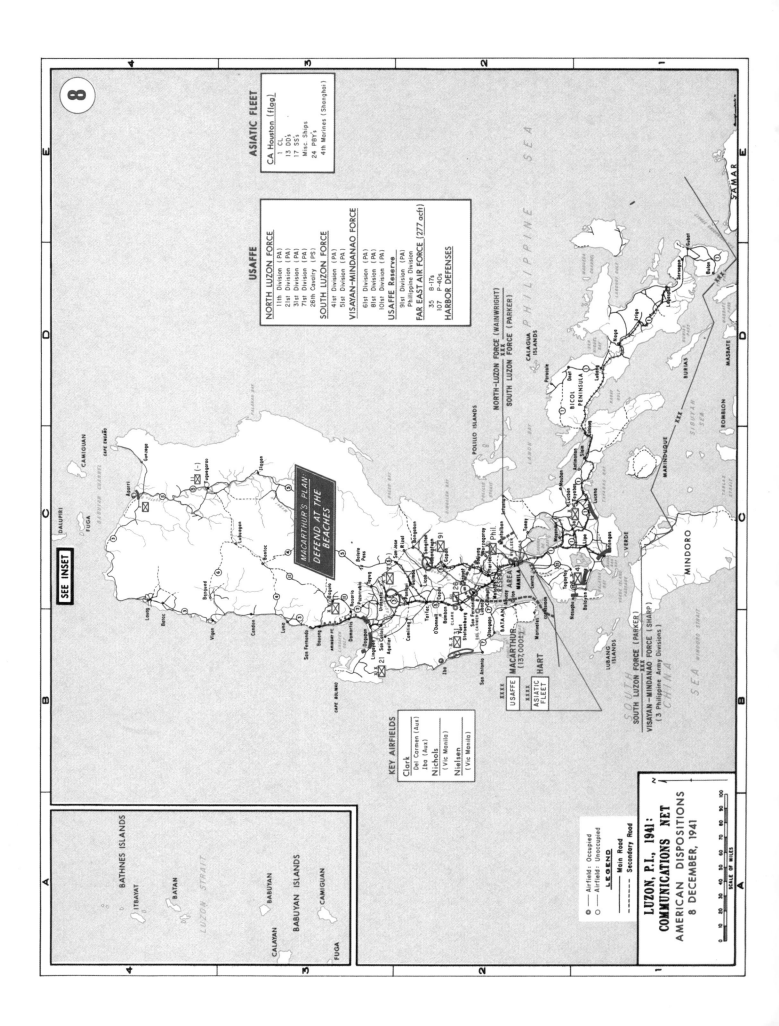

ASIATIC FLEET

CA Houston (flag)
1 CL
13 DDs
17 SSs
Misc. Ships
24 PBYs
4th Marines (Shanghai)

USAFFE

NORTH LUZON FORCE
11th Division (PA)
21st Division (PA)
31st Division (PA)
71st Division (PA)
26th Cavalry (PS)

SOUTH LUZON FORCE
41st Division (PA)
51st Division (PA)

VISAYAN-MINDANAO FORCE
61st Division (PA)
81st Division (PA)
101st Division (PA)

USAFFE Reserve
91st Division (PA)
Philippine Division

FAR EAST AIR FORCE (277 acft)
35 B-17s
107 P-40s

HARBOR DEFENSES

MACARTHUR'S PLAN: DEFEND AT THE BEACHES

SEE INSET

KEY AIRFIELDS

Clark
Del Carmen (Aux)
Iba (Aux)
Nichols
(Vic Manila)
Nielsen
(Vic Manila)

xxxx USAFFE MACARTHUR (137,000±)
xxxx ASIATIC FLEET HART

NORTH-LUZON FORCE (WAINWRIGHT)
xxx
SOUTH LUZON FORCE (PARKER)

SOUTH LUZON FORCE (PARKER)
xxx
VISAYAN-MINDANAO FORCE (SHARP)
(3 Philippine Army Divisions)

BATHNES ISLANDS
ITBAYAT
BATAN
CALAYAN BABUYAN
BABUYAN ISLANDS
CAMIGUAN
FUGA

LEGEND

⊙ — Airfield: Occupied
○ — Airfield: Unoccupied

——— Main Road
----- Secondary Road

LUZON, P.I., 1941:
COMMUNICATIONS NET
AMERICAN DISPOSITIONS
8 DECEMBER, 1941

0 10 20 30 40 50 60 70 80 90 100
SCALE OF MILES

8

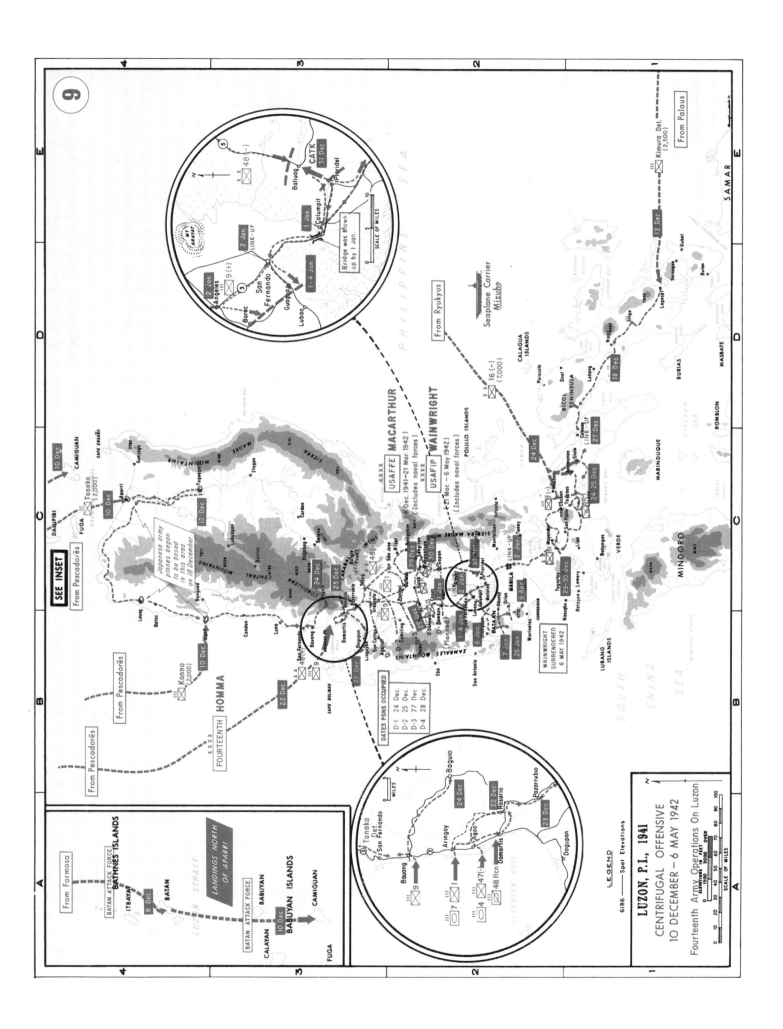

9

LUZON, P.I., 1941
CENTRIFUGAL OFFENSIVE
10 DECEMBER – 6 MAY 1942

Fourteenth Army Operations On Luzon

LEGEND

6186 —— Spot Elevations

SEE INSET

Japanese army planes began to be based in this area on 18 December.

FOURTEENTH HOMMA

USAFFE MACARTHUR
8 Dec. 1941–21 Mar. 1942
(Includes naval forces)

USAFIP WAINWRIGHT
21 Mar.– 6 May 1942
(Includes naval forces)

WAINWRIGHT SURRENDERED 6 MAY 1942

Seaplane Carrier Mizuho

From Ryukyus

From Palaus

From Pescadorēs

From Formosa

DATES PSNS OCCUPIED
D-1   24 Dec.
D-2   25 Dec.
D-3   27 Dec.
D-4   28 Dec.

CATK
31 Dec.

Bridge was blown up by 1 Jan.

PHILIPPINE SEA

SOUTH CHINA SEA

MINDORO

SAMAR

BATAAN ISLANDS

Batan Attack Force

LANDINGS NORTH OF APARRI

BABUYAN ISLANDS

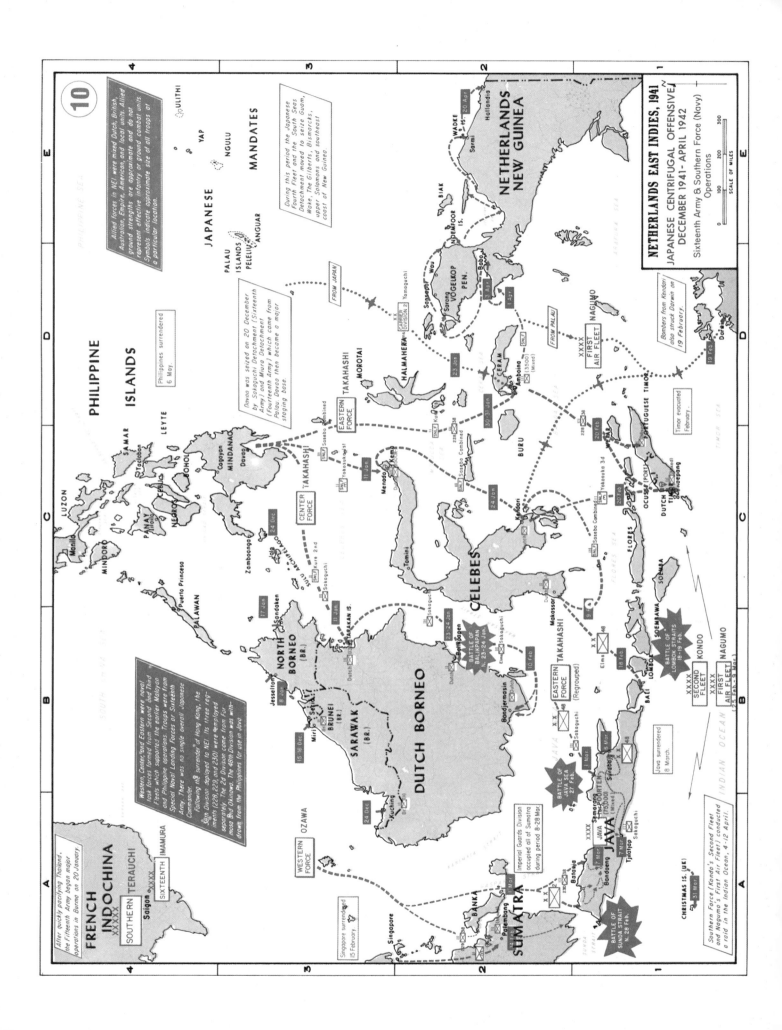

NETHERLANDS EAST INDIES, 1941

JAPANESE CENTRIFUGAL OFFENSIVE

DECEMBER 1941 – APRIL 1942

Sixteenth Army & Southern Force (Navy) Operations

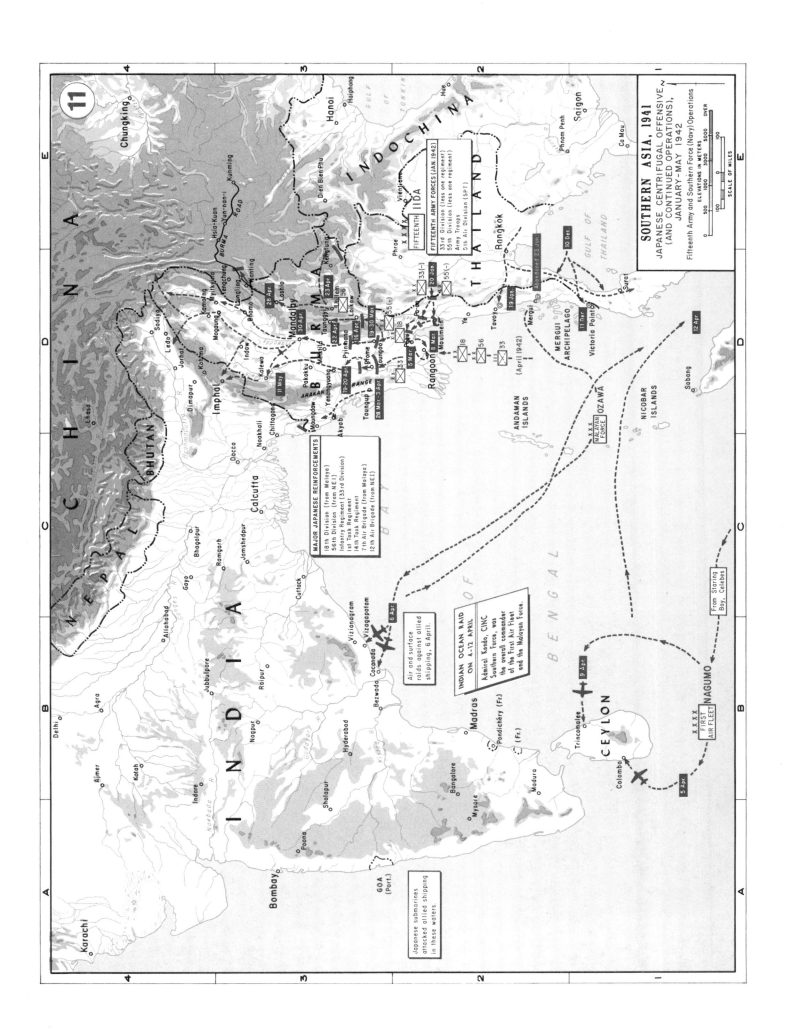

11

SOUTHERN ASIA, 1941

JAPANESE CENTRIFUGAL OFFENSIVE
(AND CONTINUED OPERATIONS),
JANUARY–MAY 1942

Fifteenth Army and Southern Force (Navy) Operations

ELEVATIONS IN METERS

500	1000	3000	5000	OVER
100				100		

SCALE OF MILES

FIFTEENTH IIDA

FIFTEENTH ARMY FORCES (JAN 1942)
33rd Division (less one regiment)
55th Division (less one regiment)
Army Troops
5th Air Division (SPT)

MAJOR JAPANESE REINFORCEMENTS
18th Division (from Malaya)
56th Division (from NEI)
Infantry Regiment (33rd Division)
1st Tank Regiment
4th Tank Regiment
7th Air Brigade (from Malaya)
12th Air Brigade (from NEI)

**INDIAN OCEAN RAID
ON 4–12 APRIL**
Admiral Kondo, CINC
Southern Force, was
the overall commander
of the First Air Fleet
and the Malayan Force.

Air and surface
raids against allied
shipping, 6 April.

Japanese submarines
attacked allied shipping
in these waters.

CHINA

Chungking

Lhasa

NEPAL

BHUTAN

Kunming

Yun-nan-i

Hsio-Kuan

BURMA ROAD

Mandalay 30 Apr

28 Apr Loshio

23 Apr Lashio 55

22 Apr Taungyi

ARAKAN YOMA RANGE

BURMA

Imphal

Kohima

Dimapur

Ledo

Sadiya

Jorhat

Mogaung

Myitkyina

Bhamo

Indaw

Kalewa

Pakokku

Yenangyaung

Pyinmana

11 May

19-20 Apr

28 Mar-3 Apr

Taungup

Prome

Toungoo

5 Mar.

Rangoon

INDOCHINA

Hanoi

Haiphong

GULF OF TONKIN

Dien Bien Phu

Vientiane

Phroe

THAILAND

Bangkok

Phnom Penh

Saigon

Ca Mau

GULF OF THAILAND

10 Dec.

Abandoned 23 Jan

19 Jan

Ye

Tavoy

Mergui

11 Mar

Victoria Point

MERGUI ARCHIPELAGO

20 Jan

333(-)

55(-)

55(e)

18

333

8 Mar Moulmein

18

56

33 (April 1942)

INDIA

Karachi

Delhi

Agra

Ajmer

Kotah

Indore

Nagpur

Raipur

Allahabad

Jubbulpore

Bhopalpur

Gaya

Ramgarh

Jamshedpur

Cuttack

Calcutta

Dacca

Noakhali

Chittagong

Akyab

Bombay

Poona

Sholapur

Hyderabad

Bangalore

Mysore

Madura

Madras

Pondichéry (Fr.)

(Fr.)

GOA (Port.)

Vizianagram

Vizagapatam

Cocanada

Bezwada

6 Apr.

BAY OF BENGAL

ANDAMAN ISLANDS

NICOBAR ISLANDS

Sabang

12 Apr.

OZAWA

MALAYAN FORCE

CEYLON

Colombo

5 Apr.

Trincomalee

9 Apr.

NAGUMO

FIRST AIR FLEET

From Staring Bay, Celebes

Surat

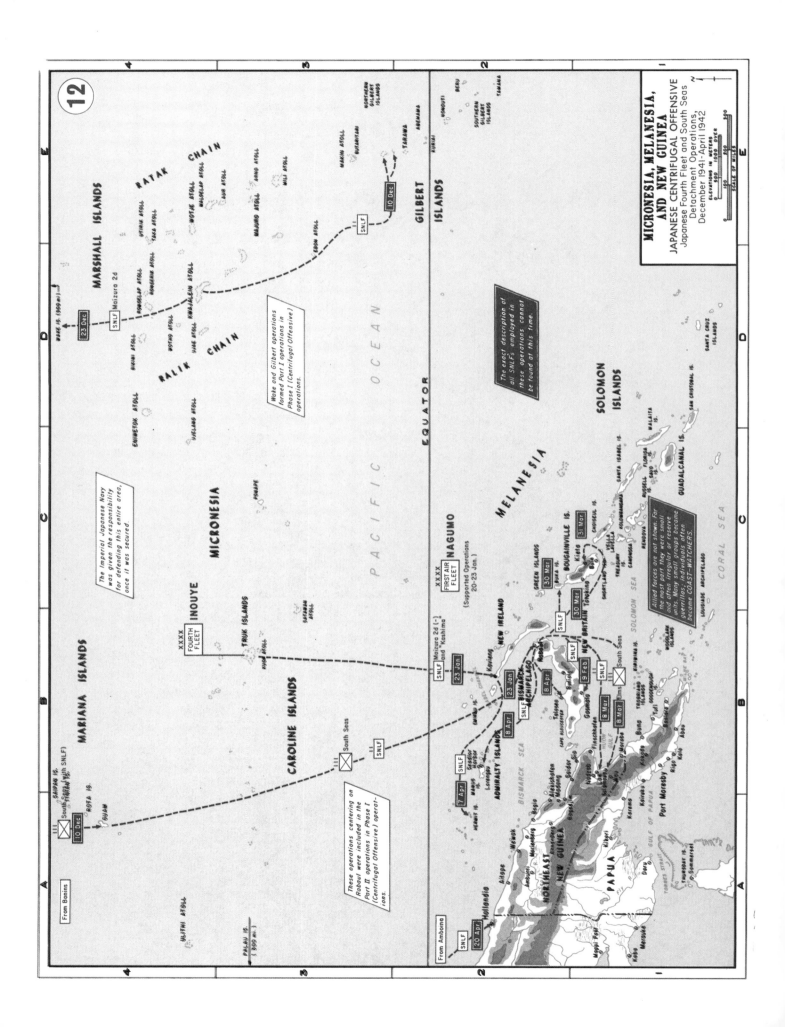

MICRONESIA, MELANESIA, AND NEW GUINEA

JAPANESE CENTRIFUGAL OFFENSIVE

Japanese Fourth Fleet and South Seas Detachment Operations, December 1941 - April 1942

These operations centering on Rabaul were included in the Part II operations in Phase I (Centrifugal Offensive) operations.

These operations centering on Phase I operations in Phase I (Centrifugal Offensive) operations.

Wake and Gilbert operations formed Part I operations in Phase I (Centrifugal Offensive) operations.

The Imperial Japanese Navy was given the responsibility for defending this entire area, once it was secured.

The exact description of all SNLF's employed in these operations cannot be found at this time.

Allied forces are not shown. For the most part they were small and often irregular or reserve units. Many small groups became guerillas; individuals often became COAST-WATCHERS.

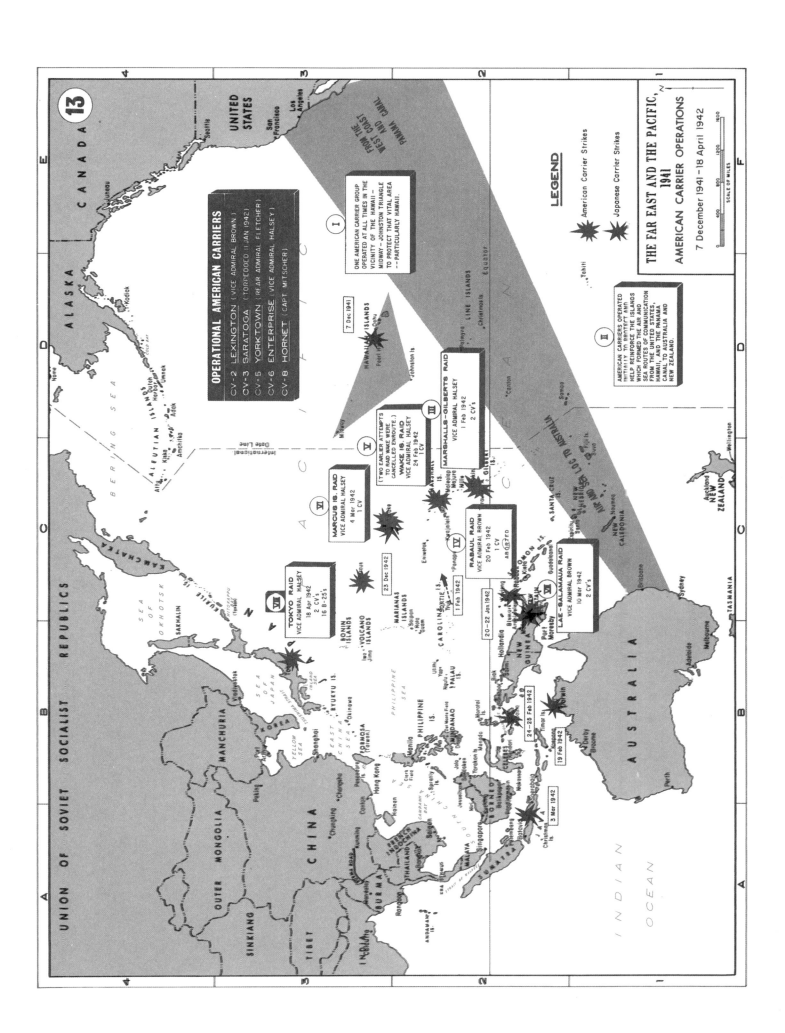

13

UNITED STATES

CANADA

ALASKA

UNION OF SOVIET SOCIALIST REPUBLICS

OPERATIONAL AMERICAN CARRIERS

CV-2 LEXINGTON (VICE ADMIRAL BROWN)
CV-3 SARATOGA (TORPEDOED 11 JAN 1942)
CV-5 YORKTOWN (REAR ADMIRAL FLETCHER)
CV-6 ENTERPRISE (VICE ADMIRAL HALSEY)
CV-8 HORNET (CAPT MITSCHER)

I — ONE AMERICAN CARRIER GROUP OPERATED AT ALL TIMES IN THE VICINITY OF THE HAWAII–MIDWAY–JOHNSTON TRIANGLE TO PROTECT THAT VITAL AREA –– PARTICULARLY HAWAII.

II — AMERICAN CARRIERS OPERATED INITIALLY TO PROTECT AND HELP REINFORCE THE ISLANDS WHICH FORMED THE AIR AND SEA ROUTES OF COMMUNICATION FROM THE UNITED STATES, HAWAII, AND THE PANAMA CANAL TO AUSTRALIA AND NEW ZEALAND.

III — MARSHALLS–GILBERTS RAID
VICE ADMIRAL HALSEY
1 Feb 1942   2 CV's

IV — RABAUL RAID
VICE ADMIRAL BROWN
20 Feb 1942   1 CV

V — WAKE IS. RAID
VICE ADMIRAL HALSEY
24 Feb 1942   1 CV
(TWO EARLIER ATTEMPTS TO RAID WAKE WERE CANCELLED ENROUTE.)

VI — MARCUS IS. RAID
VICE ADMIRAL HALSEY
4 Mar 1942   1 CV

VII — LAE–SALAMAUA RAID
VICE ADMIRAL BROWN
10 Mar 1942   2 CV's

VIII — TOKYO RAID
VICE ADMIRAL HALSEY
18 Apr 1942
2 CV's, 16 B-25's

LEGEND

✦ American Carrier Strikes

✦ Japanese Carrier Strikes

THE FAR EAST AND THE PACIFIC, 1941
AMERICAN CARRIER OPERATIONS

7 December 1941 – 18 April 1942

SCALE OF MILES
0   400   800   1200   1600

AUSTRALIA

NEW ZEALAND

CHINA

INDIAN OCEAN

PACIFIC OCEAN

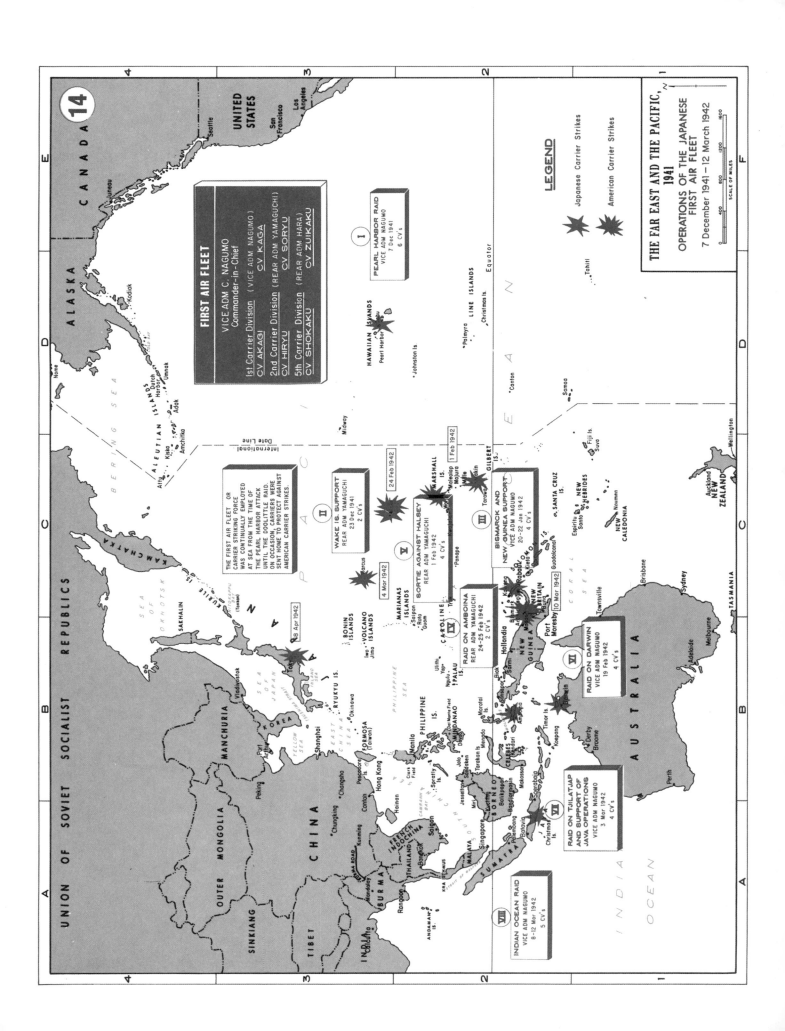

THE FAR EAST AND THE PACIFIC, 1941

OPERATIONS OF THE JAPANESE
FIRST AIR FLEET
7 December 1941 – 12 March 1942

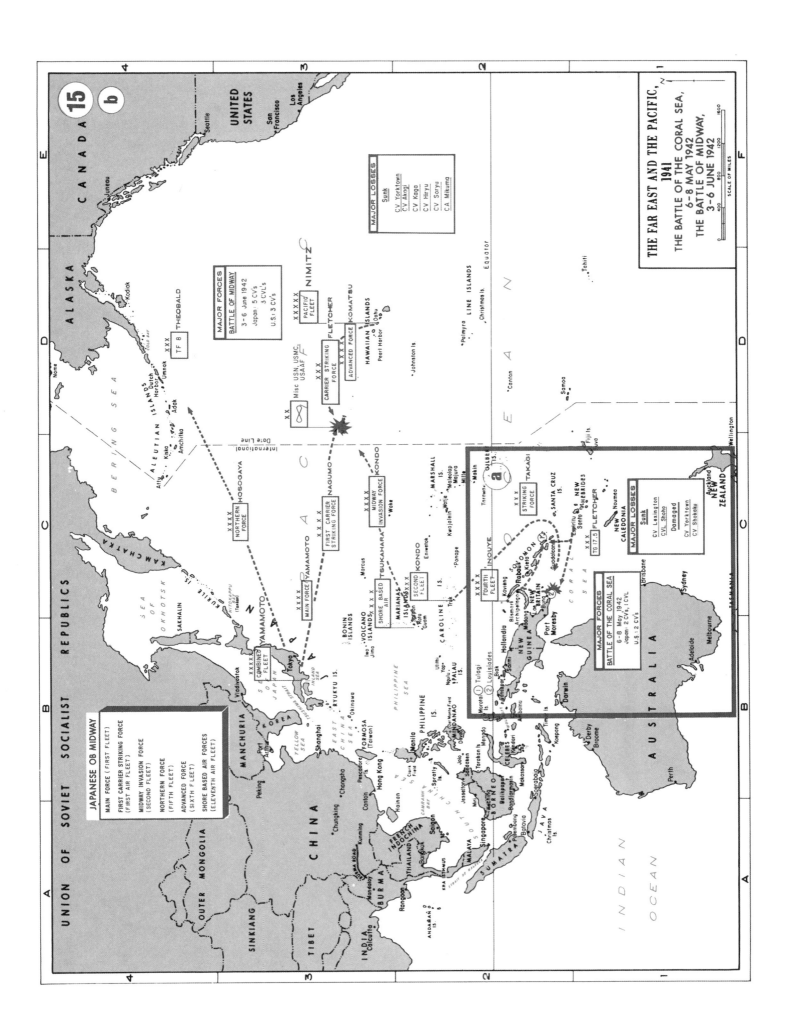

THE FAR EAST AND THE PACIFIC, 1941
THE BATTLE OF THE CORAL SEA,
6–8 MAY 1942
THE BATTLE OF MIDWAY,
3–6 JUNE 1942

SCALE OF MILES
0   400   800   1200   1600

15
b

MAJOR FORCES
BATTLE OF MIDWAY
3–6 June 1942
Japan: 5 CVs
        3 CVLs
U.S.: 3 CVs

MAJOR LOSSES
Sunk
CV Yorktown
CV Akagi
CV Kaga
CV Hiryu
CV Soryu
CA Mikuma

JAPANESE OB MIDWAY
MAIN FORCE (FIRST FLEET)
FIRST CARRIER STRIKING FORCE
(FIRST AIR FLEET)
MIDWAY INVASION FORCE
(SECOND FLEET)
NORTHERN FORCE
(FIFTH FLEET)
ADVANCED FORCE
(SIXTH FLEET)
SHORE BASED AIR FORCES
(ELEVENTH AIR FLEET)

MAJOR FORCES
BATTLE OF THE CORAL SEA
6–8 May 1942
Japan: 2 CVs, 1 CVL
U.S.: 2 CVs

MAJOR LOSSES
Sunk
CV Lexington
CVL Shoho
Damaged
CV Yorktown
CV Shokaku

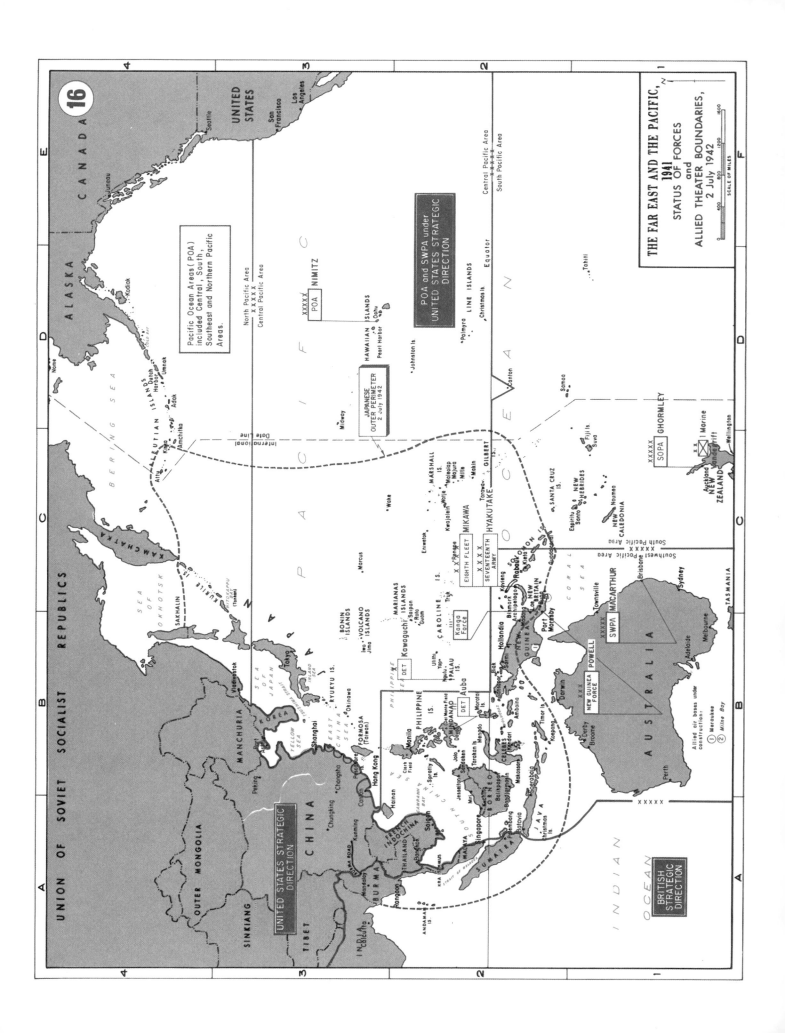

THE FAR EAST AND THE PACIFIC, 1941
STATUS OF FORCES
and
ALLIED THEATER BOUNDARIES,
2 July 1942

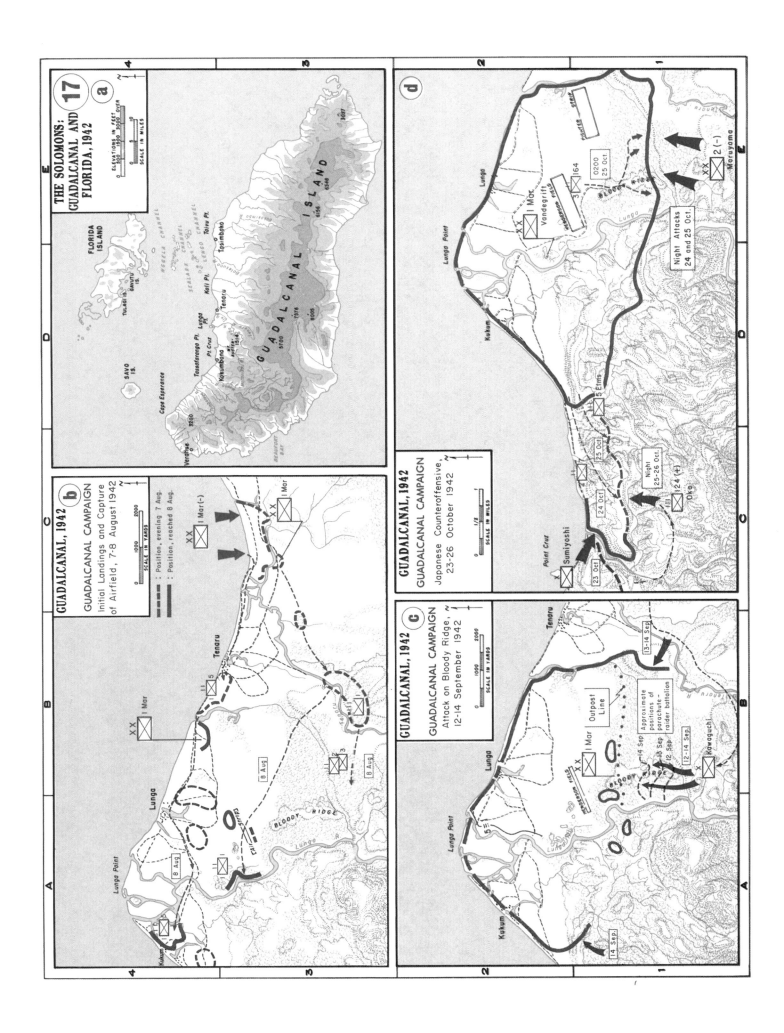

a
THE SOLOMONS: GUADALCANAL AND FLORIDA, 1942

ELEVATIONS IN FEET
500 1000 2000 3000 OVER
SCALE IN MILES

FLORIDA ISLAND

TULAGI IS.
GAVUTU IS.

NGGELA CHANNEL

SEALARK CHANNEL

FLORIDA CHANNEL

LENGO CHANNEL

SAVO IS.

Cape Esperance

Verahue

Kokumbona
Tassafaronga Pt. Lunga Pt.
Pt. Cruz
Kukumbona

Tenaru
Tasimboko

Koli Pt. Taivu Pt.

BEAUFORT BAY

G U A D A L C A N A L   I S L A N D

b
GUADALCANAL, 1942
GUADALCANAL CAMPAIGN
Initial Landings and Capture of Airfield, 7-8 August 1942

SCALE IN YARDS
0   1000   2000

: Position, evening 7 Aug.
: Position, reached 8 Aug.

Lunga Point

Kukum

Lunga

XX 1 Mar

Tenaru

5 ‖

1 Mar

1 Mar(-)

XX 1 Mar

3

8 Aug

8 Aug

8 Aug

8 Aug

BLOODY   RIDGE

Lunga

c
GUADALCANAL, 1942
GUADALCANAL CAMPAIGN
Attack on Bloody Ridge, 12-14 September 1942

SCALE IN YARDS
0   1000   2000

Lunga Point

Kukum

5 ‖

XX 1 Mar

1 Mar Outpost Line

HENDERSON FIELD

BLOODY   RIDGE

Approximate positions of parachute-raider battalion

14 Sep
13 Sep
12 Sep

14 Sep
13-14 Sep
12-14 Sep

X Kawaguchi

13-14 Sep

14 Sep.

Tenaru

d
GUADALCANAL, 1942
GUADALCANAL CAMPAIGN
Japanese Counteroffensive, 23-26 October 1942

SCALE IN MILES
0   1/2   1

Point Cruz

Sumiyoshi

23 Oct

24 Oct

25 Oct

Night 25-26 Oct.

24 Oct
Oka

25 Oct

5 Enns

Kukum

Lunga Point

Lunga

XX I Mar.

Vandegrift

3 164

I Mot.

0200 25 Oct.

HENDERSON FIELD

FIGHTER STRIP

BLOODY RIDGE

Lunga R.

Night Attacks 24 and 25 Oct.

XX 2(-)

Maruyama

17

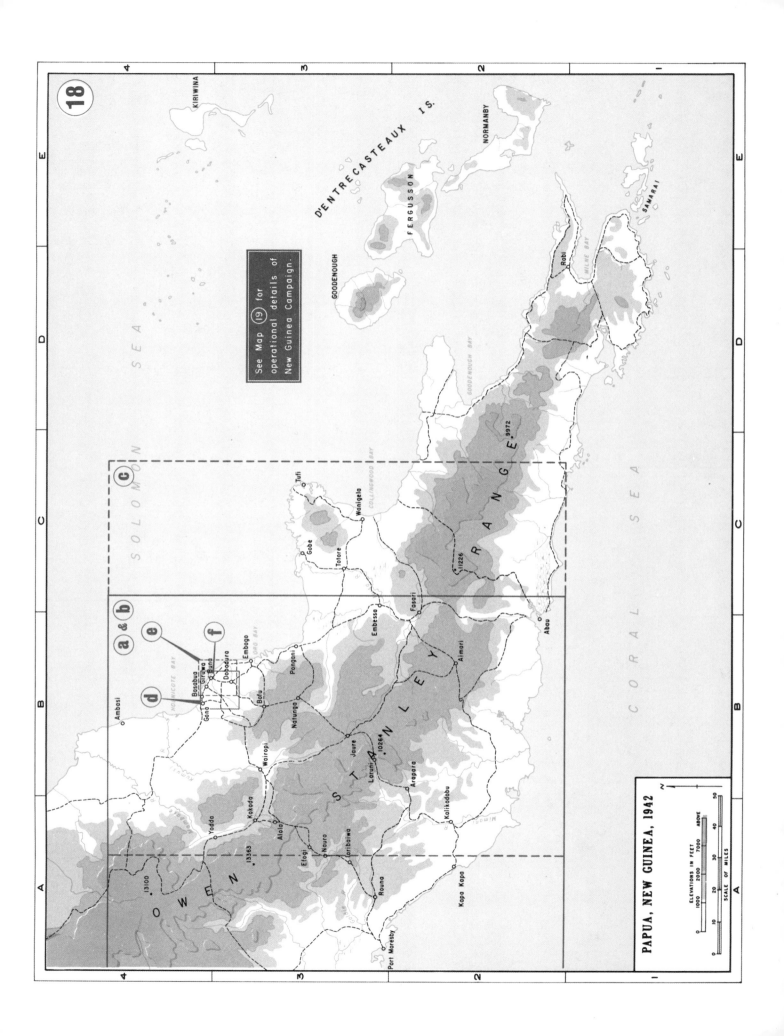

PAPUA, NEW GUINEA, 1942

ELEVATIONS IN FEET

1000 2000 7000 ABOVE

SCALE OF MILES

See Map 19 for operational details of New Guinea Campaign.

18

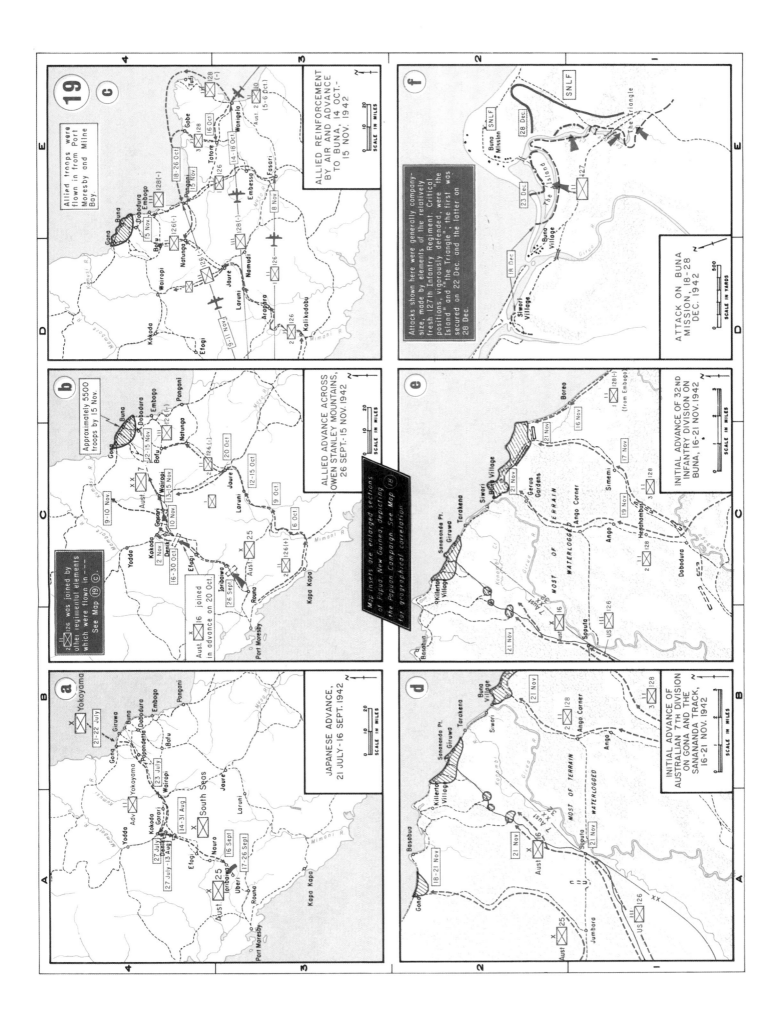

a

JAPANESE ADVANCE,
21 JULY-16 SEPT. 1942

SCALE IN MILES

b

2 126 was joined by
other regimental elements
which were flown in — — —
See Map 19 ©.

Approximately 5500
troops by 15 Nov.

ALLIED ADVANCE ACROSS
OWEN STANLEY MOUNTAINS,
26 SEPT.-15 NOV. 1942

SCALE IN MILES

Map inserts are enlarged sections
of Papua, New Guinea, depicting
the Papuan Campaign. See Map (18)
for geographical correlation.

c **19**

Allied troops were
flown in from Port
Moresby and Milne
Bay.

ALLIED REINFORCEMENT
BY AIR AND ADVANCE
TO BUNA, 14 OCT.-
15 NOV. 1942

SCALE IN MILES

d

INITIAL ADVANCE OF
AUSTRALIAN 7TH DIVISION
ON GONA AND THE
SANANANDA TRACK,
16-21 NOV. 1942

SCALE IN MILES

e

INITIAL ADVANCE OF 32ND
INFANTRY DIVISION ON
BUNA, 16-21 NOV. 1942

SCALE IN MILES

f

Attacks shown here were generally company-
size, made by elements of the relatively
fresh 127th Infantry Regiment. Critical
positions, vigorously defended, were "the
Island" and "the Triangle"; the first was
secured on 22 Dec. and the latter on
28 Dec.

ATTACK ON BUNA
MISSION, 18-28
DEC. 1942

SCALE IN YARDS

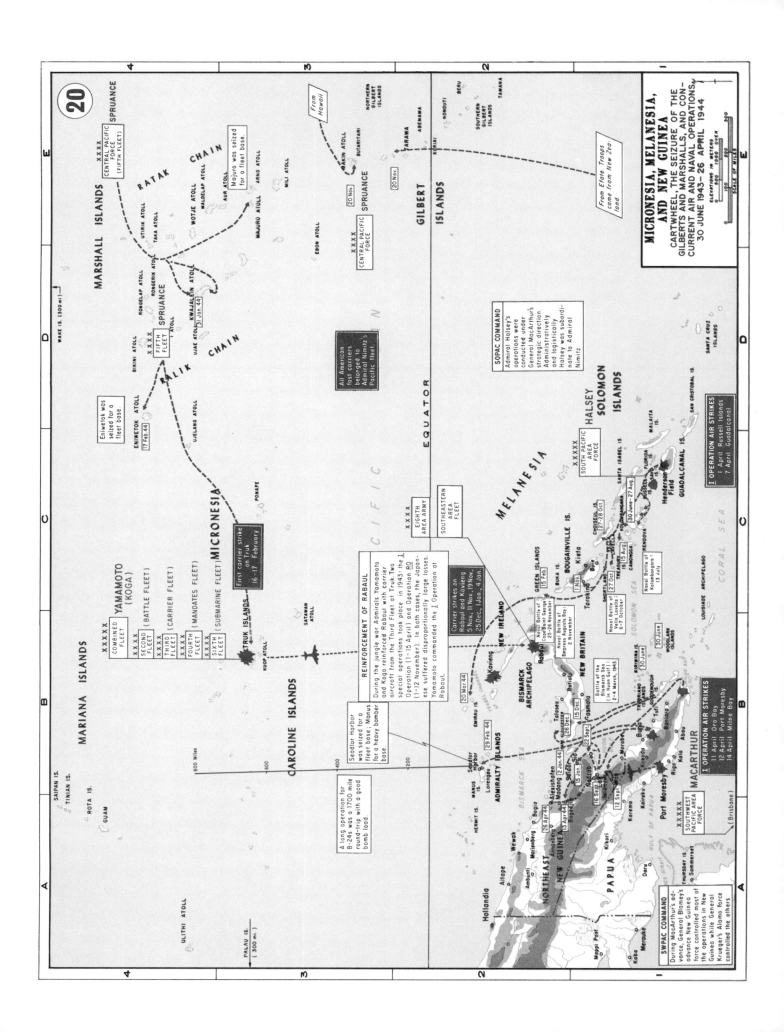

20

MARSHALL ISLANDS

RATAK CHAIN

RALIK CHAIN

XXXX
CENTRAL PACIFIC FORCE
(FIFTH FLEET)
SPRUANCE

WAKE IS. (1300 mi.)

UTIRIK ATOLL
TAKA ATOLL
RONGELAP ATOLL
RONGERIK ATOLL
BIKINI ATOLL
WOTJE ATOLL
MALOELAP ATOLL
AUR ATOLL
ARNO ATOLL
MILI ATOLL
EBON ATOLL
MAJURO ATOLL
UJAE ATOLL
KWAJALEIN ATOLL 31 Jan. 44
UJELANG ATOLL
ENIWETOK ATOLL

Majuro was seized for a fleet base.

SPRUANCE

From Hawaii
20 Nov.
20 Nov.
MAKIN ATOLL
BUTARITARI
SPRUANCE

XXXX
CENTRAL PACIFIC FORCE

Eniwetok was seized for a fleet base.
17 Feb. 44

GILBERT ISLANDS

KORIAI
TARAWA
ABEMAMA
NORTHERN GILBERT ISLANDS
BERU
NONOUTI
SOUTHERN GILBERT ISLANDS
TAMANA

From Efate Troops come from New Zealand

MARIANA ISLANDS

SAIPAN IS.
TINIAN IS.
ROTA IS.
GUAM

ULITHI ATOLL

PALAU IS.
(300 mi.)

CAROLINE ISLANDS

XXXXX
COMBINED FLEET
YAMAMOTO (KOGA)

XXXX SECOND FLEET (BATTLE FLEET)
XXXX THIRD FLEET (CARRIER FLEET)
XXXX FOURTH FLEET (MANDATES FLEET)
XXXX SIXTH FLEET (SUBMARINE FLEET)

MICRONESIA

TRUK ISLANDS

First carrier strike on Truk 16–17 February

PONAPE

KUOP ATOLL

SATAWAN ATOLL

A long operation for B-24's was 1700 mile round-trip with a good bomb load.

All American fast carriers belonged to Admiral Nimitz's Pacific fleet

EQUATOR

PACIFIC OCEAN

REINFORCEMENT OF RABAUL

During the jungle war Admirals Yamamoto and Koga reinforced Rabaul with carrier aircraft from the Third Fleet at Truk. Two special operations took place in 1943: the I Operation (1–15 April) and Operation RO (1–12 November). In both cases, the Japanese suffered disproportionally large losses. Yamamoto commanded the I Operation at Rabaul.

Seeadler Harbor was seized for a fleet base; Manus Is. for a heavy bomber base.

XXXX
EIGHTH AREA ARMY
SOUTHEASTERN AREA FLEET

Carrier strikes on Rabaul and Kavieng 5 Nov, 11 Nov, 19 Nov, 25 Dec, 1 Jan, 4 Jan.

NEW IRELAND
Kavieng
20 Mar. 44
Rabaul
NEW BRITAIN
BISMARCK ARCHIPELAGO

Naval Battle of Cape St. George 25–26 November
Naval Battle of Empress Augusta Bay: 2 November

MELANESIA

SOPAC COMMAND

Admiral Halsey's operations were conducted under General MacArthur's strategic direction. Administratively and logistically Halsey was subordinate to Admiral Nimitz.

XXXX
SOUTH PACIFIC AREA FORCE
HALSEY
SOLOMON ISLANDS

MALAITA IS.
SANTA ISABEL IS.
FLORIDA IS.
CHOISEUL IS. 27–28 Oct
VANGIKORA IS. 30 June–27 Aug
BUKA IS.
BOUGAINVILLE IS. 1 Nov
Kieta
Buin 27 Oct
Torokina
SHORTLAND IS.
TREASURY IS. 27 Oct
GREEN ISLANDS 15 Feb.
15 Aug
Naval Battle of Vella Lavella: 6–7 October
KOLOMBANGARA 13 July
Naval Battle of Kolombangara 13 July
NEW GEORGIA 30 June
RENDOVA

Henderson Field
GUADALCANAL IS.
SAN CRISTOBAL IS.
SANTA CRUZ ISLANDS

I OPERATION AIR STRIKES
1 April Russell Islands
7 April Guadalcanal

CORAL SEA

BISMARCK SEA

ADMIRALTY ISLANDS
EMIRAU IS. 29 Feb 44
HERMIT IS.
MANUS IS.
Lorengau 26 Apr 44
Seeadler Hbr.

800 Miles
600
400
200

LOUISIADE ARCHIPELAGO
WOODLARK IS. 30 June
KIRIWINA IS. 30 June

NORTHEAST NEW GUINEA
Hollandia
Aitape
Amburi
Wewak
Marienberg
Bogia
Madang
Alexishafen
Bunda
Bogadjim
Saidor 2 Jan 44
Sio
Finschhafen 2 Jun 44
Gusap
15 Jan 44
Bena
Toloso
Dumpu
Kaiapit
5 Sept
6 Oct
Lae 16 Sept
Salamaua 12 Sept
Bulolo
Kelanoa
Nadzab
Karema
15 Dec
Gasmata 15 Dec
Arawe
Cape Gloucester 26 Dec
23 Sept
Buna

Battle of the Bismarck Sea (in Huon Gulf): 2–4 March, 1943

PAPUA
GULF OF PAPUA
Port Moresby
Kikori
Tufi
Kokoda
Abau
Riga
Dorio
Samarai

Kaba
Merauke
Mappi Post

MACARTHUR

I OPERATION AIR STRIKES
11 April Oro Bay
12 April Port Moresby
14 April Milne Bay

XXXX
SOUTHWEST PACIFIC AREA FORCE
(Brisbane)

SWPAC COMMAND

During MacArthur's advance, General Blamey's advance New Guinea force controlled most of the operations in New Guinea while General Krueger's Alamo force controlled the others

MICRONESIA, MELANESIA, AND NEW GUINEA

CARTWHEEL, THE SEIZURE OF THE GILBERTS AND MARSHALLS, AND CONCURRENT AIR AND NAVAL OPERATIONS, 30 JUNE 1943–26 APRIL 1944

ELEVATIONS IN METERS
200   500   1000 OVER

100   200   300
SCALE OF MILES

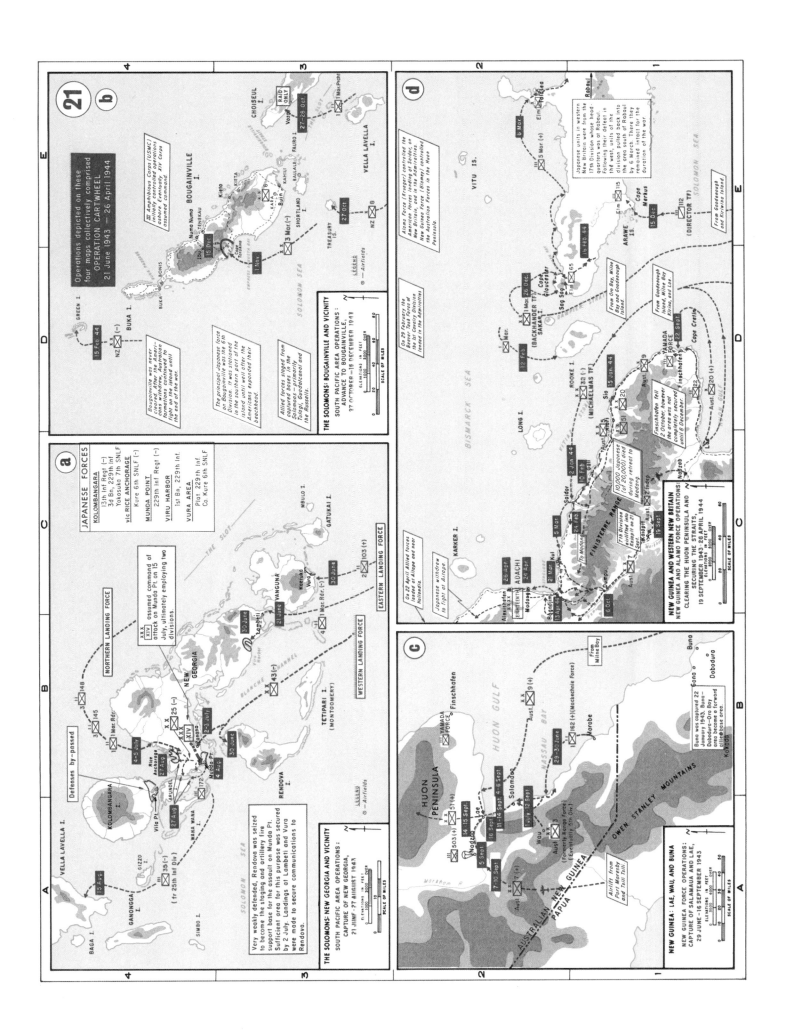

21

b

Operations depicted on these four maps collectively comprised OPERATION CARTWHEEL 21 June 1943 – 26 April 1944

II Amphibious Corps (USMC) initially controlled operations ashore. Eventually XIV Corps assumed command

Bougainville was never cleared. After the Americans withdrew, Australian formations continued to fight on the island until the end of the war.

The principal Japanese force on Bougainville was the 6th Division; it was stationed in the southern part of the island until after the Americans expanded their beachhead.

Allied forces staged from captured bases in the Solomons, primarily Tulagi, Guadalcanal, and the Russells.

THE SOLOMONS: BOUGAINVILLE AND VICINITY
SOUTH PACIFIC AREA OPERATIONS: ADVANCE TO BOUGAINVILLE, 27 OCTOBER – 15 DECEMBER 1943

a

JAPANESE FORCES

KOLOMBANGARA
13th Inf Regt (−)
3d Bn, 229th Inf
Yokosuka 7th SNLF

vic RICE ANCHORAGE
Kure 6th SNLF (−)

MUNDA POINT
229th Inf Regt (−)

VIRU HARBOR
1st Bn, 229th Inf.

VURA AREA
Plat 229th Inf
Co Kure 6th SNLF

XIV assumed command of attack on Munda Pt. on 15 July, ultimately employing two divisions.

NORTHERN LANDING FORCE

Defenses by-passed

Rendova was seized to become the staging and artillery fire support base for the assault on Munda Pt. Sufficient area for this purpose was secured by 2 July. Landings at Lambeti and Vura were made to secure communications to Rendova.

EASTERN LANDING FORCE

WESTERN LANDING FORCE

Very weakly defended, Rendova was seized to become the staging and artillery fire support base for the assault on Munda Pt. Sufficient area for this purpose was secured by 2 July. Landings at Lambeti and Vura were made to secure communications to Rendova.

THE SOLOMONS: NEW GEORGIA AND VICINITY
SOUTH PACIFIC AREA OPERATIONS: CAPTURE OF NEW GEORGIA, 21 JUNE – 27 AUGUST 1943

d

Alamo Force (Krueger) controlled the American forces landing at Saidor; on New Britain, and in the Admiralties. New Guinea Force (Blamey) controlled the Australian forces in the Huon Peninsula

On 29 February the Brewer Task Force of the 1st Cavalry Division landed in the Admiralties.

Finschhafen fell 2 October, however the area was not completely secured until 8 December.

10,000 Japanese (of 20,000) died during retreat to Madang

On 22 April Allied forces landed at Aitape and near Hollandia.

Japanese withdrew to fight at Aitape

Japanese units in western New Britain were from the 17th Division whose headquarters was at Rabaul. Following their defeat in the west, units of the division pulled back into the area south of Rabaul by 6 March. There they remained intact for the duration of the war

From Goodenough and Kiriwina Island

From Oro Bay, Milne Bay and Goodenough Island

From Goodenough Island, Milne Bay, Kiriwi, and Lae.

(DIRECTOR TF)

NEW GUINEA AND WESTERN NEW BRITAIN
NEW GUINEA AND ALAMO FORCE OPERATIONS: CLEARING THE HUON PENINSULA AND SECURING THE STRAITS, 19 SEPTEMBER 1943 – 26 APRIL 1944

c

From Milne Bay

Buna was captured 22 January 1943. Buna – Dobodura – Oro Bay area became a forward air-base area.

NEW GUINEA: LAE, WAU, AND BUNA
NEW GUINEA FORCE OPERATIONS: CAPTURE OF SALAMAUA AND LAE, 29 JUNE – 16 SEPTEMBER 1943

Airlift from Port Moresby and Tsili Tsili

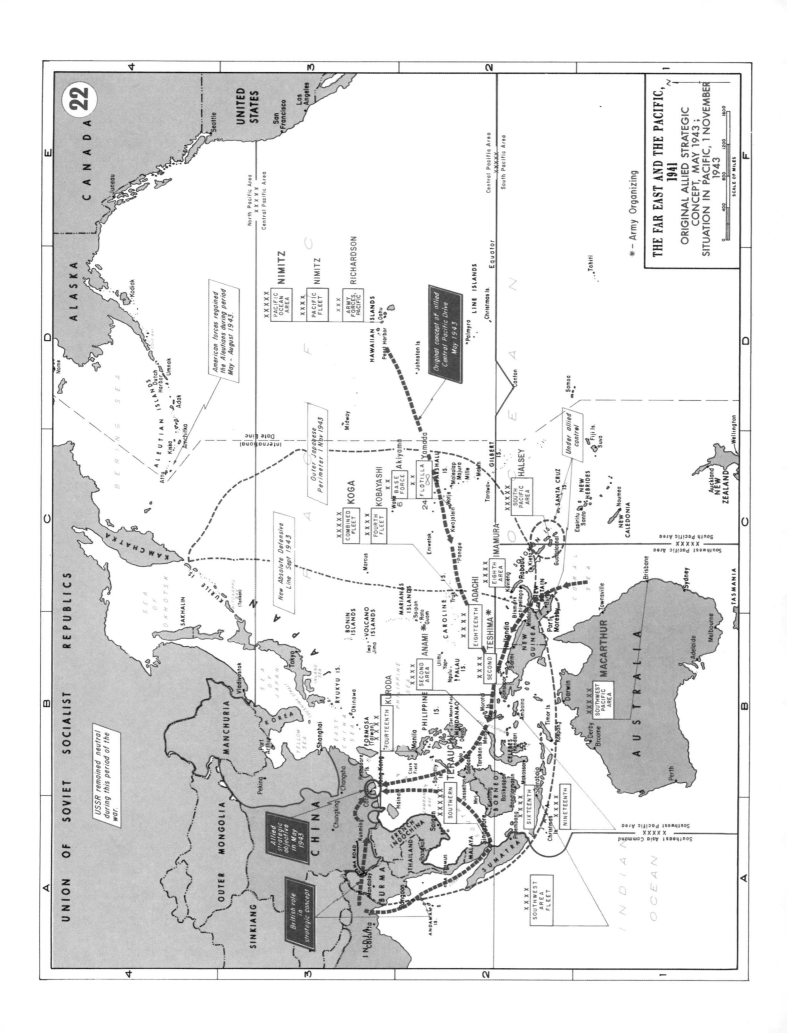

THE FAR EAST AND THE PACIFIC, 1941

ORIGINAL ALLIED STRATEGIC CONCEPT, MAY 1943; SITUATION IN PACIFIC, 1 NOVEMBER 1943

* Army Organizing

SCALE OF MILES
0   400   800   1200   1600

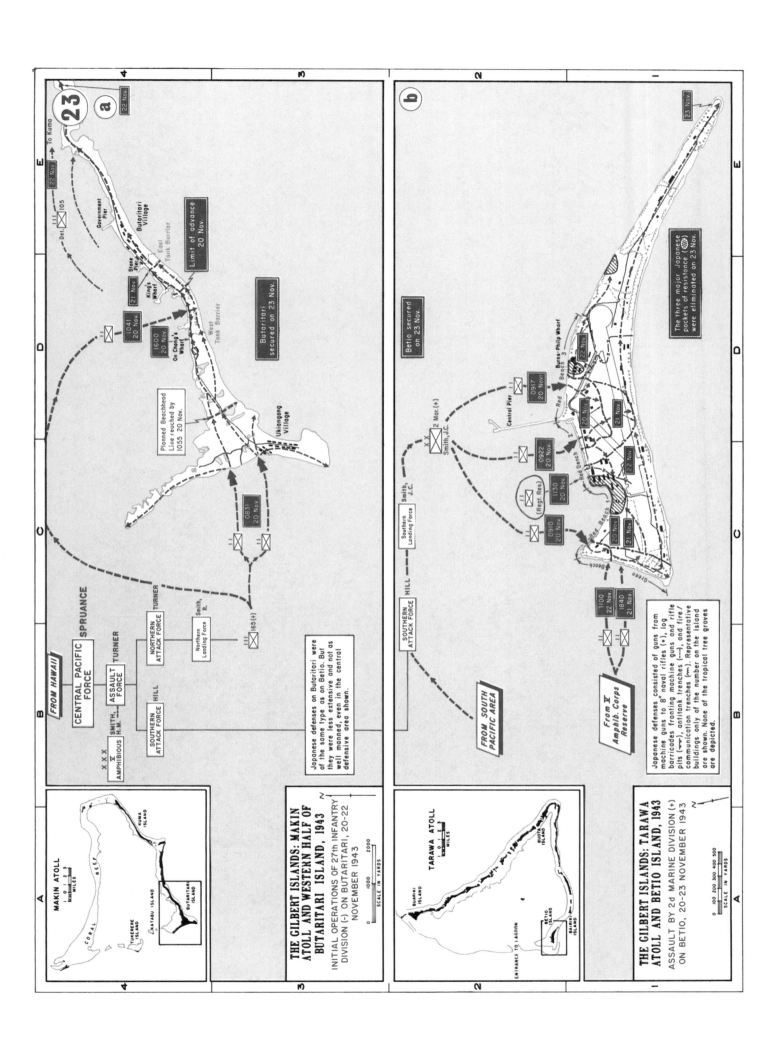

23

a

FROM HAWAII

CENTRAL PACIFIC
FORCE
SPRUANCE

XXX   SMITH, H.M.
V
AMPHIBIOUS   ASSAULT
FORCE
TURNER

SOUTHERN ATTACK FORCE ··········· SMITH, H.M.

SOUTHERN HILL

NORTHERN ATTACK FORCE ··········· TURNER

Northern Landing Force ··········· Smith, R.

Japanese defenses on Butaritari were of the same type as on Betio. But they were less extensive and not as well manned, even in the central defensive area shown.

To Kumo

22 Nov.

Det. 105

111   Det.

Government Pier

Butaritari Village

Stone Pier

King's Wharf

East Tank Barrier

21 Nov.

22 Nov.

Limit of advance 20 Nov.

West Tank Barrier

On Chong's Wharf

1600 20 Nov.

1041 20 Nov.

Planned Beachhead Line reached by 1055 20 Nov.

Butaritari secured on 23 Nov.

Ukiangong Village

083 20 Nov.

165 (+)   111

MAKIN ATOLL

MILES
0   1   2   3

KUMA ISLAND

CORAL   REEF

TUERERE ISLAND

KATABU ISLAND

BUTARITARI ISLAND

SCALE IN YARDS
0   1000   2000

THE GILBERT ISLANDS: MAKIN ATOLL AND WESTERN HALF OF BUTARITARI ISLAND, 1943

INITIAL OPERATIONS OF 27th INFANTRY DIVISION (–) ON BUTARITARI, 20-22 NOVEMBER 1943

b

FROM SOUTH PACIFIC AREA

SOUTHERN ATTACK FORCE

Southern Landing Force ········· Smith, J.C.

2 Mar.(+)   XX   Smith, J.C.

From V Amphib. Corps Reserve

Japanese defenses consisted of guns from machine guns to 8" naval rifles (•), log barricades fronting machine guns and rifle pits (▬▬), antitank trenches (▬▬), and fire/communication trenches (⌇⌇). Representative buildings only of the number on the island are shown. None of the tropical tree groves are depicted.

Betio secured on 23 Nov.

The three major Japanese pockets of resistance (▨▨) were eliminated on 23 Nov.

23 Nov.

Burns-Philp Wharf

Beach 3

22 Nov.

0917 20 Nov.

Central Pier

Red

0922 20 Nov.

20 Nov.

21 Nov.

(Regt. Res.)

1130 20 Nov.

0910 20 Nov.

Red Beach 2

Red Beach 1

20 Nov.

21 Nov.

Green Beach

1100 22 Nov.

1840 21 Nov.

TARAWA ATOLL

MILES
0   1   2   3

BUARIKI ISLAND

BUOTA ISLAND

BETIO ISLAND

BAIRIKI ISLAND

ENTRANCE TO LAGOON

THE GILBERT ISLANDS: TARAWA ATOLL AND BETIO ISLAND, 1943

ASSAULT BY 2d MARINE DIVISION (+) ON BETIO, 20-23 NOVEMBER 1943

SCALE IN YARDS
0 100 200 300 400 500

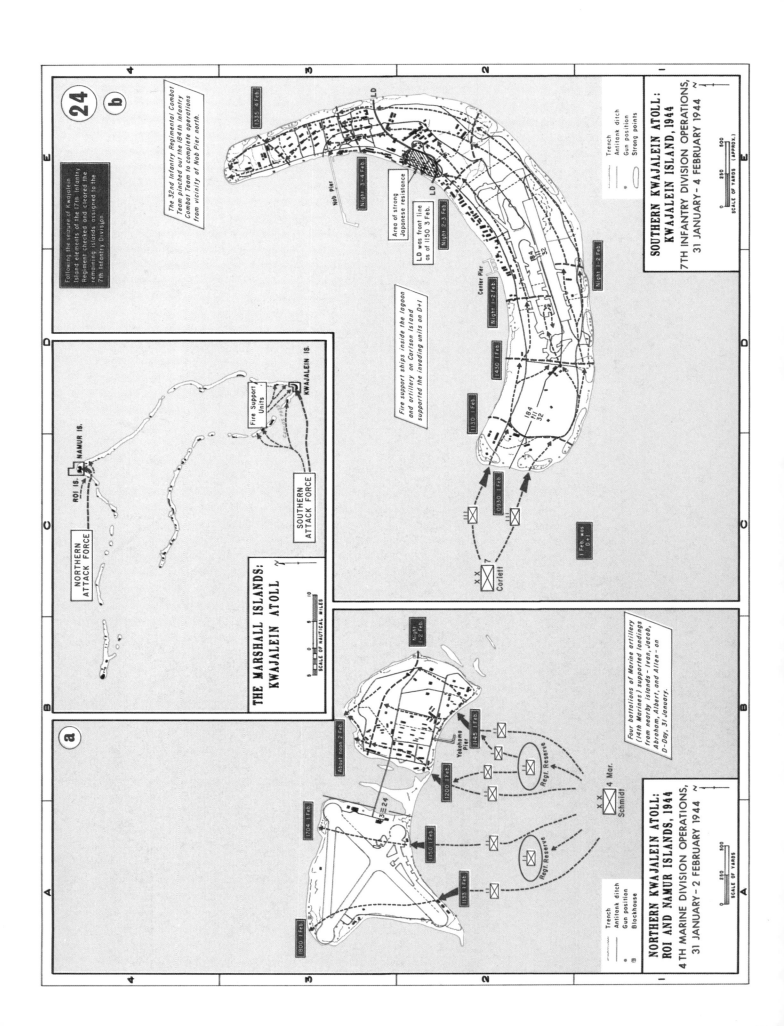

24

(b)

The 32nd Infantry Regimental Combat Team pinched out the 17th Infantry Combat Team to complete operations from vicinity of Nab Pier north.

Following the seizure of Kwajalein Island elements of the 17th Infantry Regiment checked and cleared the remaining islands assigned to the 7th Infantry Division.

1335 4 Feb.

Nab Pier

Night 3-4 Feb.

LD

Area of strong Japanese resistance

LD was front line as of 1150 3 Feb.

Night 2-3 Feb.

Center Pier

Night 1-2 Feb.

Fire support ships inside the lagoon and artillery on Carlson Island supported the invading units on D+1

1430 1 Feb.

184
Mil
32

Night 1-2 Feb.

184
32

1110 1 Feb.

Trench
Antitank ditch
Gun position
Strong points

SOUTHERN KWAJALEIN ATOLL: KWAJALEIN ISLAND, 1944
7TH INFANTRY DIVISION OPERATIONS,
31 JANUARY–4 FEBRUARY 1944

0   250   500
SCALE OF YARDS (APPROX.)

0930 1 Feb.

1 Feb. was D+1

XX 7
Corlett

(a)

NAMUR IS.

ROI IS.

Fire Support Units

KWAJALEIN IS.

CARLOS PASS.

NORTHERN ATTACK FORCE

SOUTHERN ATTACK FORCE

THE MARSHALL ISLANDS: KWAJALEIN ATOLL

5   0   5   10
SCALE OF NAUTICAL MILES

Night 1-2 Feb.

About noon 2 Feb.

Yokohama Pier

1745 1 Feb.

1200 1 Feb.

3=24

1704 1 Feb.

1150 1 Feb.

Regt. Reserve

XX 4 Mar.
Schmidt

Regt. Reserve

1133 1 Feb.

1800 1 Feb.

Four battalions of Marine artillery (14th Marines) supported landings from nearby islands – Ivan, Jacob, Abraham, Albert, and Allen – on D-Day, 31 January.

Trench
Antitank ditch
Gun position
Blockhouse

NORTHERN KWAJALEIN ATOLL: ROI AND NAMUR ISLANDS, 1944
4TH MARINE DIVISION OPERATIONS,
31 JANUARY–2 FEBRUARY 1944

0   250   500
SCALE OF YARDS

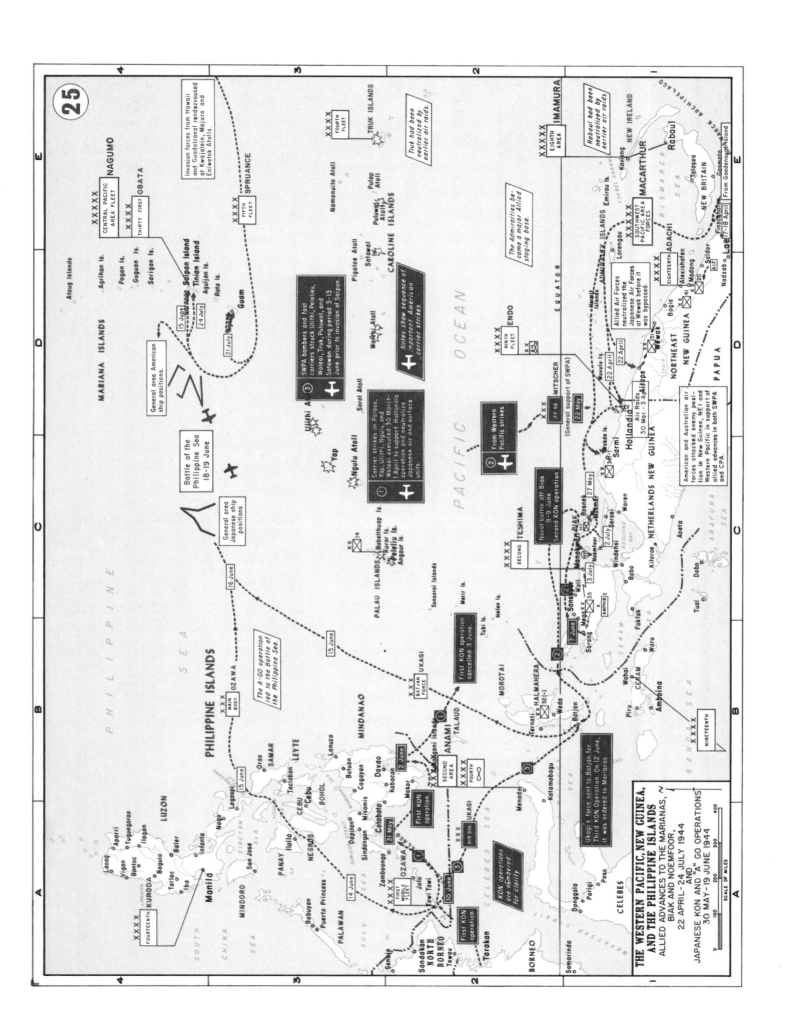

**THE WESTERN PACIFIC, NEW GUINEA,
AND THE PHILIPPINE ISLANDS**
ALLIED ADVANCES TO THE MARIANAS,
BIAK AND NOEMFOOR,
22 APRIL – 24 JULY 1944
AND
JAPANESE KON AND "A" GO OPERATIONS
30 MAY – 19 JUNE 1944

SCALE OF MILES
100   200   300   400

25

MARIANA ISLANDS

CENTRAL PACIFIC AREA FLEET NAGUMO
XXXXX

THIRTY FIRST OBATA
XXXX

Invasion forces from Hawaii and Guadalcanal rendezvoused at Kwajalein, Majuro and Eniwetok Atolls.

Atoug Islands

Agrihan Is.
Pagan Is.
Guguan Is.
Sarigan Is.
15 June Saipan Island
24 July Tinian Island
Aguijan Is.
Rota Is.
21 July Guam

General area American ship positions.

FIFTH FLEET SPRUANCE
XXXX

FOURTH FLEET
XXXX

TRUK ISLANDS

Truk had been neutralized by earlier air raids.

Namonuito Atoll

Pulap Atoll
Puluwat Atoll
Satawal

Pigalae Atoll

CAROLINE ISLANDS

Woleai Atoll

Battle of the Philippine Sea 18-19 June

General area Japanese ship positions

③ *SWPA bombers and fast carriers struck Ulithi, Peleliu, Woleai, Truk, Puluwot, and Satawan during period 3-13 June prior to invasion of Saipan.*

Notes show sequence of important American carrier strikes.

① *Carrier strikes on Palaus, Yap, Ulithi, Ngulu, and Woleai executed 30 March-1 April to support Hollandia operation and neutralize Japanese air and surface units.*

Ulithi Atoll

Soral Atoll

Yap
Ngulu Atoll

PHILIPPINE ISLANDS

The A-GO operation led to the Battle of the Philippine Sea.

MAIN BODY OZAWA
XXX

16 June

15 June

PACIFIC OCEAN

PALAU ISLANDS
Babelthuap Is.
Kuror Is.
Peleliu Is.
Angaur Is.
XX ⑭

Sonsorol Islands

Merir Is.

Helen Is.

Tobi Is.

② *From Western Pacific strikes*

EQUATOR

PHILIPPINE SEA

14 June

FOURTEENTH KURODA
XXXX

Manila
LUZON
Aparri
Tuguegarao
Ilagan
Vigan
Bangued
Baler
Baguio
Tarlac
Iba
Infanta
San Jose
Puerto Princesa

MINDORO

Legaspi
Naga

SAMAR
LEYTE
Tacloban
Catbalogan
15 June
Ormoc
Cebu
CEBU
Iloilo
PANAY
NEGROS
BOHOL
Dumaguete
Bobuyon

PALAWAN

SULU SEA

Jolo
Owi Tawi
Zamboanga

Dipolog
Misamis
MINDANAO
Cagayan
Butuan
Surigao
Davao
Kabacan
Cotabato
Makar
2 June

Sangigani Islands
TALAUD

Davao
Malalag

BATJAN FORCE UKAGI
XXX

32(-)
XXX

First KON operation cancelled 3 June

SECOND AREA ANAMI
XXXX

FOURTH ⑧⑧
XXXX

③

CELEBES SEA

Menado
Kolonodale

Kolasmobagu

Ukagi's force sent to Batjan for Third KON Operation. On 12 June, it was ordered to Marianas.

First KON operation

31 May UKAGI
AIR DIV
XXX

OZAWA ②
FIRST MOBILE FLEET
XXXX

10 June

First KON operation

① ③

KON operations are numbered for clarity.

BORNEO
Tarakan
Samarinda
Balikpapan

NORTH BORNEO
Sandakan
Tawau
Sibngu

SOUTH CHINA SEA

Samarinda

NINETEENTH
XXXX

CELEBES
Donggala
Parigi
Poso
Amboina
CERAM
Piru
Waru

BANDA SEA

Wohai
Dobo
Tual
Foktok
Kiteroo

ARAFURA SEA

NETHERLANDS NEW GUINEA

Aoeta
Bobo
Windeshi
Koloss

HALMAHERA
Weda
Ternate
Bajan

MOROTAI

SECOND TESHIMA
XXXX

Naval battle off Biak 8-9 June Second KON operation

Manokwari **BIAK**
Bosnek 27 May
Noemfoor 2 July
Warsa
Waren
Berdei

3 July
Sansapor
Sorong 7 June
Mega XX 35
x AMPHIB 2

MITSCHER
XXX TF 58
22 May

(General support of SWPA)

Hollandia
Air Raids
30 Mar. - 3 April

22 May

ENDO
XXXX
NINTH FLEET
XX ⑥⑧

Sarmi
22 April
Wakde Is.
Toem
Wewok
22 April

NORTHEAST NEW GUINEA

EIGHTEENTH ADACHI
XXXX
Alexishafen
Madang
Bogia
x 41
x 20
ALF
Nadzab Lae
Finschhafen 17-18 April
Saidor

American and Australian air forces attacked enemy positions in New Guinea, NEI and Western Pacific in support of Allied advances in both SWPA and CPA.

Allied Air Forces neutralized the Japanese Air Forces at Wewak before it was bypassed.

ADMIRALTY ISLANDS
Lorengau
Manus Island
Los Negros Is.
Emirau Is.

The Admiralties became a major Allied staging base.

SOUTHWEST PACIFIC AREA FORCES MACARTHUR
XXXXX

PAPUA

NEW IRELAND
Kavieng
Rabaul IMAMURA
EIGHTH AREA
XXXXX

Rabaul had been neutralized by earlier air raids.

NEW BRITAIN
Talasea
Gasmata
Cape Gloucester
From Goodenough Island

BISMARCK SEA

BISMARCK ARCHIPELAGO

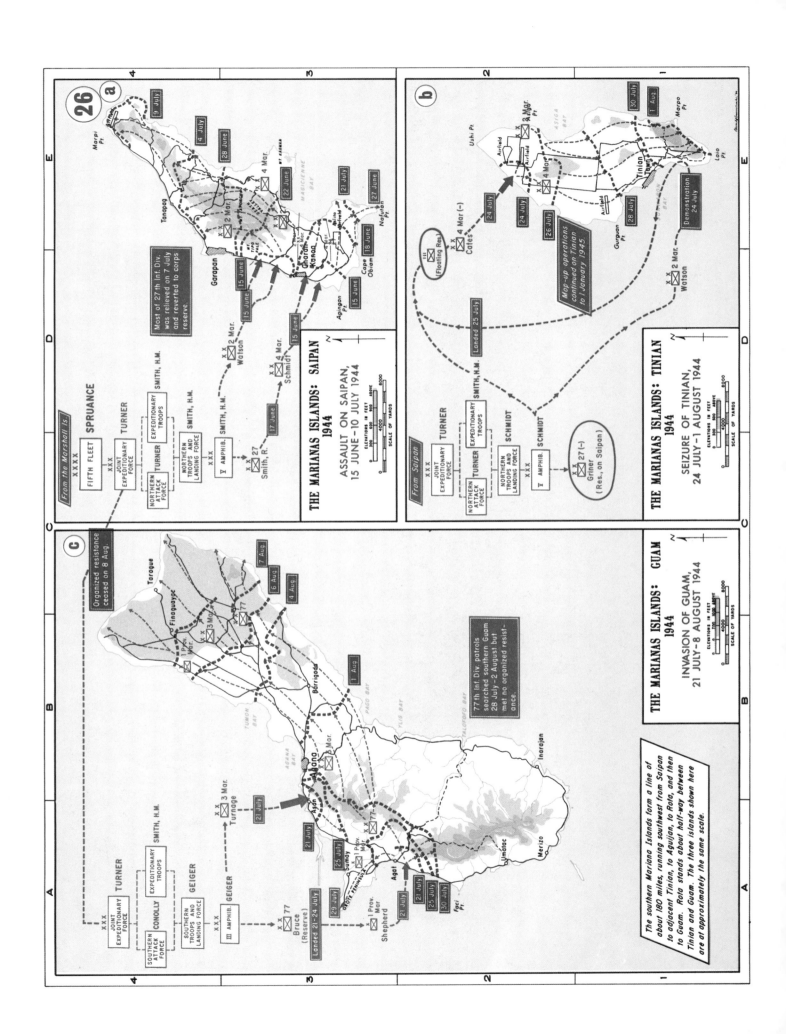

26 a

Marpi Pt.
9 July
4 July
28 June
Mt. Petosukara
22 June
XX 4 Mar.
Tanapag
XX 2 Mar.
MT. TAPOCHAU
MAGICIENNE BAY
21 July
27 June
Garapan
15 June
XX 2 Mar. Watson
Charan Kanoa
15 June
XX 4 Mar. Schmidt
15 June
18 June
Aslito Airfield
Nafutan Pt.
Agingan Pt.
15 June
Cape Obiam

Most of 27th Inf. Div. was relieved on 7 July and reverted to corps reserve.

From the Marshall Is.

SPRUANCE

FIFTH FLEET xxxx

TURNER

JOINT EXPEDITIONARY FORCE xxx

EXPEDITIONARY TROOPS	SMITH, H.M.

NORTHERN ATTACK FORCE	TURNER

NORTHERN TROOPS AND LANDING FORCE	SMITH, H.M.

V AMPHIB. SMITH, H.M.

XX 27 Smith, R.

17 June

THE MARIANAS ISLANDS: SAIPAN
1944

ASSAULT ON SAIPAN,
15 JUNE–10 JULY 1944

ELEVATIONS IN FEET
SCALE OF YARDS

---

b

Ushi Pt.
3 Mar. Pt.
30 July
1 Aug.
ASIGA BAY
Airfield
Airfield
XX 4 Mar.
XX 4 Mar.
Tinian Town
Marpo Pt.
Lalo Pt.
24 July
26 July
Gurgan Pt.
28 July
XX 2 Mar. Watson
Demonstration
24 July
Landed 25 July

III (Floating Res.)
XX 4 Mar. Cates

Mop-up operations continued on Tinian to 1 January 1945.

From Saipan

TURNER

JOINT EXPEDITIONARY FORCE xxx

EXPEDITIONARY TROOPS	SMITH, H.M.

NORTHERN ATTACK FORCE	TURNER

NORTHERN TROOPS AND LANDING FORCE	SCHMIDT

V AMPHIB. SCHMIDT

XX 27 (−) Griner (Res., on Saipan)

THE MARIANAS ISLANDS: TINIAN
1944

SEIZURE OF TINIAN,
24 JULY–1 AUGUST 1944

ELEVATIONS IN FEET
SCALE OF YARDS

---

c

Organized resistance ceased on 8 Aug.

Tarague
7 Aug
6 Aug
4 Aug
Finaguayac
XX 3 Mar.
XX 77
1 Prov. Mar.
Agana
AGANA BAY
21 July
Asan
XX 3 Mar. Turnage
TUMON BAY
Barrigada
1 Aug
PAGO BAY
TALOFOFO BAY
YLIG BAY
Sumay
XX 1 Prov. Mar.
25 July
Agat
21 July
OROTE PENINSULA
XX 77
21 July
25 July
30 July
Facpi Pt.
Shepherd
Umatac
Merizo
Inarajan

77th Inf. Div. patrols searched southern Guam 28 July–2 August but met no organized resistance.

TURNER

JOINT EXPEDITIONARY FORCE xxx

EXPEDITIONARY TROOPS	SMITH, H.M.

SOUTHERN ATTACK FORCE	CONOLLY

SOUTHERN TROOPS AND LANDING FORCE	GEIGER

III AMPHIB. GEIGER

XX 77 Bruce (Reserve)

Landed 21–24 July

THE MARIANAS ISLANDS: GUAM
1944

INVASION OF GUAM,
21 JULY–8 AUGUST 1944

ELEVATIONS IN FEET
SCALE OF YARDS

The southern Mariana Islands form a line of about 180 miles, running southwest from Saipan to adjacent Tinian, to Aguijan, to Rota, and then to Guam. Rota stands about half-way between Tinian and Guam. The three islands shown here are at approximately the same scale.

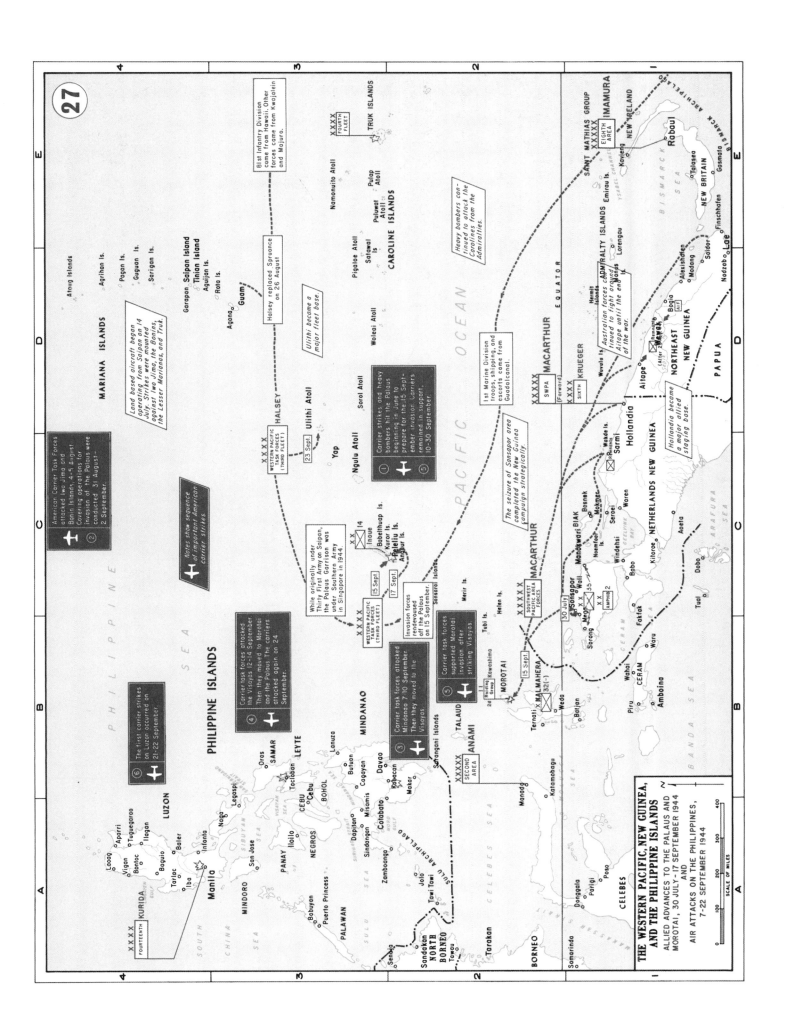

THE WESTERN PACIFIC, NEW GUINEA, AND THE PHILIPPINE ISLANDS

ALLIED ADVANCES TO THE PALAUS AND MOROTAI, 30 JULY–17 SEPTEMBER 1944
AND
AIR ATTACKS ON THE PHILIPPINES, 7–22 SEPTEMBER 1944

SCALE OF MILES
0   100   200   300   400

27

American Carrier Task Forces attacked Iwo Jima and Bonin Islands, 4-5 August. Covering operations for invasion of the Palaus were conducted 31 August–2 September.

Land based aircraft began operating from Saipan on 14 July. Strikes were mounted against Iwo Jima, the Bonins, the Lesser Marianas, and Truk.

Notes show sequence of important American carrier strikes.

81st Infantry Division came from Hawaii; Other forces came from Kwajalein and Majuro.

Ulithi became a major fleet base.

Halsey replaced Spruance on 26 August.

Heavy bombers continued to attack the Carolines from the Admiralties.

While originally under Thirty-First Army on Saipan, the Palaus Garrison was under Southern Army in Singapore in 1944.

Carrier task forces attacked the Visayas 12-14 September. Then they moved to Morotai and the Palaus. The carriers attacked again on 24 September.

Invasion forces rendezvoused off the Palaus on 15 September.

Carrier strikes and heavy bombers hit the Palaus beginning in June to prepare for the 15 September invasion. Carriers remained in support, 10-30 September.

1st Marine Division troops, shipping, and escorts came from Guadalcanal.

The seizure of Sansapor area completed the New Guinea campaign strategically.

Carrier task forces attacked Mindanao 7-10 September. Then they moved to the Visayas.

Carrier task forces supported Morotai invasion after striking Visayas.

The first carrier strikes on Luzon occurred on 21-22 September.

Australian forces continued to fight around Aitape until the end of the war.

Hollandia became a major allied staging base.

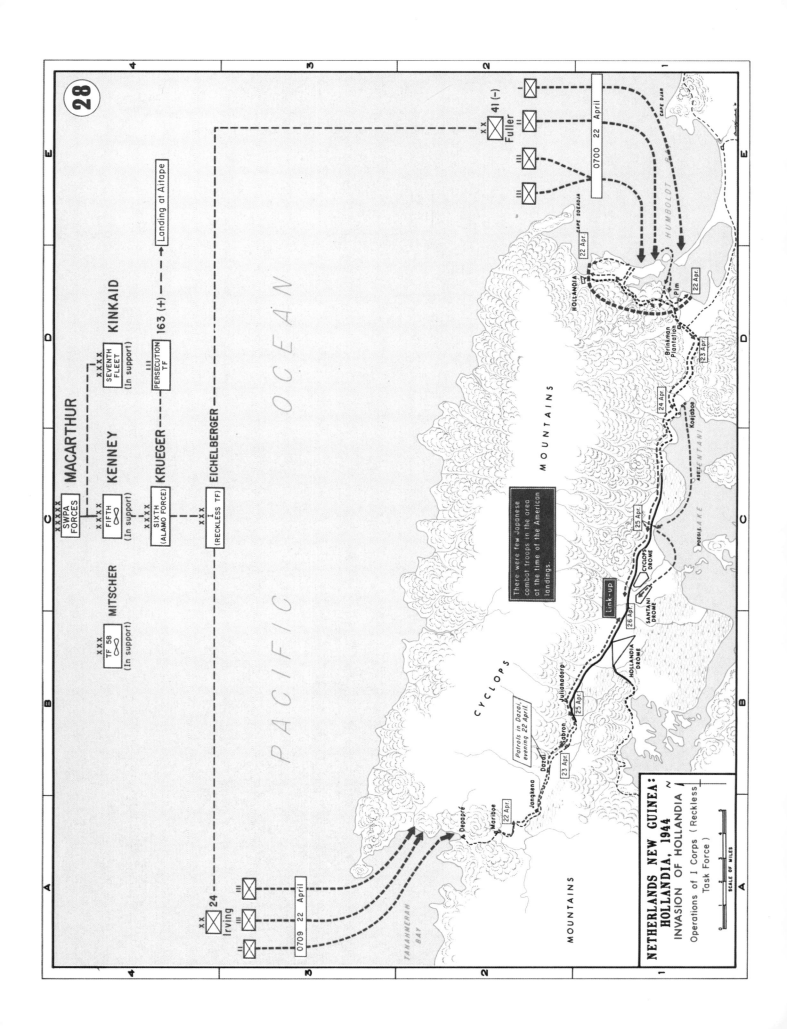

28

NETHERLANDS NEW GUINEA:
HOLLANDIA, 1944
INVASION OF HOLLANDIA

Operations of I Corps (Reckless
Task Force)

SCALE OF MILES

MACARTHUR
SWPA FORCES

MITSCHER
TF 58
(In support)

KENNEY
FIFTH
(In support)

KINKAID
SEVENTH FLEET
(In support)

KRUEGER
SIXTH (ALAMO FORCE)

PERSECUTION TF

163 (+) → Landing at Aitape

EICHELBERGER
I (RECKLESS TF)

PACIFIC

OCEAN

MOUNTAINS

CYCLOPS

MOUNTAINS

TANAHMERAH BAY

HUMBOLDT BAY

There were few Japanese
combat troops in the area
at the time of the American
landings.

24 Irving
0709 22 April

Depapré
Maribue 22 Apr
Jangkena
Dazai
Sabron 23 Apr
Julianadorp 25 Apr
HOLLANDIA DROME
SANTANI DROME
Link-up 26 Apr
25 Apr
Patrols in Dazai,
evening 22 April

CYCLOPS DROME
25 Apr
SENTANI LAKE
Koejaboe
24 Apr
23 Apr
Brinkman Plantation
HOLLANDIA
Pim 22 Apr
CAPE SOEADJA 22 Apr

Fuller 41 (−)
0700 22 April

CAPE DJAR

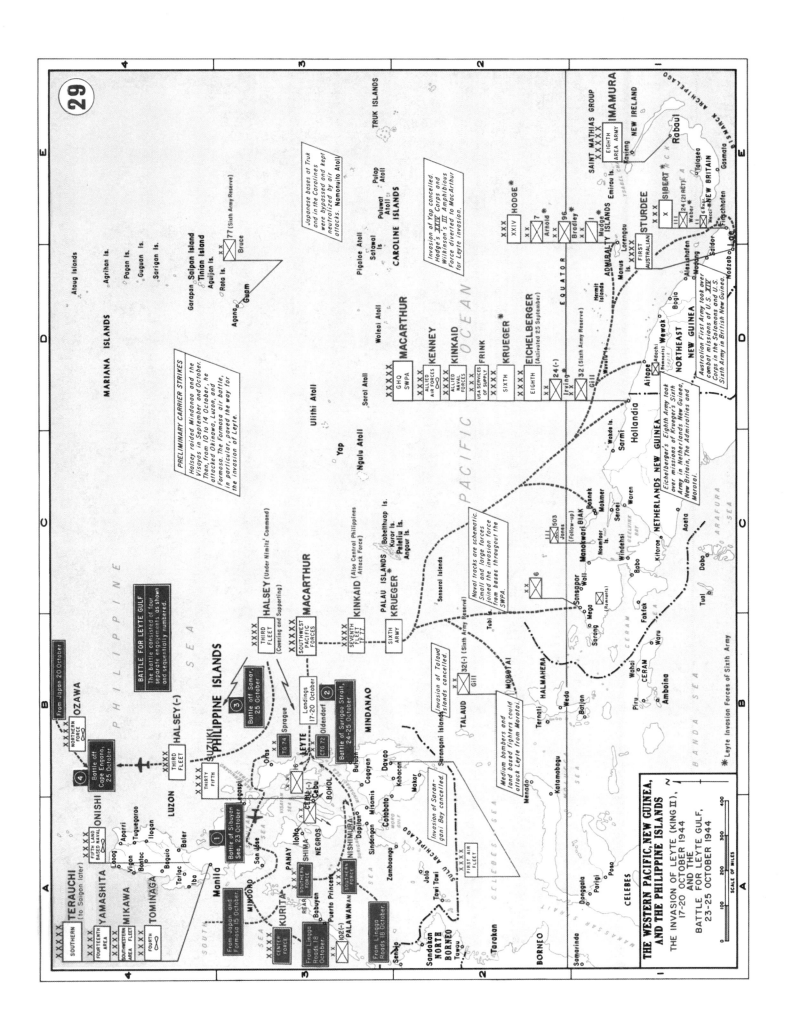

29

THE WESTERN PACIFIC, NEW GUINEA,
AND THE PHILIPPINE ISLANDS

THE INVASION OF LEYTE (KING II),
17-20 OCTOBER 1944
AND THE
BATTLE FOR LEYTE GULF,
23-25 OCTOBER 1944

SCALE OF MILES
100   200   300   400

BATTLE FOR LEYTE GULF
The battle consisted of four
separate engagements as shown
and sequentially numbered.

PRELIMINARY CARRIER STRIKES

Halsey raided Mindanao and the
Visayas in September and October.
Then, from 10 to 14 October, he
attacked Okinawa, Luzon, and
Formosa. The Formosa air battle,
in particular, paved the way for
the invasion of Leyte.

Japanese bases at Truk
and in the Carolines
were bypassed and kept
neutralized by air
attacks. Namonuito Atoll.

Invasion of Yap cancelled.
Hodge's XXIV Corps and
Wilkinson's III Amphibious
Force diverted to MacArthur
for Leyte invasion.

Naval tracks are schematic.
Small and large forces
joined the invasion force
from bases throughout the
SWPA.

Australian First Army took over
combat missions of Krueger's Sixth
Army in Netherlands New Guinea,
New Britain, The Admiralties and
Morotai.

Eichelberger's Eighth Army took
over missions of Krueger's Sixth
Army in Netherlands New Guinea,
New Britain, The Admiralties and
Morotai.

Medium bombers and
land based fighters could
attack Leyte from Morotai.

Invasion of Sarangani Bay cancelled.

Invasion of Talaud
Islands cancelled.

Invasion of Saran-
gani Islands cancelled.

* Leyte Invasion Forces of Sixth Army

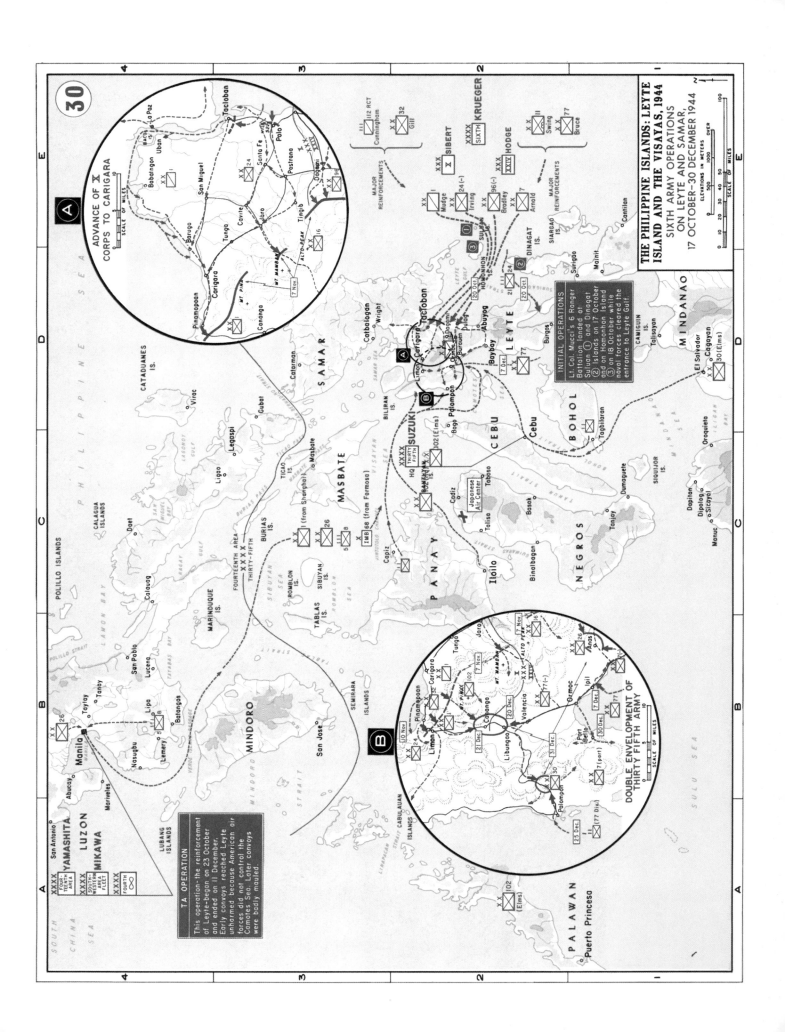

THE PHILIPPINE ISLANDS: LEYTE
ISLAND AND THE VISAYAS, 1944
SIXTH ARMY OPERATIONS
ON LEYTE AND SAMAR,
17 OCTOBER–30 DECEMBER 1944

ADVANCE OF X
CORPS TO CARIGARA

INITIAL OPERATIONS

Lt. Col. Mucci's 6 Ranger
Battalion landed at
Suluan ① and Dinagat
② Islands on 17 October
and on Homonhon Island
③ on 18 October while
naval forces cleared the
entrance to Leyte Gulf.

DOUBLE ENVELOPMENT OF
THIRTY FIFTH ARMY

TA OPERATION

This operation—the reinforcement
of Leyte—began on 23 October
and ended on 11 December.
Early convoys reached Leyte
unharmed because American air
forces did not control the
Camotes Sea. Later convoys
were badly mauled.

30

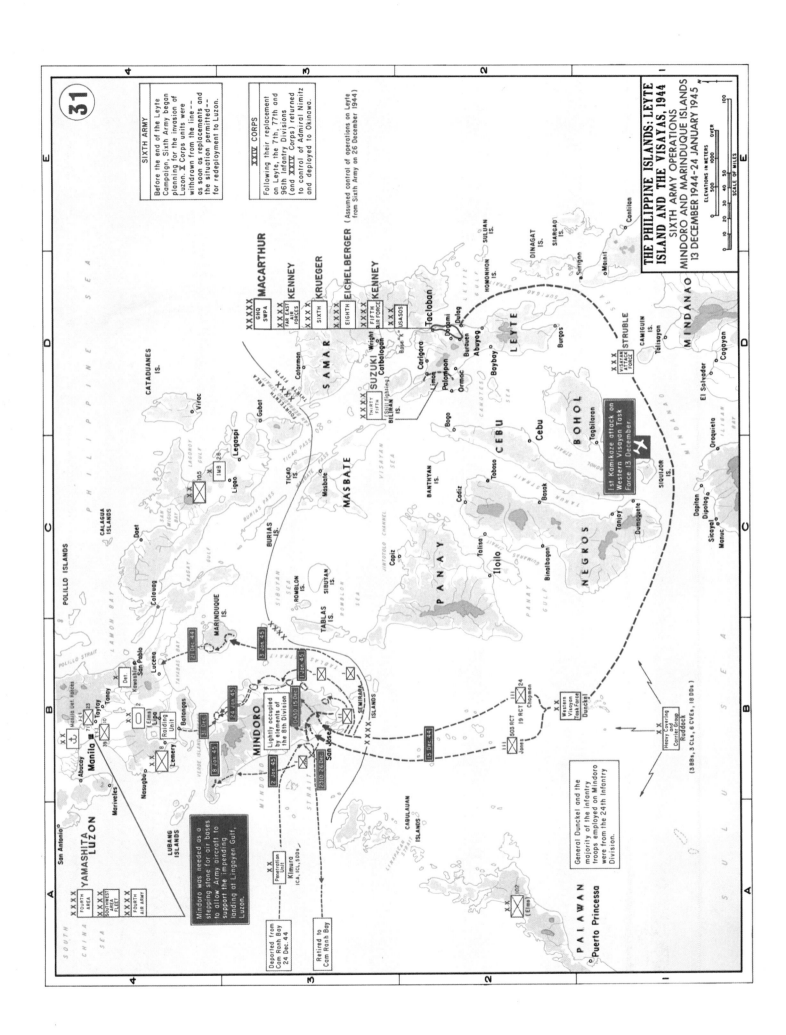

31

SIXTH ARMY

Before the end of the Leyte Campaign, Sixth Army began planning for the invasion of Luzon. X Corps units were withdrawn from the line-- as soon as replacements and the situation permitted-- for redeployment to Luzon.

XXIV CORPS

Following their replacement on Leyte, the 7th, 77th and 96th Infantry Divisions (and XXIV Corps) returned to control of Admiral Nimitz and deployed to Okinawa.

THE PHILIPPINE ISLANDS: LEYTE ISLAND AND THE VISAYAS, 1944
SIXTH ARMY OPERATIONS
MINDORO AND MARINDUQUE ISLANDS
13 DECEMBER 1944-24 JANUARY 1945

ELEVATIONS IN METERS

| 500 | 1000 | OVER |

SCALE OF MILES

Mindoro was needed as a stepping stone for air bases to allow Army aircraft to support the impending landing at Lingayen Gulf, Luzon.

General Dunckel and the majority of the infantry troops employed on Mindoro were from the 24th Infantry Division.

(Assumed control of operations on Leyte from Sixth Army on 26 December 1944)

1st Kamikaze attack on Western Visayan Task Force 13 December.

Departed from Cam Ranh Bay 24 Dec. 44

Retired to Cam Ranh Bay

Penetration Unit
Kimura
ICA, ICL, 5DDs

Heavy Covering and Carrier Group
Ruddock
(3 BBs, 3 CLs, 6 CVEs, 18 DDs)

Western Visayan Task Force
Dunckel

STRUBLE

VISAYAN ATTACK FORCE

XXXXX GHQ SWPA — MACARTHUR
XXXXX FAR EAST AIR FORCES — KENNEY
XXXX SIXTH — KRUEGER
XXXX EIGHTH — EICHELBERGER
XXXX FIFTH AIR FORCE — KENNEY
USASOS

THIRTY FIFTH — SUZUKI (fighting)

FOURTEENTH AREA — THIRTY FIFTH

YAMASHITA
LUZON

XXXX FOURTH AREA
XXXX SOUTHWEST AREA FLEET
XXXX FOURTH AIR ARMY

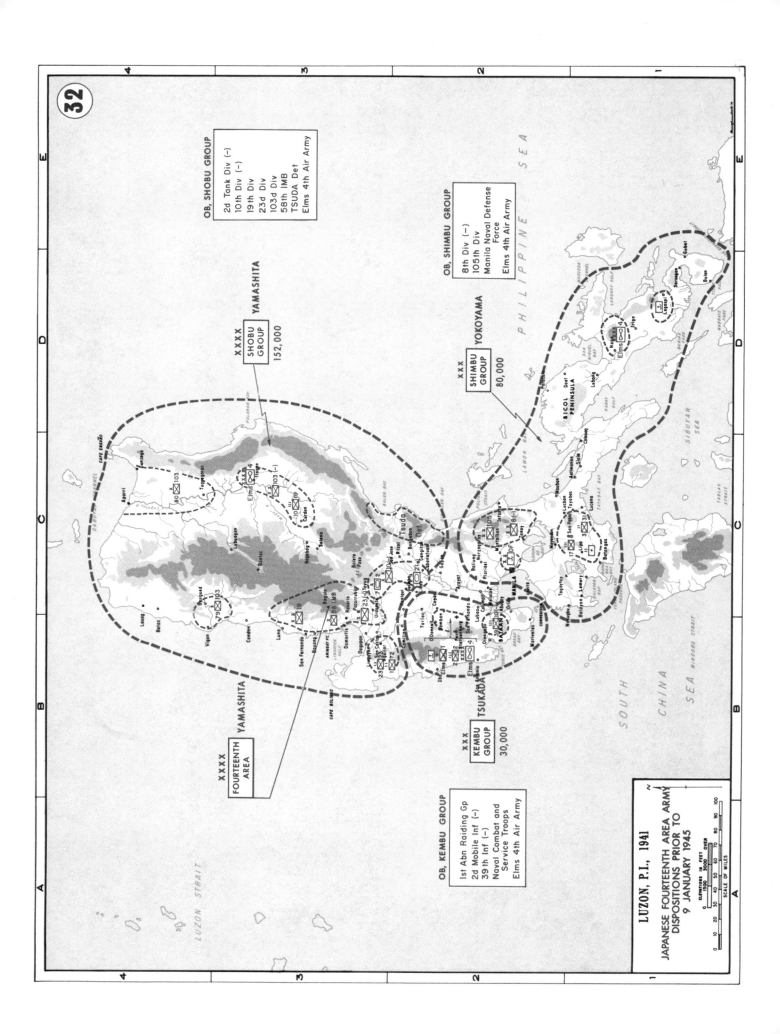

LUZON, P.I., 1941

JAPANESE FOURTEENTH AREA ARMY DISPOSITIONS PRIOR TO 9 JANUARY 1945

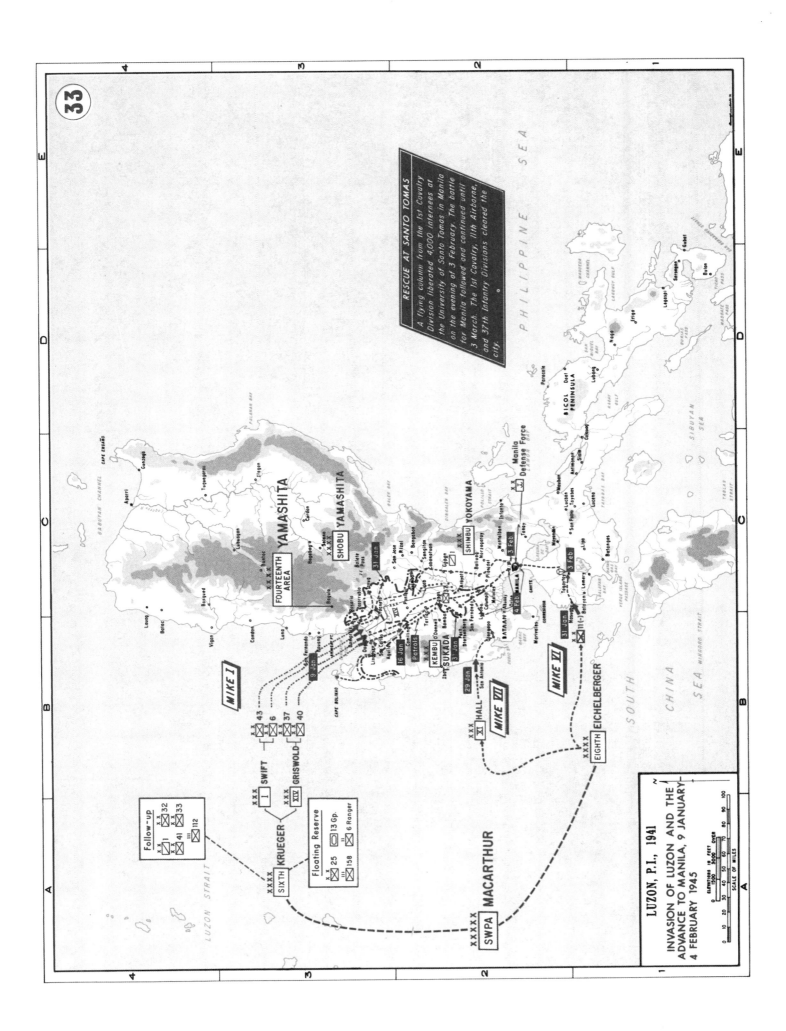

33

RESCUE AT SANTO TOMAS

A flying column from the 1st Cavalry Division liberated 4,000 internees at the University of Santo Tomas in Manila on the evening of 3 February. The battle for Manila followed and continued until 3 March. The 1st Cavalry, 11th Airborne, and 37th Infantry Divisions cleared the city.

PHILIPPINE SEA

YAMASHITA

YAMASHITA

FOURTEENTH AREA

SHOBU YAMASHITA

SHIMBU YOKOYAMA

Manila Defense Force

BICOL PENINSULA

SIBUYAN SEA

31 Jan

16 Jan

Patrols

KEMBU

SUKADA

3 Jan

3 Feb

4 Feb MANILA

3 Feb

BATAAN

29 Jan

31 Jan

MIKE I

SWIFT

43

6

GRISWOLD

37

40

MIKE VII

HALL

MIKE VI

EICHELBERGER

EIGHTH

SOUTH CHINA SEA

LUZON STRAIT

Follow-up

| 32 |
| 33 |
| 1 |
| 41 |
| 112 |

KRUEGER

SIXTH

Floating Reserve

| 13 Gp. |
| 6 Ranger |
| 25 |
| 158 |

MACARTHUR

SWPA

N

LUZON, P.I., 1941

INVASION OF LUZON AND THE ADVANCE TO MANILA, 9 JANUARY–4 FEBRUARY 1945

ELEVATIONS IN FEET

SCALE OF MILES

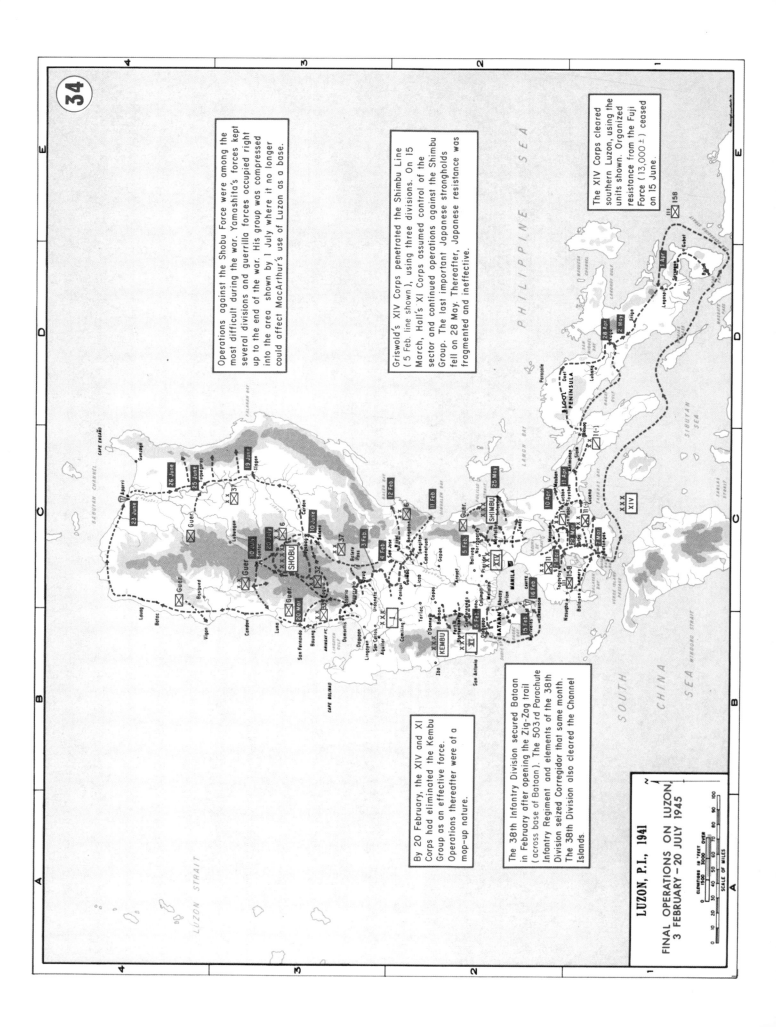

Operations against the Shobu Force were among the most difficult during the war. Yamashita's forces kept several divisions and guerrilla forces occupied right up to the end of the war. His group was compressed into the area shown by 1 July where it no longer could affect MacArthur's use of Luzon as a base.

Griswold's XIV Corps penetrated the Shimbu Line (5 Feb line shown), using three divisions. On 15 March, Hall's XI Corps assumed control of the sector and continued operations against the Shimbu Group. The last important Japanese strongholds fell on 28 May. Thereafter, Japanese resistance was fragmented and ineffective.

The XIV Corps cleared southern Luzon, using the units shown. Organized resistance from the Fuji Force (13,000 ±) ceased on 15 June.

By 20 February, the XIV and XI Corps had eliminated the Kembu Group as an effective force. Operations thereafter were of a mop-up nature.

The 38th Infantry Division secured Bataan in February after opening the Zig-Zag Trail (across base of Bataan). The 503rd Parachute Infantry Regiment and elements of the 38th Division seized Corregidor that same month. The 38th Division also cleared the Channel Islands.

LUZON, P.I., 1941

FINAL OPERATIONS ON LUZON,
3 FEBRUARY – 20 JULY 1945

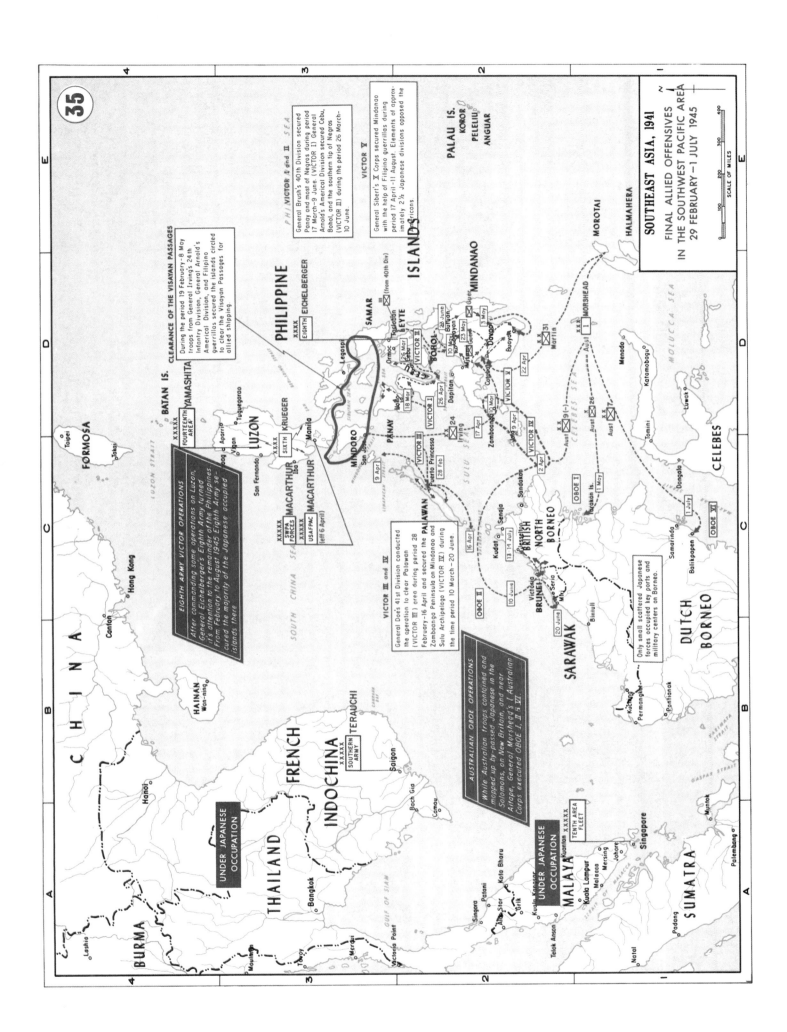

35

SOUTHEAST ASIA, 1941

FINAL ALLIED OFFENSIVES
IN THE SOUTHWEST PACIFIC AREA
29 FEBRUARY–1 JULY 1945

SCALE OF MILES

EIGHTH ARMY VICTOR OPERATIONS

After commanding some operations on Luzon, General Eichelberger's Eighth Army turned its attention to the remainder of the Philippines. From February to August 1945 Eighth Army secured the majority of the Japanese occupied islands there.

CLEARANCE OF THE VISAYAN PASSAGES

During the period 19 February–8 May troops from General Irving's 24th Infantry Division, General Arnold's Americal Division, and Filipino guerrillas secured the islands circled to clear the Visayan Passages for allied shipping.

PHILIPPINE SEA

General Brush's 40th Division secured Panay and most of Negros during period 17 March–9 June (VICTOR I) General Arnold's Americal Division secured Cebu, Bohol, and the southern tip of Negros (VICTOR II) during the period 26 March–10 June.

VICTOR V

General Sibert's X Corps secured Mindanao with the help of Filipino guerrillas during period 17 April–11 August Elements of approximately 2½ Japanese divisions opposed the Americans.

VICTOR III and IV

General Doe's 41st Division conducted the operation to clear Palawan (VICTOR III) area during period 28 February–16 April and secured the Zamboanga Peninsula on Mindanao and Sulu Archipelago (VICTOR IV) during the time period 10 March–20 June.

AUSTRALIAN OBOE OPERATIONS

While Australian troops contained and mopped up by-passed Japanese in the Solomons, on New Britain, and near Aitape, General Morshead's I Australian Corps executed OBOE I, II & VI.

Only small scattered Japanese forces occupied key ports and military centers on Borneo.

UNDER JAPANESE OCCUPATION

UNDER JAPANESE OCCUPATION

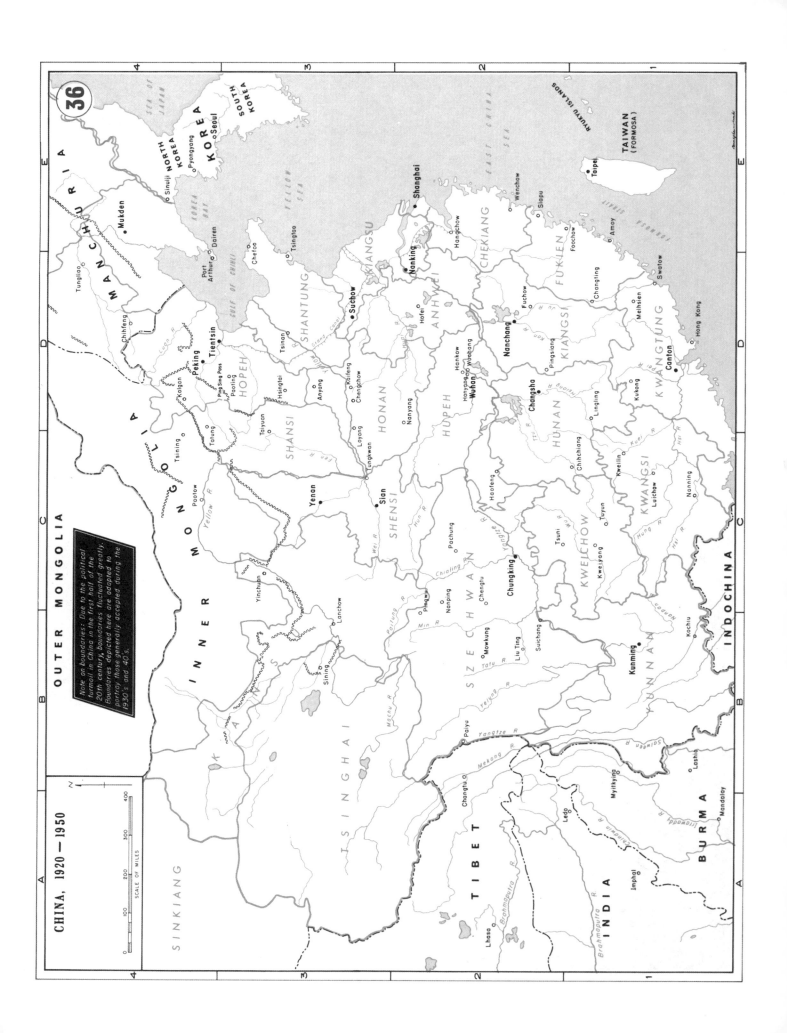

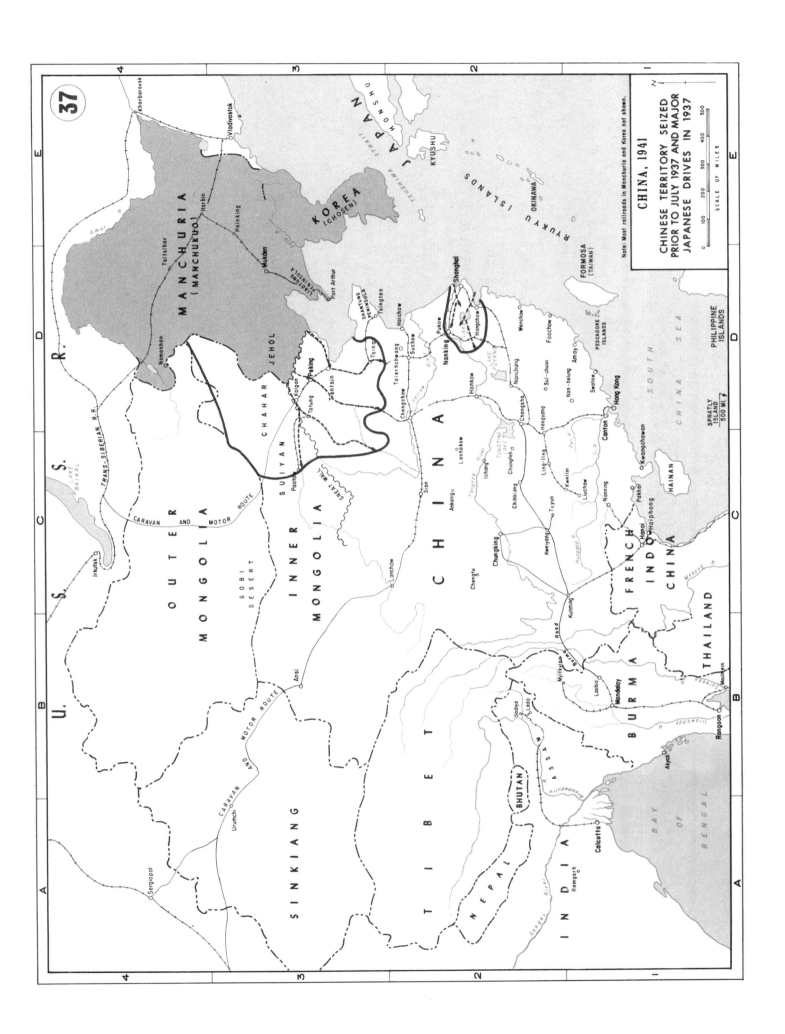

CHINA, 1941

CHINESE TERRITORY SEIZED
PRIOR TO JULY 1937 AND MAJOR
JAPANESE DRIVES IN 1937

Note: Most railroads in Manchuria and Korea not shown.

SCALE OF MILES

0   100 200 300 400 500

37

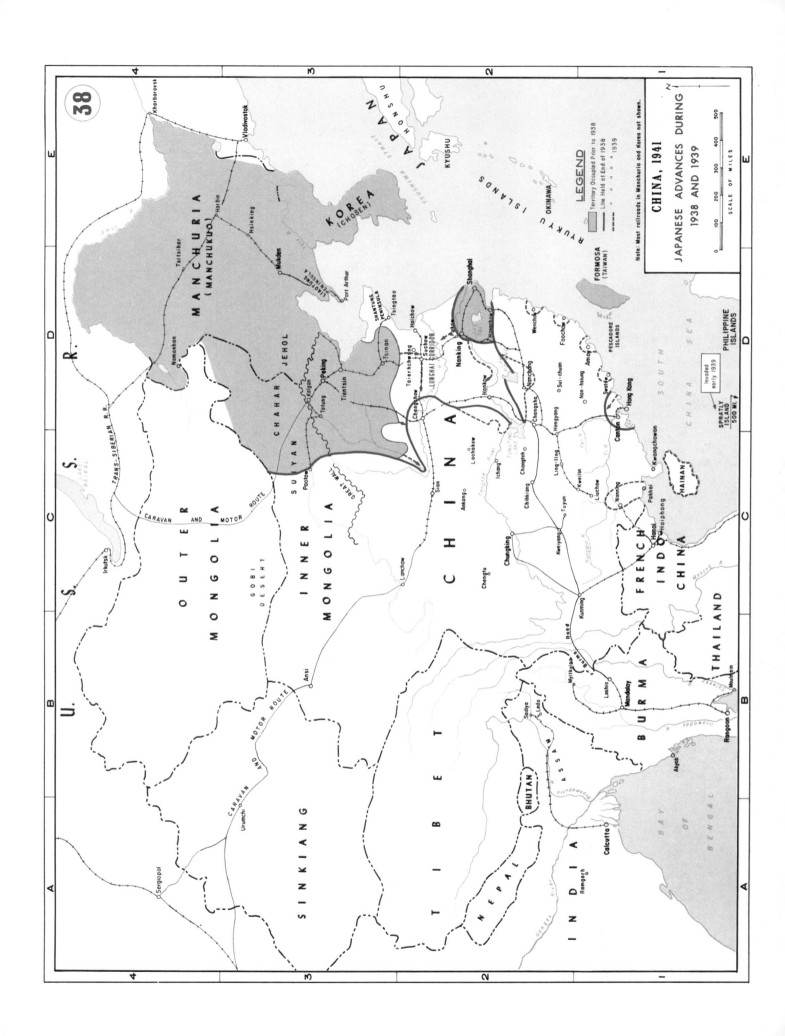

38

CHINA, 1941
JAPANESE ADVANCES DURING
1938 AND 1939

Note: Most railroads in Manchuria and Korea not shown.

LEGEND

Territory Occupied Prior to 1938
Line Held at End of 1938
"   "   "   "   "   1939

SCALE OF MILES

0   100   200   300   400   500

U. S. S. R.

LAKE BAIKAL

Irkutsk

Sergiopol

TRANS-SIBERIAN R.R.

Khabarovsk

Vladivostok

Amur R.

MANCHURIA
(MANCHUKUO)

Tsitsihar

Nomonhan

Harbin

Hsinking

Mukden

Port Arthur

LIAOTUNG PENINSULA

KOREA
(CHOSEN)

JAPAN

JAPAN SEA

HONSHU

TSUSHIMA STRAIT

KYUSHU

OKINAWA

RYUKYU ISLANDS

FORMOSA
(TAIWAN)

PESCADORE ISLANDS

SOUTH CHINA SEA

PHILIPPINE ISLANDS

Invaded early 1939

SPRATLY ISLAND 500 MI.

OUTER MONGOLIA

GOBI DESERT

CARAVAN AND MOTOR ROUTE

Ansi

Urumchi

CARAVAN AND MOTOR ROUTE

SINKIANG

INNER MONGOLIA

SUIYAN

CHAHAR

JEHOL

Kalgan

Totung

Pootow

Peking

Tientsin

GREAT WALL

Sian

Lanchow

CHINA

Chengtu

Chungking

Chengtu

Amang

Ichang

Loohokow

Yangtze River

Chungteh

Chihkiang

Tuyun

Kweiyang

Kunming

Burma Road

TIBET

BHUTAN

NEPAL

Ganges River

Ramgarh

Calcutta

INDIA

Sadiya

Ledo

Lashio

Mandalay

Myitkyina

ASSAM

Brahmaputra

Aiyab

BURMA

Moulmein

Rangoon

Irrawaddy

BAY OF BENGAL

THAILAND

Salween R.

Mekong R.

FRENCH INDO CHINA

Hanoi

Haiphong

Hongha R.

HAINAN

Pakhoi

Kwangchow

Nanning

Luchow

Kweilin

Ling-ling

Hengyang

Changsha

TUNGTING LAKE

Siang R.

Non-hsiang

Sui-chum

Nanchang

Hankow

LUNGHAI CORRIDOR

SUCHOW CORRIDOR

Suchow

Taierhchwang

Chengchow

Honanfu

Nanking

Shanghai

TAI HU

Hangchow

Wenchow

Foochow

Amoy

Swatow

Canton

Hong Kong

Kwangchow

Haichow

Tsingtao

Tsinan

SHANTUNG PENINSULA

Yellow R.

Hankow

Yellow Sea

Sergiopol

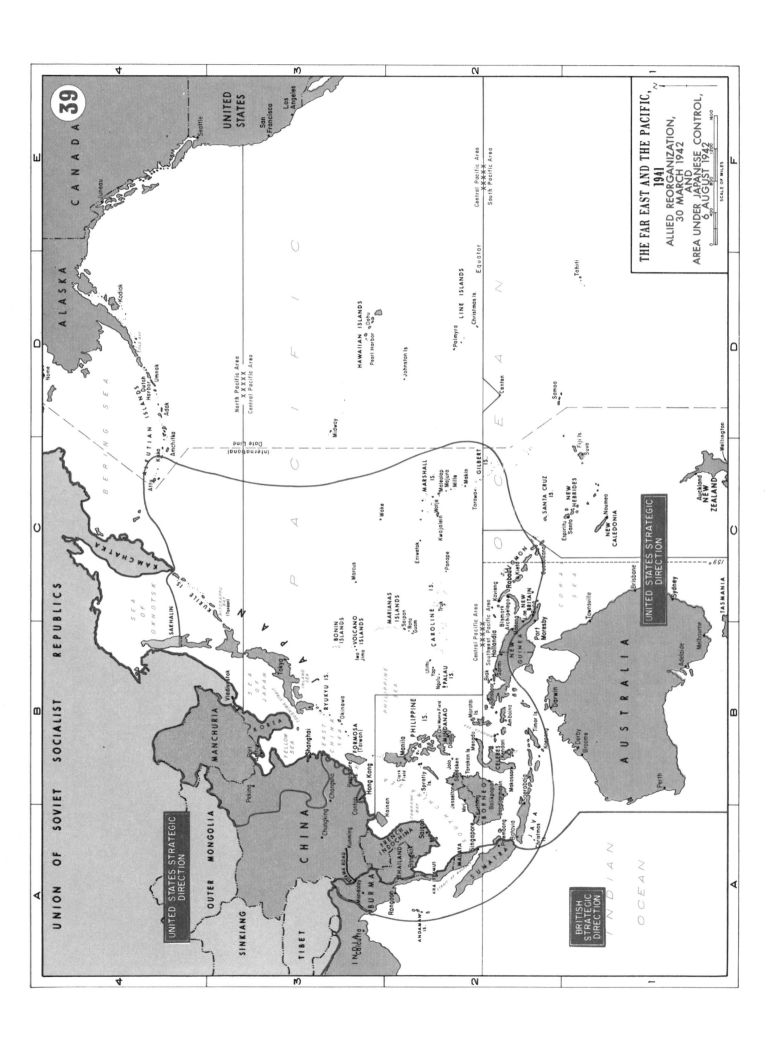

THE FAR EAST AND THE PACIFIC,
1941
ALLIED REORGANIZATION,
30 MARCH 1942
AND
AREA UNDER JAPANESE CONTROL,
6 AUGUST 1942

SCALE OF MILES

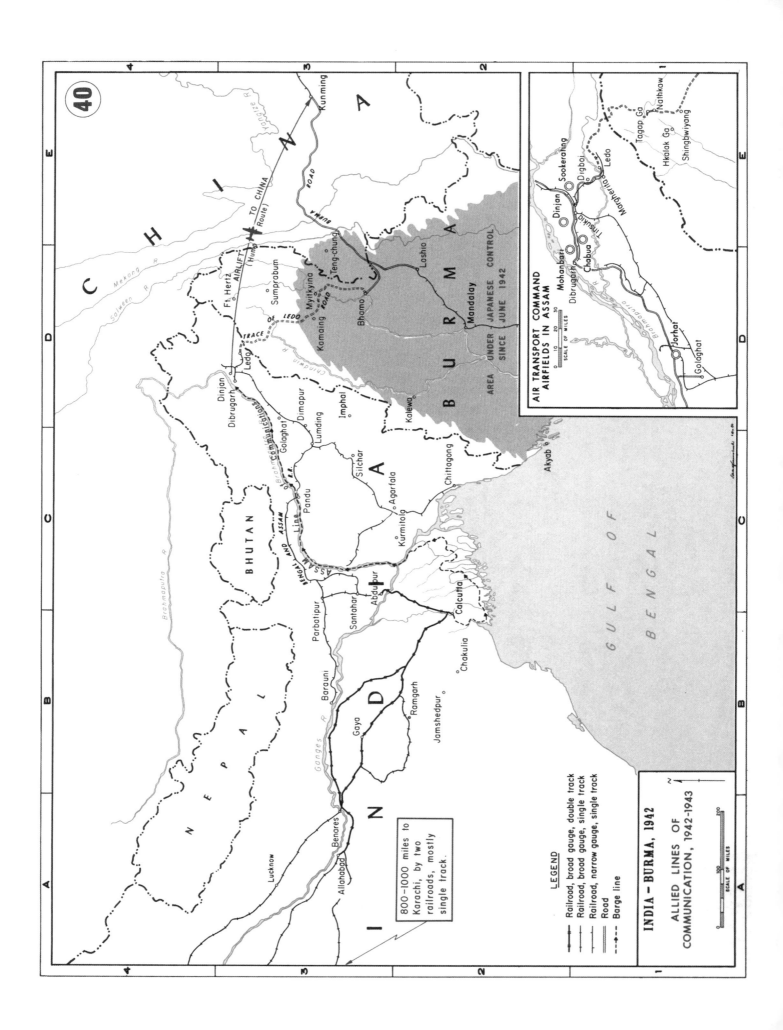

INDIA – BURMA, 1942

ALLIED LINES OF
COMMUNICATION, 1942-1943

LEGEND

Railroad, broad gauge, double track
Railroad, broad gauge, single track
Railroad, narrow gauge, single track
Road
Barge line

800-1000 miles to
Karachi, by two
railroads, mostly
single track.

AIR TRANSPORT COMMAND
AIRFIELDS IN ASSAM

SCALE OF MILES
0 10 20 30

40

CHINA

Kunming

TO CHINA
(Hump Route)
AIRLIFT
Ft. Hertz

BURMA ROAD

Sumprabum

Myitkyina
Teng-chung

Bhamo

Lashio

Mandalay

Kamaing

LEDO ROAD

TRACE OF LEDO

Ledo

Kalewa

AREA UNDER JAPANESE CONTROL SINCE JUNE 1942

Mekong R.
Salween R.
Yangtze R.
Chindwin R.

Dinjan
Dibrugarh

Golaghat
Dimapur
Lumding
Imphal

Brahmaputra R.

Silchar

Bengal and Assam Line
Assam R.R.

Pandu

Agartala

Chittagong

Akyab

GULF OF BENGAL

NEPAL

BHUTAN

Brahmaputra R.

ASSAM

Kurmitola

Parbatipur
Santahar

Abdulpur

Calcutta

Chakulia

Barauni

Ramgarh

Jamshedpur

Ganges R.

Gaya

INDIA

Lucknow

Allahabad
Benares

SCALE OF MILES
0   100   200

N

Mohanbari
Dinjan
Sookerating
Digboi
Ledo

Margherita
Tagap Ga
Nathkaw
Hkalak Ga
Shingbwiyang

Tinsukia
Dibrugarh
Chabua

Jorhat
Golaghat

Brahmaputra

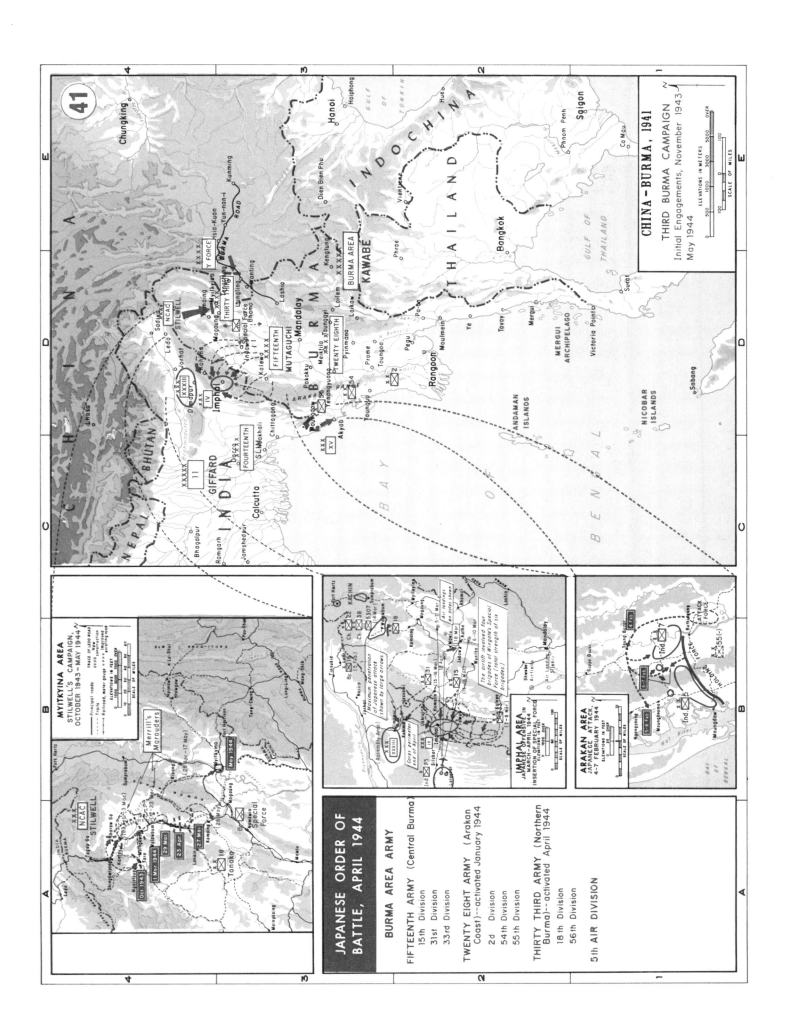

41

CHINA-BURMA, 1941

THIRD BURMA CAMPAIGN
Initial Engagements, November 1943 - May 1944

ELEVATIONS IN METERS

SCALE OF MILES

MYITKYINA AREA,
STILWELL'S CAMPAIGN,
OCTOBER 1943-MAY 1944

ELEVATIONS IN FEET

SCALE OF MILES

Merrill's Marauders

IMPHAL AREA
MARCH-APRIL 1944
INSERTION OF SPECIAL FORCE

ELEVATIONS IN FEET

SCALE OF MILES

The airlift involved four brigades of Wingate's Special Force (total strength of six brigades).

Maximum penetration of Japanese attack shown by large arrows.

ARAKAN AREA
JAPANESE ATTACK,
4-7 FEBRUARY 1944

ELEVATIONS IN FEET

SCALE OF MILES

JAPANESE ORDER OF BATTLE, APRIL 1944

BURMA AREA ARMY

FIFTEENTH ARMY (Central Burma)
15th Division
31st Division
33rd Division

TWENTY EIGHT ARMY (Arakan Coast)—activated January 1944
2d Division
54th Division
55th Division

THIRTY THIRD ARMY (Northern Burma)—activated April 1944
18th Division
56th Division

5th AIR DIVISION

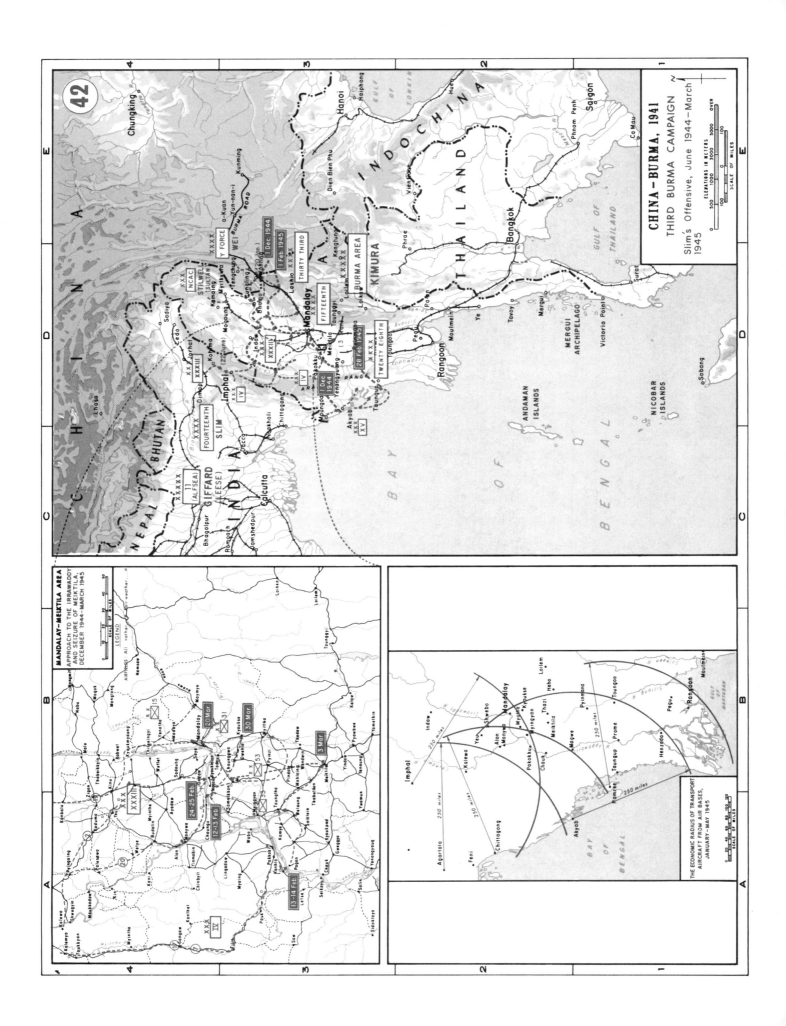

CHINA-BURMA, 1941
THIRD BURMA CAMPAIGN
Slim's Offensive, June 1944–March 1945

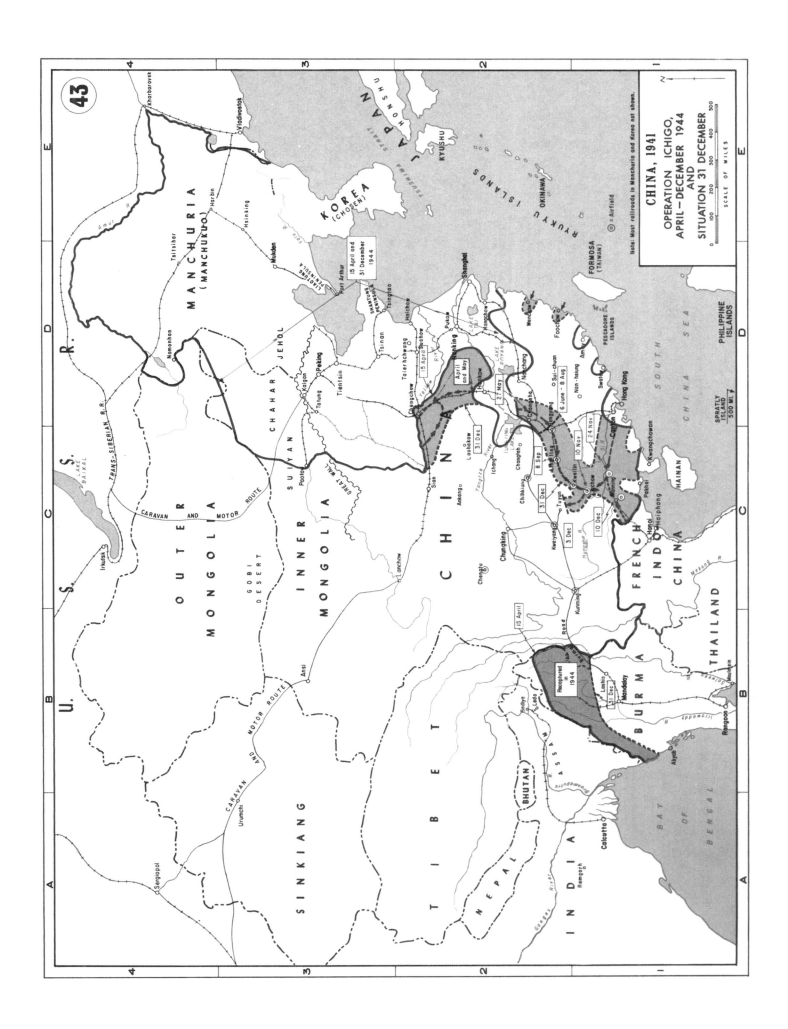

CHINA, 1941
OPERATION ICHIGO,
APRIL – DECEMBER 1944
AND
SITUATION 31 DECEMBER

Note: Most railroads in Manchuria and Korea not shown.

⊙ = Airfield

SCALE OF MILES
0   100   200   300   400   500

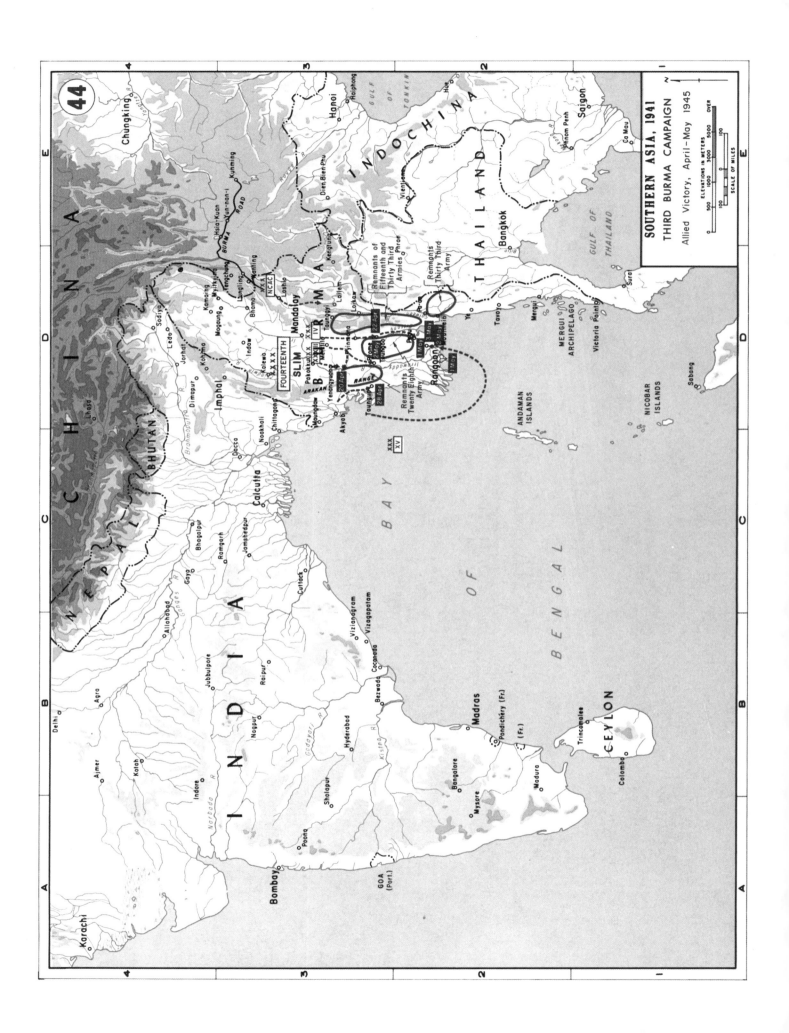

SOUTHERN ASIA, 1941
THIRD BURMA CAMPAIGN

Allied Victory, April–May 1945

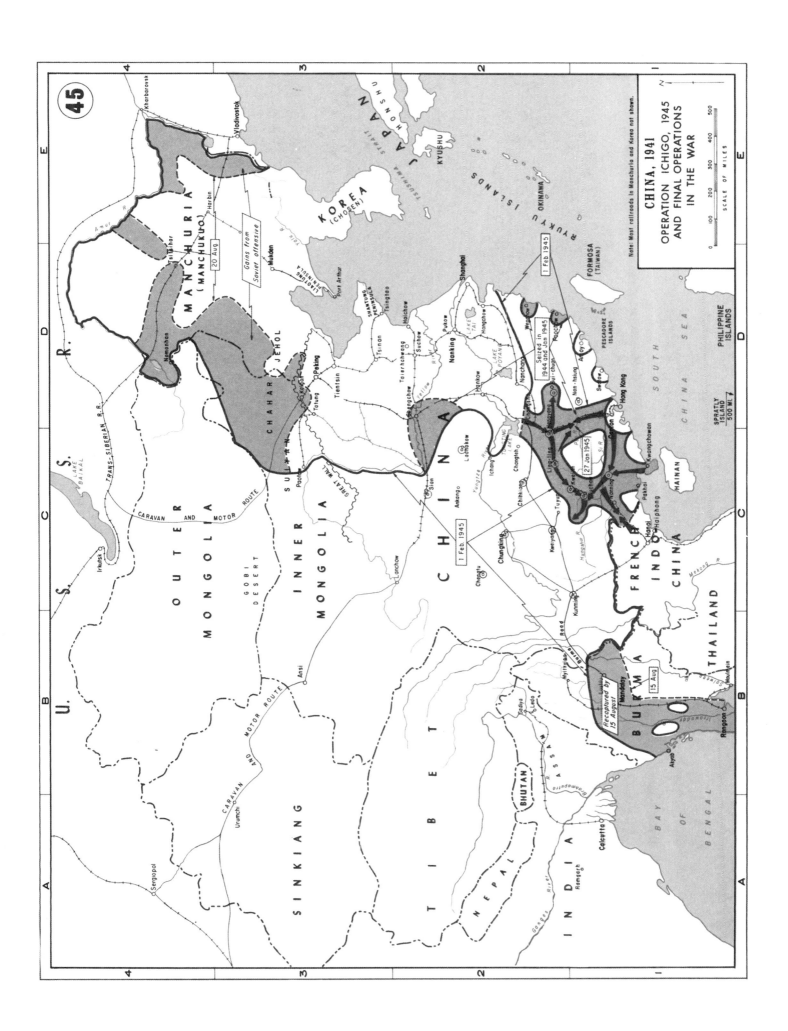

CHINA, 1941

OPERATION ICHIGO, 1945
AND FINAL OPERATIONS
IN THE WAR

Note: Most railroads in Manchuria and Korea not shown.

SCALE OF MILES
0   100   200   300   400   500

45

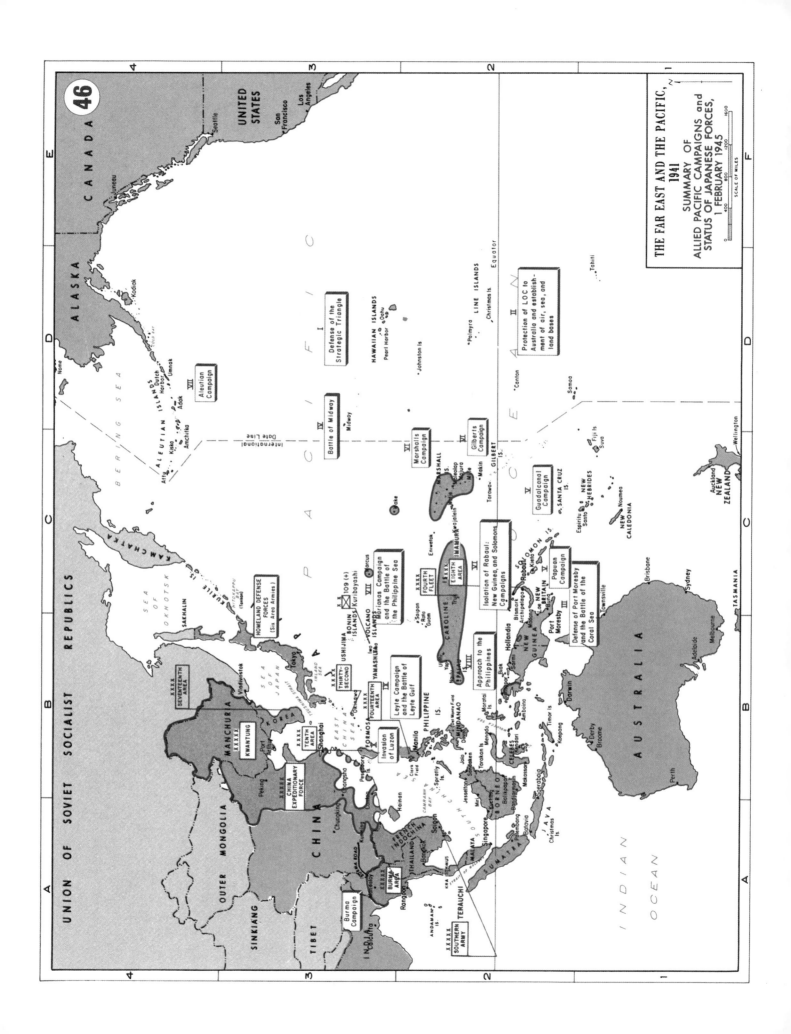

THE FAR EAST AND THE PACIFIC, 1941

SUMMARY OF
ALLIED PACIFIC CAMPAIGNS and
STATUS OF JAPANESE FORCES,
1 FEBRUARY 1945

SCALE OF MILES

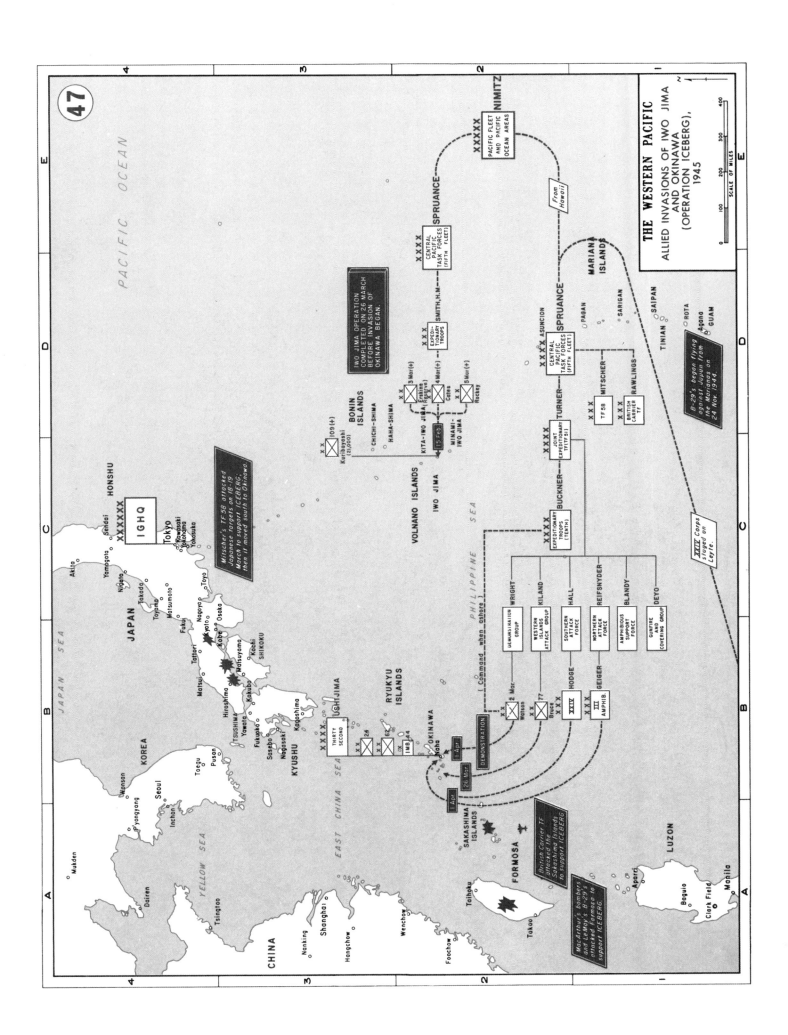

THE WESTERN PACIFIC

ALLIED INVASIONS OF IWO JIMA
AND OKINAWA
(OPERATION ICEBERG), 1945

SCALE OF MILES
0   100   200   300   400

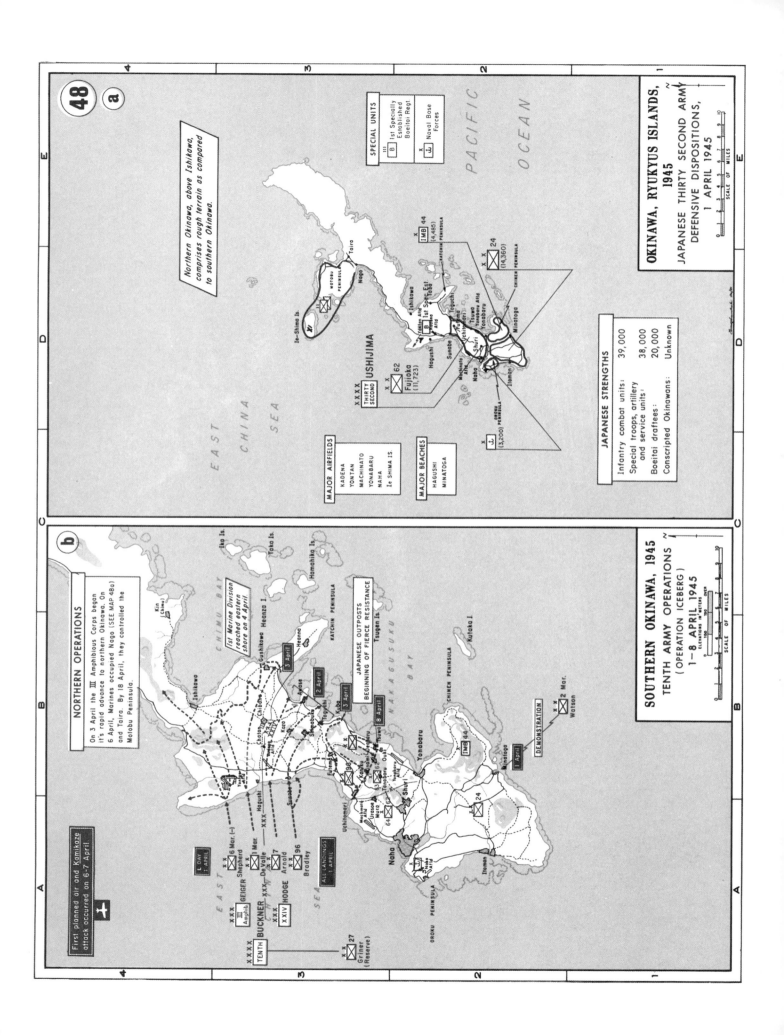

48

a

Northern Okinawa, above Ishikawa, comprises rough terrain as compared to southern Okinawa.

PACIFIC

OCEAN

EAST

CHINA

SEA

USHIJIMA

XXXX
THIRTY
SECOND

62
Fujioka
(11,723)

SPECIAL UNITS

III
B 1st Specially
Established
Boeitai Regt

x
J Naval Base
Forces

1MB 44
(4,485)

XX 24
(14,360)

x
J (3,200)
ORORU
PENINSULA

MAJOR AIRFIELDS

KADENA
YONTAN
MACHINATO
YONABARU
NAHA
Ie SHIMA IS

MAJOR BEACHES

HAGUSHI
MINATOGA

JAPANESE STRENGTHS

Infantry combat units: 39,000
Special troops, artillery
 and service units: 38,000
Boeitai draftees: 20,000
Conscripted Okinawans: Unknown

**OKINAWA, RYUKYUS ISLANDS,
1945**

JAPANESE THIRTY SECOND ARMY
DEFENSIVE DISPOSITIONS,
1 APRIL 1945

SCALE OF MILES

b

First planned air and Kamikaze
attack occurred on 6-7 April

NORTHERN OPERATIONS

On 3 April the III Amphibious Corps began
it's rapid advance to northern Okinawa. On
6 April, Marines occupied Nago (SEE MAP 48a)
and Taira. By 18 April, they controlled the
Motobu Peninsula.

CHIMU
BAY

Ie Is.

Taka Is.

Hamahika Is.

KATCHIN PENINSULA

Kin
(Chimu)

1st Marine Division
reached eastern
shore on 4 April.

3 April

2 April

JAPANESE OUTPOSTS
BEGINNING OF FIERCE RESISTANCE

Tsugen Is.

5 April

8 April

NAKAGUSUKU
BAY

Ikutaka I.

CHINEN PENINSULA

XXXX
TENTH
BUCKNER

XX
27
Griner
(Reserve)

XXX
III
Amphib
GEIGER

XX
6 Mar (−)
Shepherd

XX
1 Mar
Del Valle

XXX
XXIV
HODGE

XX
7
Arnold

XX
96
Bradley

L DAY
1 APRIL

ALL LANDINGS
1 APRIL

Ishikawa

Gushikawa

Heanza I.

Heanna

1MB 44

Yonabaru

Shuri

24

2 Mar
Watson

1 April

DEMONSTRATION

Naha

Itoman

ORORU PENINSULA

EAST

CHINA

SEA

SOUTHERN OKINAWA, 1945

TENTH ARMY OPERATIONS
(OPERATION ICEBERG)
1-8 APRIL 1945

ELEVATIONS IN METERS

SCALE OF MILES

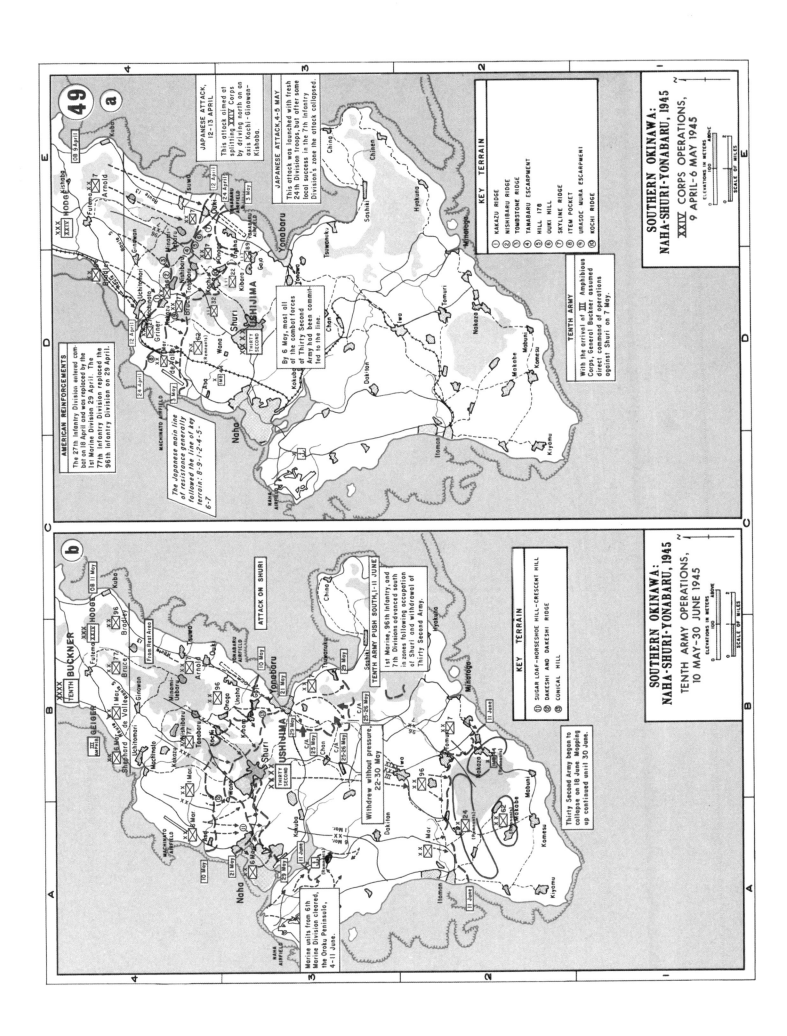

49

a

SOUTHERN OKINAWA:
NAHA-SHURI-YONABARU, 1945
XXIV CORPS OPERATIONS,
9 APRIL-6 MAY 1945

ELEVATIONS IN METERS
0   100   ABOVE

SCALE OF MILES
0   1   2

KEY TERRAIN

① KAKAZU RIDGE
② NISHIBARU RIDGE
③ TOMBSTONE RIDGE
④ TANABARU ESCARPMENT
⑤ HILL 178
⑥ OURI HILL
⑦ SKYLINE RIDGE
⑧ ITEM POCKET
⑨ URASOE MURA ESCARPMENT
⑩ KOCHI RIDGE

TENTH ARMY

With the arrival of III Amphibious Corps, General Buckner assumed direct command of operations against Shuri on 7 May.

AMERICAN REINFORCEMENTS

The 27th Infantry Division entered combat on 18 April and was replaced by the 1st Marine Division 29 April. The 77th Infantry Division replaced the 96th Infantry Division on 29 April.

The Japanese main line of resistance generally followed the line of key terrain: 8-9-1-2-4-5-6-7

JAPANESE ATTACK, 12-13 APRIL

This attack aimed at splitting XXIV Corps by driving north on an axis Kochi-Ginowan-Kishaba.

JAPANESE ATTACK, 4-5 MAY

This attack was launched with fresh 24th Division troops, but after some local success in the 7th Infantry Division's zone the attack collapsed.

By 6 May, most all the combat forces of Thirty Second Army had been committed to the line.

b

SOUTHERN OKINAWA:
NAHA-SHURI-YONABARU, 1945
TENTH ARMY OPERATIONS,
10 MAY-30 JUNE 1945

ELEVATIONS IN METERS
0   100   ABOVE

SCALE OF MILES
0   1   2

KEY TERRAIN

⑪ SUGAR LOAF-HORSESHOE HILL-CRESCENT HILL
⑫ DAKESHI AND DAKESHI RIDGE
⑬ CONICAL HILL

TENTH ARMY PUSH SOUTH, 1-11 JUNE

1st Marine, 96th Infantry, and 7th Divisions advanced south in zones following occupation of Shuri and withdrawal of Thirty Second Army.

ATTACK ON SHURI

Withdrew without pressure, 22-30 May.

Thirty Second Army began to collapse on 18 June. Mopping up continued until 30 June.

Marine units from 6th Marine Division cleared the Oroku Peninsula, 4-11 June.

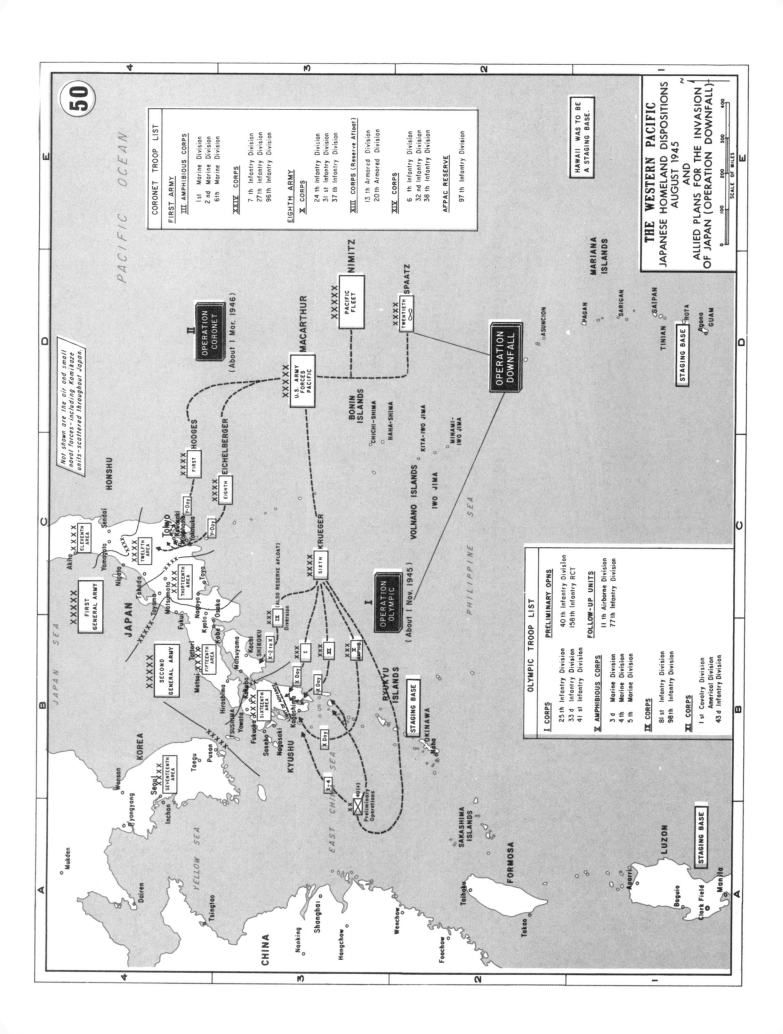

50

PACIFIC OCEAN

Not shown are the air and small naval forces—including Kamikaze units—scattered throughout Japan.

CORONET TROOP LIST

FIRST ARMY

III AMPHIBIOUS CORPS
- 1st Marine Division
- 2nd Marine Division
- 6th Marine Division

XXIV CORPS
- 7th Infantry Division
- 27th Infantry Division
- 96th Infantry Division

EIGHTH ARMY

X CORPS
- 24th Infantry Division
- 31st Infantry Division
- 37th Infantry Division

XIII CORPS (Reserve Afloat)
- 13th Armored Division
- 20th Armored Division

XIV CORPS
- 6th Infantry Division
- 32nd Infantry Division
- 38th Infantry Division

AFPAC RESERVE
- 97th Infantry Division

OPERATION CORONET
II
(About 1 Mar. 1946)

MACARTHUR

NIMITZ
XXXXX PACIFIC FLEET

XXXX TWENTIETH SPAATZ

XXXXX U.S. ARMY FORCES PACIFIC

XXXX FIRST HODGES

XXXX EIGHTH EICHELBERGER

XXXX SIXTH KRUEGER

HONSHU

ELEVENTH AREA XXXX
Akita Sendai

TWELFTH AREA XXXX
Tokyo Kawasaki Yokohama Yokosuka

THIRTEENTH AREA XXXX
Niigata Toyo Matsumoto

FIRST GENERAL ARMY XXXXX

JAPAN

FIRST ARMY XXXXX

Yamagata
Nagaoka
Takada
Toyama
Nagano
Nagoya
Osaka
Kyoto
Kobe
Fukui

SECOND GENERAL ARMY XXXXX

FIFTEENTH AREA XXXX
Tottori
Matsue

SIXTEENTH AREA XXXX

SHIKOKU
Kochi
Matsuyama

Hiroshima
Takamatsu

SUSHIMA
Yawata

Fukuoka XXXX

Sasebo
Nagasaki

KYUSHU
Kagoshima

KOREA

SEVENTEENTH AREA XXXX
Seoul
Inchon
Pyongyang
Wonsan
Taegu
Pusan

Mukden
Dairen
Tsingtao

OPERATION DOWNFALL

OPERATION OLYMPIC
I
(About 1 Nov. 1945)

OLYMPIC TROOP LIST

I CORPS	PRELIMINARY OPNS
25th Infantry Division	40th Infantry Division
33d Infantry Division	158th Infantry RCT
41st Infantry Division	
	FOLLOW-UP UNITS
V AMPHIBIOUS CORPS	11th Airborne Division
3d Marine Division	77th Infantry Division
4th Marine Division	
5th Marine Division	

IX CORPS	
81st Infantry Division	
98th Infantry Division	

XI CORPS	
1st Cavalry Division	
Americal Division	
43d Infantry Division	

BONIN ISLANDS
CHICHI-SHIMA
HAHA-SHIMA

VOLNANO ISLANDS
KITA-IWO JIMA
IWO JIMA
MINAMI-IWO JIMA

PHILIPPINE SEA

EAST CHINA SEA

RYUKYU ISLANDS

STAGING BASE
OKINAWA
Naha

SAKASHIMA ISLANDS

FORMOSA
Taihoku
Takao

LUZON
STAGING BASE
Aparri
Baguio
Clark Field
Manila

MARIANA ISLANDS
ASUNCION
PAGAN
SARIGAN
TINIAN SAIPAN
STAGING BASE ROTA
GUAM Agana

HAWAII WAS TO BE A STAGING BASE.

JAPAN SEA

YELLOW SEA

CHINA
Nanking
Shanghai
Hangchow
Wenchow
Foochow

THE WESTERN PACIFIC
JAPANESE HOMELAND DISPOSITIONS
AUGUST 1945
AND
ALLIED PLANS FOR THE INVASION
OF JAPAN (OPERATION DOWNFALL)

SCALE OF MILES
0 100 200 300 400

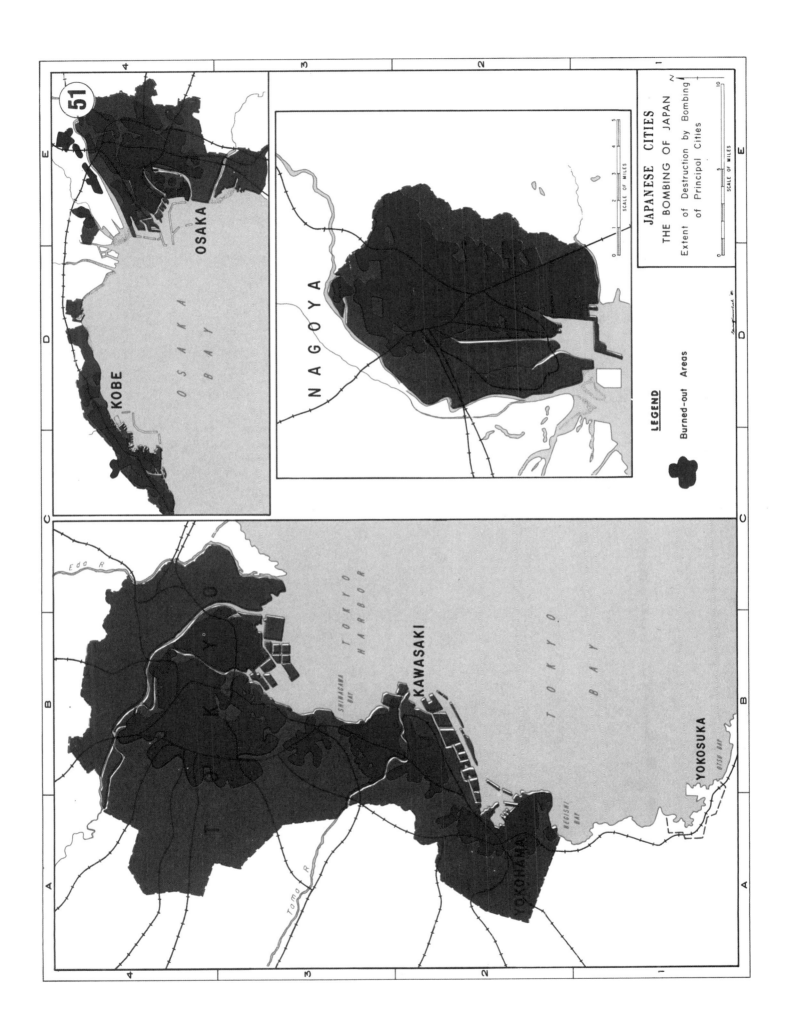

JAPANESE CITIES
THE BOMBING OF JAPAN

Extent of Destruction by Bombing
of Principal Cities

LEGEND

Burned-out Areas

51

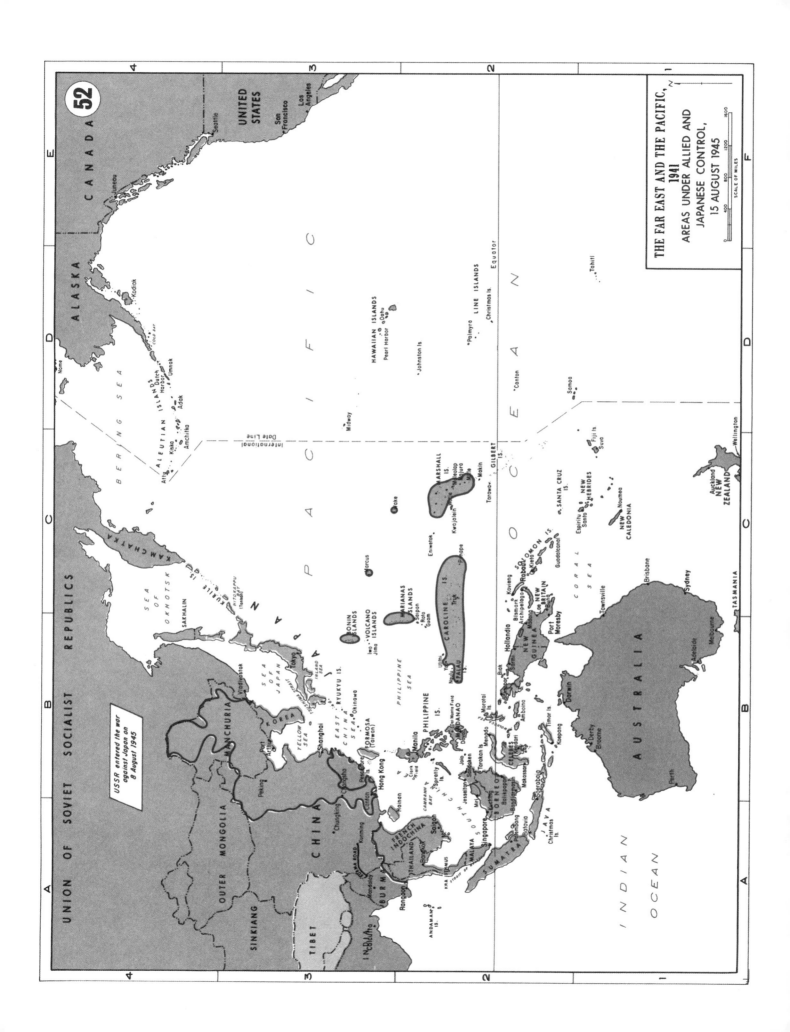

THE FAR EAST AND THE PACIFIC,
1941
AREAS UNDER ALLIED AND
JAPANESE CONTROL,
15 AUGUST 1945

SCALE OF MILES

USSR entered the war
against Japan on
8 August 1945

52

The West Point

Written by men who have served on the faculty of the United States Military Academy, this unprecedented series of books and atlases weaves the complexities of individual historical conflicts into a broader fabric, chronicling the turbulent periods of civilization. Utilizing their expertise as scholars and soldiers, the authors shed light on the crucial events and factors that shaped the planning and execution of the world's great military campaigns. Each of the following volumes focuses on a specific era of warfare, bringing you into the thick of battle to give you a clear and accurate picture of men at war.

Definitions and Doctrine of the Military Art

As a unique dictionary of military language, this book provides comprehensive definitions of all the technical terms found throughout the other volumes. It includes information on tactics, strategies, levels of command, logistics, administration, technology, military theory, and doctrine as they applied in the past and as they apply today.

Ancient and Medieval Warfare

Focusing on the Greek, Macedonian, Roman, and Byzantine wars, this volume provides an overview of more than two millennia of military evolution. It traces the development of warfare from the closed ranks of the Greek phalanx to the medieval use of cavalry, catapults, and bowman.

The Wars of Napoleon

This fascinating study takes the reader from the early years of Napoleon's career to the Emperor's defeat at Waterloo. It is a penetrating look at the technology, tactics, logistics, strategy, and outstanding generalship that created an empire stretching from the Atlantic coast to the Russian Steppes, from the North Sea to the Mediterranean.

Accompanying Campaign Atlas Available.

The Dawn of Modern Warfare

Providing a survey of five centuries of Western warfare, this volume begins with the emergence of man from the stagnation of medieval warfare and concludes with the events that preceded the French Revolution. It is a fascinating examination of the period in which Great Captains from Gustavus Adolphus to Frederick of Prussia stormed across the battlefield, ultimately restoring flexibility and balance to the practice of war.

Early American Wars and Military Institutions

This book sheds light on the formative years of the American military system. From this struggling young nation's fight for independence to its display of professionalism in the Mexican War, it examines the social, political, economic, and geographic factors that determined the development of America's military policy and, in so doing, influenced the course of history yet to come.

Military History Series

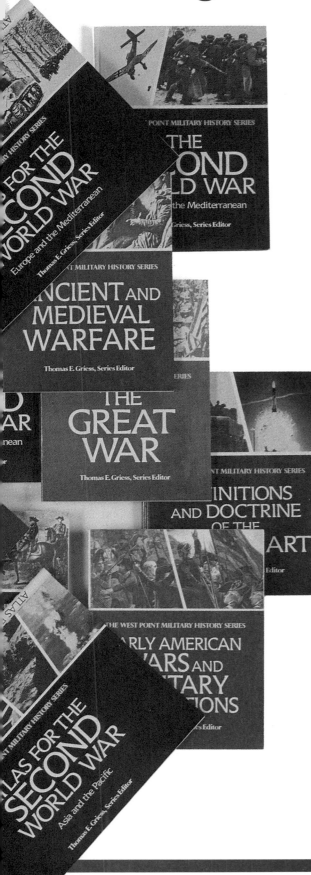

The American Civil War

As the nation divided, North against South, a great test of wills was played out in the battlefields of America's heartland. Resuming the narrative of the nation's military evolution, this campaign-by-campaign account of the Civil War examines the economic, social, political, and military aspects of this turbulent period.

Accompanying Campaign Atlas Available.

The Great War

Fought on an unprecedented scale, World War I marked the end of the old military order and the beginning of the era of mechanized warfare. This is a thorough examination of the campaigns of "the war to end all wars." It analyzes the development of military theory and practice from the prewar period of Bismarck's Prussia to the creation of the League of Nations.

Accompanying Campaign Atlas Available.

The Second World War: Europe and the Mediterranean

From the prewar development of the German war machine to the ultimate victory of the Allied coalition, this volume offers an in-depth analysis of the major battles that raged on the Western and Eastern Fronts. It examines the major strategies, the innovative tactics, and the new generation of weapons—along with the people who used them to control the European Theater of War.

Accompanying Campaign Atlas Available.

The Second World War: Asia and the Pacific

Beginning with a look at the readiness of the Imperial Japanese Army and Navy and the United States armed forces, this book gives a detailed account of the Allies' brutal five-year struggle with Japan. It examines the interrelationship of land, sea, and air forces as they battled over the vast reaches of the Pacific Theater of War.

Accompanying Campaign Atlas Available.

The Arab-Israeli Wars, The Chinese Civil War, and The Korean War

Since 1945, a number of major wars have greatly influenced contemporary military theory. This volume analyzes the strategies and tactics used in several of the Arab-Israeli conflicts, the Chinese Civil War, and the Korean War.

Accompanying Campaign Atlas Available.

Avery Publishing Group   350 Thorens Avenue • Garden City Park, NY 11040